FORD~BASED KIT CARS

PIERCE RIEMER
&
STEPHEN MILLS

ISLE COLLEGE
RESOURCES CENTRE

Foulis

Haynes
®

C20155

First published 1988

A FOULIS Book

Published by:
Haynes Publishing Group
Sparkford, Yeovil, Somerset BA22 7JJ, England

Haynes Publications Inc.
861 Lawrence Drive, Newbury Park,
California 91320 USA

Library of congress catalog card number 88-81072

British Library Cataloguing in Publication Data

Riemer, Pierce
Ford based kit cars.
1. Ford cars
I. Title   II. Mills, Stephen
629.2'222

ISBN 0-85429-623-9

Editor: Robert Iles
Printed in England by: J.H. Haynes & Co. Ltd.

Contents

Acknowledgements

Bill Battey, Derek Bentley, Rob Bloom, David Bradley (750MC), Alan Breeze, Dick Buckland, Don Collins, Frank and Martin Collins, EJ Day, Richard Disbrow, Nick Durow, Mike Eydmann, Alan Frener, Roger Garland, Anne Hill, Peter Hulse, Russell James, Chris Jacobs, John Jobber, Brian Johns, David Jones, David Malins, Scott MacMillan, Jem Marsh, Christopher Paterson (BRSCC), David Pepper, Derek Robinson, Anthony Taylor, Rob Whitwell, Roger Woolley.

Our thanks also go to the many manufacturers, organisations, owners clubs and individuals who freely gave their time and expertise during the preparation of this book.

Dedication

Dedicated to Zoe, Russell and John.

Foreword

There are no half measures in either design or engineering standards where today's kit cars are concerned.

The sophisticated 'State of the Art' methods of producing body panels in modern materials would quickly dispel any pre-conceived ideas of the kit car constructor being forced to use second grade 'plastic' components. High standards of finish are now achievable in glass fibre and Kevlar with built-in accuracy as good as the metal counterparts. As a kit producer myself, I know that this is what the customers demand.

Intelligent use of an existing chassis from a donor car, or the deployment of a specially designed and constructed framework, has brought an enlightened attitude to what now is a rapidly growing industry.

The range of design options is enormous, enabling a family man on a restricted budget to produce a tailor-made vehicle for both everyday duties and weekend recreation; alternatively, a sports car or off-road enthusiast can indulge in their pastime in a very economical way.

Pierce Riemer and Stephen Mills have devoted much time and travel to research this book. From the many kit cars both available today and surviving from yesteryear, Pierce and Stephen have compiled this fascinating collection using their own photographs, and writing from their own very extensive knowledge of the subject.

The day of the credible kit car really is here!

Derek Rickman

Introduction

The British kit car industry has existed for a lot longer than many people realise and although at times, its roots may seem a little obscure, they can be traced back over many years. Ever since the introduction of the motor car, individuals and small companies have been modifying them to meet special needs or a buyer's particular requirements. In the early days of motoring, it was not uncommon for rolling chassis, with or without any bodywork, to be produced. These were supplied to coach-builders for the fabrication and fitting of the bodywork of the customer's choice. Initially this tended to be limited to the more expensive end of the market but as "motoring for the masses" gradually became a reality, even the more humble offerings of the motor industry became the recipients of coach-built bodywork. At one extreme were Bentleys and Rolls Royces, whilst at the other was the little Ford Model Y. Each was available in chassis form, ready for the fitting of the bodywork of the customer's choice. Although these were not "kit cars" in the accepted sense, this tradition of individually built cars was to survive in Britain even in later years when domestic manufacturers were turning out thousands of cars destined for the man in the street.

Even when the motor industry was in full swing, producing countless vehicles, from sports cars to limousines, there were always the individuals who felt that, for a variety of reasons, the best car was the one they built themselves. Britain has a long history of "Special" builders, determined men, who were convinced that the best car was one constructed with their own hands. Many of these early Special builders were involved in various forms of motor sport and the products of their labours could be seen thundering around Brooklands or fighting it out on hill-climbs and trials. It was hardly surprising that a certain percentage of these cars would end up doubling as road transport for their owners. Inevitably a few cars were copied, but there was little serious commercial exploitation. In pre-war days, there were still plenty of British manufacturers producing sports cars who were able to satisfy the sporting aspirations of most people.

The majority of pre-war Specials were only "one-offs", never intended for any kind of production, however, in them were the first seeds from which the large and varied kit car industry, that was to come in later years, was to grow.

We have taken a look at the early days of the industry, a period that has failed to receive much written coverage and indeed, only little recognition of its importance. The activities that started after World War II and carried on throughout the 1950s and 60s, helped to establish a solid base of experience from which many of today's ultra-sophisticated kit cars eventually sprang. It has not always been an easy path. Many companies have foundered on the way, but out of their failure, others were able to take note, learn their lessons, and ultimately produce cars that were able to challenge, and even exceed, the products of the conventional producers. With a few notable examples, all of these early companies have long since departed, but many of their products still survive, now maintained and cared for by appreciative individuals and owner clubs. If anything, we detected something of an increase in interest in the early cars, such as Rochdale, Typhoon, Falcon, and so on. Remarkably, some of these cars are actually being redesigned and reworked by manufacturers, intending to use them as the basis of new projects.

The "industry" is perhaps something of a misnomer, as it has always consisted of comparatively small companies, varying in numbers, over the years. Even the largest of the kit car manufacturers is not, or has ever been, in the same league, in terms of sheer volume, as the conventional producers. Having said that, the industry has never really set out to compete in terms of sheer numbers, relying on its inherent flexibility to fill gaps in the market place.

Over the years, they have produced a variety of specialist cars that were being denied to the public, usually on the grounds of economics. Conventional producers, in general, do not like a very wide product range, preferring to target their activites on the most lucrative, high-volume sectors of the market. On the other hand, many kit car producers have specifically aimed at the smaller, more specialised areas ignored by the "big boys". Whereas it is possible for a kit car manufacturer to make a living in these areas, they would clearly be of little interest to the major motor manufacturers. This has been one of the reasons for the industry's growth in recent years. As types and styles of cars from the multinationals has reduced, so there has been a corresponding increase in the variety and types being produced in kit form. Clearly, the kit car industry is providing a much greater degree of choice, usually at more tolerable prices.

Over the years, the activity in the industry has, at different times, both increased and decreased. Various outside factors have influenced these fluctuations. Such things as Purchase Tax, VAT, compulsory vehicle testing and the threat of Type Approval, have all played their part. In general, after every lull, has come a corresponding increase, each one seemingly greater than the last. Currently, the industry seems to be on something of a high, with increasingly sophisticated and professionally-produced products coming from a multitude of companies. Even greater things are rumoured for the future.

Our selection of recently produced kit cars does not purport to be a complete market run-down of every Ford based/powered product on the market. We have tried to pick what we consider to be some of the most interesting, in both mechanical and visual terms, and the exclusion of any particular car does not imply any criticism of it. Clearly, only a finite number could be included.

Why did we limit our project to Ford based/powered kit cars? As in so many other fields of automotive activity, Ford components have played an enormous part. If the Ford 8/10 chassis and running-gear had not been available in such profusion during the 1950s, it seems unlikely that the kit car industry would have evolved to anything like the size that it is today. Out of this mass of, often quite crude, kit cars and Specials, the present industry grew. Today, Ford components make a sensible choice from a number of angles. Firstly, Ford donor cars, in the shape of the Escort, Cortina, Capri, and Granada ranges, are so easily available. The sheer volume inevitably means that prices are often low, an ideal base for a kit car. Secondly, Ford mechanical components are, almost invariably, very reliable. In many cases, they will outlive the bodywork of the car. This means that with a modicum of rebuilding, most of the mechanical parts can be transferred without incurring much additional expense. Even when the car's bodywork is beyond saving, the mechanical parts often have a considerable amount of mileage left in them.

Other advantages are the easy availability of Ford parts, this helping to minimise the problems of keeping the car on the road. Virtually every town has a Ford parts supplier and nearly every garage in the country is familiar with the repair and maintenance of Ford parts.

For the performance buff, Ford engines offer a sensible route to take. Tuning gear exists for practically every type of Ford engine ever made. It is therefore a straightforward matter to take a standard Ford drive-train, and systematically increase its state of tune, as and when required. As a result of Ford's involvement in a variety of other spheres, such as rallying, tuning equipment is now easily available and well developed.

The industry is in a constant state of change, with projects changing hands, companies merging and moving, and products continually being upgraded and improved. As a result, the latter half of this book can be regarded as no more than a snapshot in time. You will find few references to prices or addresses as these constantly alter and would therefore be meaningless. If the desire to build a kit car takes hold, we would recommend you to look at one of the excellent magazines that now cover the subject. *Kit Cars and Specials, Kit Car,* and *Which Kit,* all do a very good job of reviewing the ever-changing scene, and it is partly due to their independent comment that the kit car industry is now largely populated with such well designed and built cars.

Today, the kit car scene certainly presents an interesting and colourful picture, with an incredible range of variety. In an age when conformity, usually as a result of economic pressures, seems to creep into every aspect of daily life, it is comforting to know that there is still a chance of escape into the varied and exciting world of the kit car.

1

The industry's early days

The first real kit cars began to emerge shortly after World War II. There was then a new incentive, for in addition to the diehard band of Special builders, there were a large number of young men looking for fast, sports-type road cars. The main problem was that, as a result of the war, sports cars were both hard to get hold of and consequently expensive. What most young men didn't have was money! What they did have was enthusiasm and it was out of this, that the first kit car producers were born. These companies were some of the earliest to utilise the "new" fibreglass compositions, for automotive use. This was to set the trend and opened the flood gates for a host of other small firms such as Deep-Sanderson, Bond, Delta, GSM, Heron, Shirley, Rochdale, Ashley, VW, HG, Elva, Diva, Fairthorpe, Gilbern, Turner, Ogle, Ginetta, Gordon-Keeble, Marcos, TVR and many others.

One of the earliest companies of note was Bucklers. They started by constructing space-frame chassis that would accept the Ford 10 engine, gearbox and much of the running-gear. This was clothed in a two-seater sports body. Not content with this, they also began to offer a number of suspension and performance options. Bucklers produced a number of different chassis at various times. Some were specifically designed to accept shells being produced by other manufacturers. For instance, the DD2 was originally designed to take the Microplas

Mistral body. This was also available to accept body shells from Ashley Laminates, Falcon and Auto Kraft. Other chassis options included the Mk XVII which was specifically for the 7' 10" wheelbase Ashley GT, the DD2/Falcon III for the Falcon Caribbean, and the GT I/R for the Rochdale GT. One of Buckler's specialities was the independent swing axle independent front suspension, this using coil-overs instead of the transverse spring.

Apart from the space-frames they also produced a number of backbone chassis, as well as some with de Dion rear-ends. As well as taking the E93A, 100E and later, 105E engines, options also included MG and Coventry Climax. Buckler chassis cost between £70 and £100, depending upon type and specification. In addition, they also produced a large range of competition parts, such as racing engines, gears, and camshafts. The company managed to survive up to 1962 and when they finally ceased trading, around 5–600 cars had been built.

Whereas Bucklers tended to be better known for their chassis and mechanical components, around the same period, the Rochdale Company started to become noticed for their bodies. The Company was founded in 1948 by panel beaters Harry Smith and Frank Butterworth, under the name of Rochdale Motor Panels. The original stimulus came from their involvement in the 750 Motor Club, their first bodies being ash-framed and aluminium panelled, designed to fit the Austin 7 chassis. A number of other aluminium bodies followed however, 1952 saw the appearance of the first fibreglass body shell (the Mk VI) designed to fit various chassis, with the 1172 cc Ford unit. This was followed in 1954 by the C and F types. The next offering to come out of Rochdale, was the Sports Tourer (ST), specifically designed to fit the plentiful Ford chassis. Around this time, Harry Smith realised that there was a much wider market to be tapped for a 2+2 saloon body, the result being the appearance in 1956, of the GT model. This was quite a comprehensive kit for the time, and included wheel arches, bulkhead, floor, dash and battery box in situ. In addition, doors (complete with windows) were also fitted. Once again, the GT was designed to fit the Ford chassis. This was to prove to be Rochdale's greatest success, with more than 1000 kits being sold between 1956 and 1961. Meanwhile, 1959 saw the launch of the Riviera, this being essentially a convertible version of the GT. Surprisingly, it had only limited success, only around 40 being built.

These cars formed the solid foundation for what was to become, perhaps, the company's best remembered car, the Olympic, the first models appearing late in 1960. Initially, it was only available as a complete body/chassis unit, intended to take the major components from several different donors, including the Ford 8/10. Later, complete kits also became available with the 105E Anglia engine offered. The Olympic was poised on the brink of great success when, early in 1961, a disastrous fire completely destroyed the factory. It was not until 1962, that limited production was able to resume. The Racing Car Show of 1963 saw the Mk II version appear, similar in looks to the

Mk I, but with a much redesigned chassis and suspension. The front suspension was now based on that of the Triumph Spitfire, this replacing the Morris 1000-type torsion bar set-up used in the Mk I. The standard power-plant was the 1500 cc Ford 116E engine (with modified cylinder head), however late 1963 saw the 1500 GT engine being listed as an option. The Phase II sold steadily throughout the next few years, however by the mid 1960s, a number of supply problems, compounded with poor sales, resulted in the car being offered in bodyshell form only. Around 1970, sales had effectively stopped, although it was still possible to obtain new shells to special order. Although no production figures exist, reliable sources have estimated that around 50 alloy body shells, approximately 100 of the Mk VI, C, F and ST, combined, over 1000 GTs, 40 Rivieras, 250 Phase I and 150 Phase II Olympics were built. Those that survived, especially the Olympics, are now beginning to be appreciated for the fine cars that they undoubtedly were. Their styling has been likened by some writers as being similar to that of the TVR products of the time, however certain Teutonic influences also appear to have had some hand in the styling.

What started out as a hobby for Major Arthur Mallock eventually became a small, but notable, company, over the years building a number of interesting cars.

Following the end of World War II, Mallock began building Austin 7-based specials and this, after innumerable modifications and alterations, formed the basis of the 1172 cc Ford powered Mallock U2. This was originally powered by the E93A engine but this was later updated to the 100E specification and raced with some success. This configuration was eminently suitable for the new Formula Junior. Mallock went on to produce a small number of U2s in "kit" form, some of which found themselves on the road. The chassis was available for £48 or, complete with body panels, £75. By now the powerplant was based on the 105E Anglia engine and in tuned form, was capable of over 120 mph. Various

Turner Sports Cars of Wolverhampton produced their little two-seater cars in both fully-built and kit form. Although primarily intended for the running-gear from the Austin A30 and later the A35, a number were fitted with 1172 cc Ford parts. Surviving examples, especially of the Ford-powered, are rare.

Ford engine options followed, cars being built up to the late 1970s. Although Mallocks were few in number, they are fondly remembered as both rapid and enjoyable track and road cars. Mallock are still active in racing, with Mallock cars still scoring successes on the race tracks. One of their specialities is now suspension tuning, not merely for their own cars, but for any type, including kit cars. They also supply various race-orientated parts including full ground-effect chassis, as well as brake and steering parts.

One of the foremost names to emerge during the immediate post-war period was that of Colin Chapman. He started out, in 1947, building little trials cars, based on the ubiquitous Ford chassis and running gear. Perhaps the most notable car to come out of this period was the Lotus 6, which was the first kit-based car and the forerunner of the legendary Lotus 7. The latter was originally designed and built by Chapman, primarily for racing use, however it was not long before the popular little cars found themselves on the roads. The 7 was based on a multi-tubular space-frame chassis and this, when combined with a skimpy, aluminium

body, ensured that it was a very light car. Some later versions, powered by the Ford 100E engine and three-speed gearbox, were good for over 80 mph. With a modicum of tuning work, 100 mph was not unrealistic. In addition, the road holding and handling was excellent. In 1960, three versions of the Seven kit were available. The Seven (F model) used the Ford 100E engine and gearbox and cost £587, the Seven A took the BMC A series parts and the Lotus C, used the Coventry Climax engine. These comprehensive kits were available from Lotus Engineering in Tottenham Lane. From these humble beginnings, Lotus Cars would eventually emerge.

In 1954, Peter Pellandine was busy with a number of things, one of which was building Austin 7 Specials. As a result of his experiments, he began producing fibreglass bodies, intended for the Austin 7 chassis. This proved to be so successful that he formed a business partnership with Keith Waddington, and the Loughton-based Ashley Laminates came into being.

Their first production body was, as were most of the others of the time, an open, two-seater sports body, destined for the Austin 7 chassis. The venture met with a good deal of success, however in 1951, Pellandine left to set up the well-known Falcon Shells. The Mk I Falcons were, perhaps not surprisingly, of similar design to that of the Ashley, although of longer wheelbase. Ashley continued under the control of Keith Waddington and in 1958, produced a new bodyshell, known as the 1172, designed to fit the 7′ 6″ wheelbase Ford chassis. Once again, it was a sleek, open, two-seater sports body, and featured a front-hinged bonnet section with faired-in headlights. An option of a detachable hard top was also available.

1959 saw the range extended by the addition of two new bodies, the 1172 Ninety, and Ninety Four. These were designed to fit the 7′ 6″ and 7′ 10″ wheelbase Ford chassis, respectively. Further improvements were announced to the bodies at the 1960 Racing Car Show, the shells now coming complete with bonded-in bulkheads, larger doors, and bigger boot lids for the open models.

November 1960 saw another newcomer, the Sportiva, although this was essentially the same body with a redesigned front end. 1961 saw the arrival of a new 8' wheelbase chassis, designed to accept the mechanical parts from the E93A. It included an independent front suspension set-up, pedals and master cylinders, rear suspension units, transmission tunnel, Panhard and radius rods. The end for the kits was, however, coming into sight, as gradually the emphasis had been shifting towards the production of hard tops and body panels for the Austin-Healey Sprite. Within a few years, the body shells and related parts had, like so many others, disappeared from the scene.

The latter half of the 1950s saw a great upsurge in the interest in kit cars, although many of these consisted of replacement bodies, as opposed to the modern body/chassis concept. A multitude of manufacturers began to produce a wide variety of fibreglass bodies with which to tempt the general public. Some offerings were very stylish, others less than successful.

The majority of these kits were aimed at the younger age bracket, this being reflected in the predomination of small, two-seater sports bodies that were offered. The majority of these were based on only two types of donor vehicle, both of them cheap and plentiful. One was the little Austin 7 and the other was the Ford 8 and 10 range. The latter had remained virtually unaltered mechanically since the 1930s and as a result, scruffy examples were available very cheaply. For those who could not run to the cost of an MG, Jaguar or similar (and many couldn't), a fibreglass body fitted to an old Ford rolling chassis often provided the answer. As with any kit car project, the end result was only as good as the man who built it and consequently, cars were built that reflected the whole spectrum of abilities, from first class engineering to downright dangerous! There were examples that were based on meticulously rebuilt and updated Ford running gear and, at the other extreme, those where the bodywork

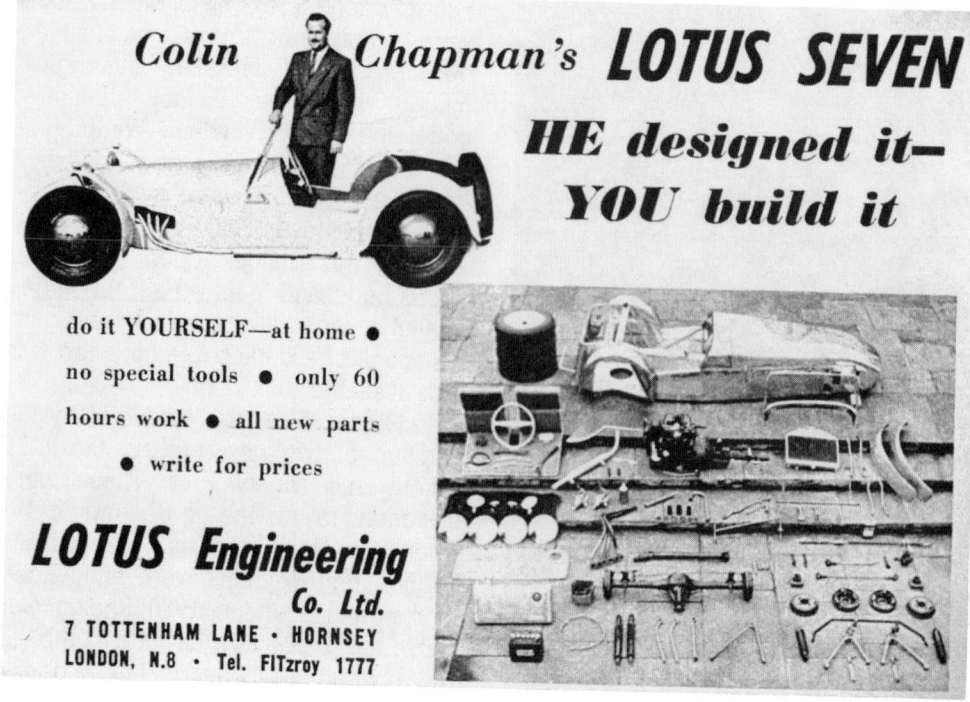

Colin Chapman's LOTUS SEVEN

HE designed it— YOU build it

do it YOURSELF—at home •

no special tools • only 60

hours work • all new parts

• write for prices

LOTUS Engineering Co. Ltd.

7 TOTTENHAM LANE · HORNSEY
LONDON, N.8 · Tel. FITzroy 1777

A 1959 advertisement for Colin Chapman's Lotus Seven kit. The comprehensive kit supplied virtually everything necessary to build an impressive road/track car. Notice the use of a lightweight aluminium body in an era when most manufacturers were switching to fibreglass.

had simply been chiselled off and a crude fibreglass shell dropped on top. Most examples came somewhere in between these two extremes.

The majority of cars built during this early period retained much of the running gear as Ford made it. The 1172 cc sidevalve engine, three-speed gearbox and torque-tube transmission might have been cleaned and painted, but were often left unmodified. For those however, with sporting pretensions, there was plenty of scope for updating and modifying the mechanical components, either for more speed or improved handling. Fords of this period still retained transverse springing and beam front axles, a legacy of their 1930s heritage and although admittedly things were improved by the use of a lightweight body, handling was not always what it might have been.

A number of manufacturers were well aware of the handling limitations but clearly, many buyers of the period were unwilling or unable to pay for the extra cost of a suitable replacement chassis. As a result, something of a compromise was reached with a number of systems designed to update the suspension, appearing on the market. Probably the most famous was developed (originally during the 1930s) by Leslie Ballamy. His system was known as, the "Supersprung Suspension" and was sold by the hundred. It consisted of an independent front suspension set-up, based on a split beam axle, modified so that it pivoted around a central point (the swing-axle conversion). Many of Ballamy's ideas were as a result of his racing activities using a much-modified Popular. His car, naturally, used the independent front suspension, his own 15 inch wheels (as opposed to the usual 17 inch), track increasing spacers and a host of other modified pieces. The engine was super-charged by means of a Godfrey blower. Various independent comments of the period claimed that his suspension system "put the Popular in the sports car class" which, considering the high centre of gravity, was no mean feat.

Ballamy also went on to produce the LMB Lightweight replacement chassis which was of a ladder configuration and used two deep section rectangular tubes with four inch diameter cross-members. Rack and pinion steering was used and, of course, a swing axle IFS.

Ballamy was not alone with his independent suspension, a number of other kit manufacturers also offering the split-axle conversion. Elliot Brothers Ltd (EB), for example, would supply a split-beam axle conversion with a pair of coil-over Woodhead-Monroe units replacing the transverse spring. All of the necessary modified parts were included in the price of £23/15s.

For the more modest amount of £15/15s, ex-BRM chief, Raymond Mays would supply you with one of his "Fluid Cushion" suspension set-ups. This retained the transverse springing but used an anti-roll bar at the front and tubular shock absorbers on all four corners.

Whichever system was utilised, a dramatic and often necessary improvement in road holding and handling were invariably noted. This was especially true where a lightweight replacement body-shell had replaced the steel Ford body.

Once the handling had been improved, it was time to consider the power output. Tuning was often a low budget affair consisting of a number of fairly simple steps. The compression ratio was often boosted, either by skimming the original or fitting a replacement high compression head. Carburation was another area for improvement, the usual step being the fitting of twin carburettors, such as SUs, mounted on a simple replacement manifold. This was often complemented by the addition of a tubular exhaust manifold and straight through silencer.

For those with deep pockets, a wide range of tuning parts was available. The well-known Aquaplane Company could supply a wealth of performance parts for either racing or fast road use. Their lists included manifolds, carburettors, high compression heads and lightened flywheels. In addition, they supplied much needed uprated oil and water pumps. Other modifications that could be carried out included the fitting of oversized inlet valves, used on conjunction with opened out throats in the block.

These basic steps, when carried out correctly, could produce quite sizeable increases in power and where the weight of the car had been dramatically reduced by the fitting of a lightweight shell, performance was often on a par with some of the sports cars of the period.

One of the most expensive power-boosting steps that could be taken was the fitting of an overhead inlet valve conversion head. These were available for around £60 from a number of sources such as Elva and Willment Speed Shop. The conversion was both quick and simple and gave a sizable increase in power. The advantages of such a set-up included the use of larger inlet valves, almost direct flow into the combustion chambers and individual inlet ports. Fitted with one of these heads, many lightweight Ford Specials became real fliers!

Not surprisingly, with an increase in power, other weak links in the drive train appeared. Heavy duty clutches and HD high friction brake linings were offered by a number of manufacturers to help overcome some of the problems. In addition, Lasford Ltd manufactured differentials and "axle ends" for independent suspension for Ford-based sports and racing cars. These were available for both the E93A and the 100E ranges.

One of the most interesting and innovative companies of this early period was ELVA, founded by Frank Nichols, who had been responsible for building the CSM special, based on a Ford 10. The first ELVAs (Elle va, She goes) were built in 1955, mainly intended for racing. The chassis was a multi-tubular affair, similar to the Lotus Seven. The ELVA used a Ford 10-based engine, converted to use overhead inlet valves, as opposed to side valves, a modification that the company

was to become well known for. This type of conversion became quite popular for performance use both, on and off the track. In later years Cosworth tuned 105E Anglia engines were used.

A body or a kit?

During this early period, kit cars were somewhat arbitrarily, split into five different types. Then, as now, not many fitted neatly into specific categories, however it generally helped to characterise them.

"Complete" kits, were those that contained virtually all of the necessary mechanical and body parts, perhaps with the exception of the drive-train. In some

What appears to be a somewhat modified Falcon Mk III. The body shell was designed to fit the 7' 6" wheelbase Ford 8 and 10 chassis (1933 to 1959) and was described in period advertisements as "ravishingly beautiful". The kit was very comprehensive, including many extras.

cases, even the engine was supplied, the customer merely having to carry out the final assembly. The situation was similar to that currently encountered with some of the more comprehensive kits, the buyer substituting his labour for the manufacturer's (helping to keep the price down, as well as avoiding tax on the completed vehicle).

"Semi" kits, as the name implies, were those that supplied the basic parts such as the body and chassis assembly, but required the majority of the mechanical parts from, usually, the Ford 8 or 10 range. A typical example was Watford's "Cheetah". Often, kits fell somewhere between these two groups.

The majority of kits produced were intended for road use, however a number were designed with competition use in mind. "Racing" kits included for example the Terrier, such cars being raced in a number of different formulae. Although they were essentially track cars, inevitably many did see a certain amount of road use. Once again, the dividing line was often blurred.

"Replacement body shells" to fit the Ford chassis were subdivided into two categories, being composed of either "Plastic" or "Non-plastic bodies". The former clearly included the majority of the fibreglass shells produced over a number of years by a multitude of different manufacturers, and the latter, to the relatively few cars that used aluminium bodies, such as the Buroche. Notable advancements in fibreglass technology, resulted in many hard top bodies emerging during the early 1960s.

Clearly, there were a number of different possible approaches to kit car building during the 1950s and early 1960s. Perhaps the most important choice facing the builder was whether to go for a body and chassis from one of the suppliers, or to adopt the more conservative approach and "re-body" a standard Ford 8 or 10 chassis. The latter was obviously cheaper although it clearly imposed certain limitations. As mentioned previously, in many people's eyes, Ford's transverse sprung suspension was at its best, only tolerable, and to many Special builders, was quite

unacceptable for any serious sporting or fast road use. Obviously, re-bodying an old, unmodified Ford chassis limited any sporting aspirations that the owner might have, but for normal road use, may have been quite acceptable. Body roll and handling were generally improved by the replacement of the steel body with a light shell.

For serious work, a replacement chassis often proved a better bet, as these were generally stronger, sometimes lower, lighter and often came with a split beam axle front suspension set-up. A number of companies would supply both bodies and chassis, some with the circuit in mind and others aimed at road use. Several manufacturers, such as Falcon Shells and Watford Sports Cars (who produced the "Cheetah") manufactured a twin-tube chassis which accepted most of the Ford rolling parts. The Cheetah chassis was specifically designed to accept the Ford mechanical parts and was constructed from three-inch diameter side-members, braced by a pair of tubular cross-members, a rectangular cross-member and two channel sections. A steel hoop also supported the scuttle area, providing additional support for the body shell. Built for the 7' 6" wheelbase shells, the chassis came complete with aluminium floor pan and was available with a swing axle conversion or a solid front axle, located by means of a Panhard rod (as was the rear axle). The chassis was designed to accept any post-1938 Ford 8 or 10 parts, and sold for £70. The fibreglass body cost a further £130.

Falcon had originally entered the market producing fibreglass body shells and went on to produce the 100E powered Caribbean, the 2+2 Bermuda as well as a "competition shell". The Bermuda came later, being in essence, a four-seater Caribbean. 1962 saw the arrival of the "improved" Mk IV Caribbean, now coming complete with glass side windows, polished framing, built-in dash panel and glove box, plus a sleeker front end with a polished grille. The kit also included a lined hard top, lights, door locks and many other essential bits and pieces. Falcon shells were well known for their quality and at

The Typhoon used a tubular steel chassis of Tornado's own design, with 3 inch diameter main tubes, front swing-axle system, with the running-gear from the Ford 8/10. Different wheelbases were offered, to accept either the 2- or 4-seater bodies.

the time, advertised "production car finish for your special". During the company's life, they produced over 2000 bodies and kits, finally going out of business in 1964.

Walklett Brothers little Ginetta also used a tube frame in conjunction with a stressed aluminium skin, floor and bulkheads. It would take the running-gear from any 1938–1953 Ford and, in 1958 cost £156.

Space-frame chassis were even available, the Speedex Sirocco making use of their "Mercury" unit. Other manufacturers had their chassis made by outside firms, for example, the Super Accessories "Super Two" used two-inch square-section tube chassis, with independent front suspension, made by the well-known Bowden company. Super Accessories were based in Bromley and also sold a wide range of parts and equipment for Austin 7 and Ford 10 Special builders. The Super Two kit sold for a very reasonable £99, the two-seater sports body being specially made by Hamblin. The little cars proved to be quite popular, and between 1960 and 1965, around 200 were sold. Only a few have managed to survive the ravages of time, however one beautifully restored example recently surfaced in the pages of a national magazine.

Another good reason for considering a replacement chassis was that, clearly, it would guarantee a good fit! Many body shells were designed to fit both the 7' 6" and 7' 10" wheelbase Ford chassis. This could be accomplished by fitting the body to the chassis, marking the rear wheel centres and cutting out the rear wheel openings to suit. Needless to say, the overall effect, both in terms of appearance and workmanship, was not always what had been hoped for!

One of the most stylish and popular kits of the period was the Typhoon, this being available as a well-made body and chassis combination. It was built by the Tornado Company, originally founded by Bill Woodham, and used Tornado's own chassis, costing in 1959, £70. It featured telescopic suspension units and was generally considered to be a well-designed and well-made unit. The body cost £130, was constructed from eleven separate mouldings and came equipped with most of its hinges, trim, locks, etc. It would accept components from any of the post–1938 Ford 8 or 10 range, the end result being a very stylish 2+2. Between 1957 and 1963, a total of around 350 Typhoons were sold. From 1957, Tornado produced their own tubular ladder chassis which used three-inch diameter main frame tubes. It featured a swing-axle

16

system fitted with Armstrong telescopic dampers and coil springs. Two sub-frames were used, one at the rear to carry the petrol tank and provide support for the rear body mountings, and one at the front to mount the radiator and forward body section. It was available either in a 7' 3" wheelbase version to accept two-seater bodies, or in 8' 1" for four-seaters.

Between 1960 and 1962, Tornado also produced the Tempest, this using a similar sports-body to the Typhoon, but powered by the 997 cc ohv Anglia engine. Once again, Tornado produced their own chassis, now with Triumph front suspension and brakes. The rear-end of the Mk I model used a live axle with coil-over units, whereas the Mk II had an independent set-up of Tornado's own design. Only 10 cars were built during the Tempest's short life. Both the Typhoon and the Tempest could be ordered in either open, or hard top versions, with different wheelbases for either the two-seater or 2+2 forms. A few full four-seater bodies were also produced.

An interesting variation was the Sportsbrake, an estate bodied variant. The appropriate top half of the body could be supplied separately, enabling the conversion of any of the existing cars, or alternatively, could be ordered as a complete new body. The Sportsbrake, although few in number, probably provided the inspiration for many of the sports estates that were to follow, such as the Scimitar GTE.

Tornado's other model was the Talisman, a four-seater sports saloon produced between 1961 and 1964. This used a 3.5 inch diameter tubular chassis, with Triumph front suspension and braking system. The rear-end used the Tornado independent system. Power for the Mk I version was provided by the 1340 cc Classic engine, and for the Mk II, the 1498 cc unit. The engines were unique to the Talisman, being specially modified for the company by Cosworth. A special cam was fitted, along with a modified cylinder head. The "Tourer" model used a single carburettor whereas the GT was fitted with a pair of Weber units. A total of 186 cars were produced by the time the company finally ceased operations. The Talisman in particular, is now becoming quite a sought-after car, the performance and handling of the lightweight (13 cwt) car, having made quite a name for itself at the time, both on the road and on the race track.

Sometimes it was possible to obtain a chassis from one source and combine it with a body from another. For instance, a very acceptable car could be built using Falcon Shell's Mk II two-seater sports body, mounted on an ELVA chassis. The final decision often came down to finance.

Kits and body shells were, for the main part, aimed at the sports car market. There were a surprisingly large number of manufacturers who produced two-seater sports-type bodies, designed to accept the mechanical parts from the Ford 8 and 10 range. Concordette Developments made the Concord, Convair Developments produced the Convair, AKS, the Continental, and the Walklett Brothers manufactured the Fairlite and Ginetta range. The Fairlite was made by the Walkletts as a shell only, although Fairlite was a separate company. The shell was the same as the Ginetta G3. Other examples included Nickri Laminates Spyder, Champion and Alpine; Nordic Panels, Excell; Rochdale's GT and Riviera; and Ashley's 1172.

Body shells to fit the Ford chassis abounded, from companies all around the country. For instance, TWM Engineering of Newark-on-Trent, (who were in business from the late 1950s to the early 1960s) produced their own kit (with an identical body shell to a number of other manufacturers) costing £85, designed to fit the Ford 7' 6" Ford 10 chassis. A BMC-based kit was also offered. In addition, they also marketed a new, boxed chassis, complete with mounts, for £29/10s, cross-flow radiators for £6/15s and screen for £18. Unlike a number of their competitors, they also supplied weather protection in the form of a hard top for £25, a hood for £18 and optional side-screens. In addition, there was also a "Deluxe" body shell available for £135. The TWM could be completed for around £550, depending on the engine option, and had a claimed top speed of around 100 mph. The road holding and braking of the completed car was very good.

The Fairthorpe Company was to become another of the industry's long-term survivors, being founded in the 1950s by Air Vice-Marshall Donald "Pathfinder" Bennet. Over the years, the company produced a number of different models such as the Atom, Electron, Electron Minor, Rockette and, of course, the Zeta. Although the Zeta was the only car to use a Ford drive-train as standard, a surprising number of other models eventually found themselves with Ford engines. For instance, a number of Electron Minors, although intended for Standard 8 drive-trains, were fitted with the 105E Anglia engine, and a few Rockettes, with 1500 cc units. The bodies for most of the early Fairthorpes were based on that of the Electron Minor, including that of the Zeta.

For performance buffs of the era, perhaps the ultimate machine was in fact, the Zeta, this brute being powered by a Raymond Mays Ford Zodiac engine. A single carburettor version, as well as twin and six carburettor versions were offered, the latter costing £868 and giving a top speed of 145 mph! The Zeta proved to be a bit of a handful and consequently a total of only 14 were built.

Another company active in the field, was the Watling Car Company. They were one of the less well known manufacturers, mainly because the majority of their early products were specifically built for racing. The Hertfordshire based company later became well established, producing sports bodies and chassis, as well as boats and caravans. In 1960, Watling began offering several cars in kit form, using their own tubular steel ladder frame chassis. Their GT body shell, which resembled a cross between an early Marcos and a hard top E-type Jaguar, could be ordered with the chassis, complete with Ford 100E engine and gearbox, for £610, or with the E93A unit, for £550. If the "new" Anglia ohv engine was adopted the price was £625. The customer obviously had the choice of supplying his own running-gear, the kit, less drive-train, being available for £330. The Watling cars were fairly well advanced for that time, and featured such touches as steering and pedals that were fully adjustable (during the construction) to suit a variety of owners. Two body shapes were produced, one modelled on the Aston Martin and one of the Ferraris of the period.

Although most bodies and kits were produced for the road, a number were available specifically for racing. One notable example was the 1172 Terrier, of the Terrier Cars and Engineering Company of Thornwood. Throughout the 1959 season, the Mk II version won all but one of its races and in 1960, held the 1172 Formula lap record at Silverstone, Oulton Park, Snetterton and Brands Hatch! The car was available, complete with 100E engine and gearbox, for £527, or with the customer supplying the mechanical parts, for £440. The sophisticated little car used a lightweight 6' 10" wheelbase tubular chassis, with coil springs and double wishbone front suspension. Hydraulic brakes were used, as was rack and pinion steering.

Another notable race-orientated car was the Gemini. This early 1960s racer was very successful in the Formula Junior class, the kit, with the 105E engine, costing £925, a great deal of money in 1960. A lightweight space frame chassis was used in conjunction with a single-seat alloy body.

Racing also had a direct influence on some of the road-going cars of the time. For instance, Buroche produced an exceedingly sleek, alloy-bodied kit car which resembled a 1950s Grand Prix racer. Various body options costing between £61 to £121 were available, as were a number of chassis options.

One company which has always been active in racing, in one way or another, was Ginetta. Ginetta was founded by the four Walklett Brothers, and is still very much alive and kicking today. The first Ginetta was based on a Wolsely Hornet, this early Special being called the Ginetta G1, and it was the brothers' experience with this car that eventually led them to design one to sell to the public. The result was a multi-tubular space-framed car, known as the G2, which had a similar layout to the Lotus 6 and utilised many of the mechanical parts from the 103E Popular. Following the success of this, the Walklett's decided that a more sophisticated follow-up was called for. Their new venture was called the G3 and featured a fibreglass coupe body, the car selling well. The successor to the G3 made its public debut at the 1961 Racing Car Show. By now, a Ford Anglia rear axle was being used, located by trailing arms and suspended on coil-over units. The redesigned chassis carried a two-seater sports body, power coming from the 105E Anglia motor. The 1340 cc Classic engine was also listed as an option. 1963 saw the appearance of the G5, this powered by the 1498 cc Cortina engine. Good sales were, once again, achieved, when the cars, powered by 1600 cc pushrod Ford engines, began beating far more expensive sports cars at a number of racing venues. By 1967 sales were up to 500.

Later years saw the arrival of the G10, which was a two-door sports car powered by an American Ford V8 of 4.7 litre capacity. Unfortunately, despite its obvious racing potential, the car was too

expensive, only a dozen being built. The G11 faced similar problems, this being replaced by the G12 which was a mid-engined, independently sprung coupe. Early versions were powered by 1000 cc Cosworth engines and later ones by, Lotus-Ford twin-cams. The G13 was avoided because of superstition! 1973 saw the launch of the G21 which could accommodate the 3 litre Essex V6. Ginetta have never disappeared from the scene and are still one of the most active and innovative manufacturers. As in their early days, many of their cars are still to be found on the race track.

During this period, many companies came and just as quickly, went. For instance, the Birmingham-based company of Dellow, who had been producing little trials and road cars based on the Ford 10, finally went out of business in 1957. In the same year, TVRs began to increase in popularity, producing either completed cars or kits, the latter obviously avoiding purchase tax. Production was low, at only two or three a month, however there was a choice of power-plants. One option was the Coventry Climax and the other, the ever-popular 1172 cc Ford. The latter was also available in supercharged form, relying on a Shorrock unit. 1959 saw the Grantura Mk II appear, this being available with the 100E engine. This was soon superseded by the new 997 cc ohv Anglia engine and later, to be joined by the 1340 cc Classic unit. The cars had multi-tubular chassis as well as independent suspension all around. Front disc brakes were also offered as an option. In the following years, TVRs ceased to be available in kit form, the company deciding to concentrate solely on the production of complete cars.

Although sports-type bodies accounted for most of the market, saloons aimed at the family man were produced by a few manufacturers, such as Auto Bodies of Oldham, who produced Mk I, II and III models. Westlite was another manufacturer whose products were aimed beyond the sports-body market. They produced a full five-seater, with a fibreglass body that was self-coloured in either white, green or red. Their kit

A 1960 2-seater Tempest complete with hard top. This particular car is in left-hand drive form and is about to be shipped to the USA. Only a few were built. (David Mallins)

Ford based kit cars
/
The industry's
early days

included all the doors, hinges, locks, as well as a tubular steel chassis, complete with battery platform, bulkhead and "wheel extension castings". The kit price was £100, the car using either the Ford 8 or 10 as a donor.

A few other alternatives to sports bodies were available at various times, such as the station wagon body produced, in 1961, by Naco Plastics. The replacement body fitted the Ford 8 or 10 chassis, the end result resembling the later 100E Estates. A saloon body from Car Conversions also came onto the market around this time. This too, fitted straight onto the Ford chassis, the finished car looking something like a Hillman Imp.

A rather more exotic "saloon" was the Speedex Sirroco, this featuring a space-frame chassis and gull-wing doors. The mechanical parts, however, were not so exotic, coming mainly from the E93A! A number of 2+2s were offered by other manufacturers and although rear seating was sometimes very cramped, it was adequate for carrying children.

Another firm of note was Gilbern Cars, who were founded in 1959, their first offering being the Gilbern GT Mk I which was powered by either Coventry Climax or BMC engines. By the mid 1960s they were producing, on average, three complete cars a week which were sold mainly in kit form. By the middle of 1966 a new model was launched known as the Genie. This was available to take either Ford or BMC mechanical components. The Ford option allowed the use of a number of parts from the Ford Zodiac, this including the V6 engine and four-speed manual gearbox. This unit produced around 140 bhp which gave the Gilbern a top speed in the 120 mph bracket and a respectable 0-60 time of 9 seconds. The Genie, despite being a lightweight and

stylish performer, suffered from a less than perfect body finish, this manifesting itself as slight body rippling. This marred an otherwise very well designed little car. In 1969 a fuel injected version of the Genie was launched and this continued in production up to 1970 when it was replaced by the new Invader. Despite the different names, the cars were virtually identical. An estate version appeared in 1971. This period saw the sales beginning to decline in the face of competition from some of the sports saloons being produced by the larger manufacturers. April 1973 saw the final blow arrive in the shape of the new Value Added Tax. This brought the price of the Gilbern up to that of many mass-produced performance cars. This competition, together with new safety and pollution legislation finally finished off the company.

Despite the many company disappearances during this period, it was still a busy time. A survey taken in January 1961 indicated that there were somewhere between 20–25000 kit cars and Specials on British roads. If "conventional" cars that had been modified by changing the engine or altering the suspension by the use of such things as swing-axle independent set-ups were included, the figure rose to an astonishing 100,000!

There were plenty of options in 1961. Alexander Engineering were producing the Turner as a kit or "a tuned kit" and, Tornado were selling the Typhoon in

A 2-seater Typhoon, pictured in 1959/60. Notice the period pieces such as special wheel and hub-caps, complete with Tornado logos. (David Mallins)

"semi-kit" form, as well as the 105E-engined Tempest. The Marcos GT was available, constructed from laminated plywood and fibreglass, a concept that was to make Marcos famous. The kit sold for £798 with an untuned engine, but with a Wilen-tuned racing 105E unit, an extra £120 was added. The Walkletts were active with the Ginetta G4, and Elva were selling their kit at a price of £725.

Replacement "plastic" bodies were still available from a number of sources, despite the disappearance of a number of manufacturers. Newcomers and variants on the scene included Sabre, Vixen, Towend (with their 581), AKS, HG, and Auto Bodies. Falcon shells were still busy, their new project using a tubular space-frame, 105E engine, and a variation of their famous sports body. For racing, the

A rare surviving TWM, which once again, used the Ford 10 chassis and drive-train. In its day, the TWM "Deluxe" body shell cost £135 and the completed car, around £550. The car was one of the multitude of sports-bodied kits of the time, but was much more comprehensively equipped and well finished than many of its counterparts.

Terrier was still available in body/chassis form for £182, or set-up for Formula racing, for £527.

The activity carried over into 1962, with updated products from a number of manufacturers. Chapman's Lotus Super Seven appeared on the scene, with the option of a Cosworth-Ford Classic 1340 cc engine, with twin choke Weber carburettors and a four branch exhaust manifold. With 85 bhp on tap, the lightweight car would easily exceed 100 mph and give a 0–60 time of less than 7 seconds. Available in kit form, it cost £599. In the same year Falcon introduced the improved four-seater Bermuda and the Caribbean Mk IV.

Just how many kits, in total, were built is not known, largely because the market at the time was so fragmented, consisting of so many small firms. Clearly, some were sold in much greater profusion than others. What is a little sad is that so few of the early kit cars seem to have survived the passage of time, many of them disappearing from the roads during the 1960s.

There were some significant changes taking place in the kit car industry during the early part of the 1960s with many of the manufacturers of both body shells and complete cars disappearing from the scene. During this period, many of the cars, upon which the industry had formerly based their kits, began to disappear in increasing numbers. A combination of the new MOT tests and a general dissatisfaction with the by now, antiquated looking upright Fords, led to their rapid disappearance from the roads. The public no longer wanted such old fashioned cars, preferring the much more modern looking products such as the Mini, Morris Minor and of course the newer Fords. With the disappearance of the Ford 8 and 10 range went much of the kit car market.

Things were not totally static however and this period saw a number of attempts at the production of what appeared to be rather more sophisticated cars. Some manufacturers still attempted to use the Ford chassis. For instance, 1962 saw the arrival of EB (Staffs) Ltd's Debonair SI. This consisted of a "Gran Turismo" 2+2 body (costing £148) which fitted the 7' 6" chassis. EB would also supply a boxed chassis for £28 and for a further £11, an independent front suspension conversion. The car used 15 inch wheels which also helped to hide its origins. Apart from the body, the kit included winding windows, push button door locks, glass, doubled-skinned doors, bonnet and boot lid. The body came complete with dashboard, bulkhead, inner wheel arches, brackets and bumpers. A long list of

optional extras such as manifolds, seats, wheels and radiators was also available.

A number of estate car conversions also appeared on the scene, aimed at the family man. Conversion Car Bodies could supply an estate body for £156 designed to fit the Ford chassis. In this case the 17" wheels were retained.

Above and left: **The track/road-going 1961 Fairthorpe Electron Minor of Martin Collins, secretary of the Fairthorpe Sports Car Club. Some of the original cars used the 997 cc 105E Anglia engine and gearbox, however this particular car is powered by an Escort 1300 cc unit. The rear axle is also of the same origin, however the front suspension is Triumph derived, now fitted with Ford wheel adaptors.**

Although by this time, a number of sports body manufacturers had gone out of business, there were still a number of new models arriving on the scene. In 1962, for instance, Ginetta were offering the basic G3 body (for £59) or the G4. The latter retailed for £697 and could be powered by either the 105E Anglia or 1340 cc Classic engines. Ashley were supplying their new Sportiva 2+2 sports body, this fitting the Popular chassis.

As the 1960s drew on, new companies continued to arrive on the scene whilst others faded. One of the newcomers was Piper Cars who came into being in 1966, building racing cars and carrying out engine conversions. Their first cars were built soley for the race track and were capable of accepting engines from 1300 cc four-cylinders up to 3.5 litre V8s. A full space-frame chassis was used. 1967 saw the new Piper GT launched, of which a total of only six were built, some being powered by 1600 GT Cortina engines. A number of refinements and alterations were made, based on the experience gained with these cars and Ford engines adopted as the norm. In 1968 the kit cost £1355, with a special trim option also offered, putting it at the fairly expensive end of the market. Apart from the engine and gearbox, other Ford components included the rear axle which was a Corsair unit. Although production rates were still low, the future looked promising, however the company's fortunes began to change following the death of one of the partners in a road accident. This was followed by a protracted strike which stopped the supply of engines. Eventually the company was wound up in 1971 and although a number of efforts were made to keep it going, they ultimately ended in failure. Yet another company faded from the scene.

Interest began to revive during the early 1970s with a number of new kit car products appearing. These were intended to utilise the large number of rusty Anglias and Cortinas that were now around. It became possible, for example to buy a rusty, but mechanically sound 105E Anglia for as little as £20. This could be stripped, any necessary refurbishment carried out (often quite minimal) and the parts fitted into one of Geoff Jago's Jeep kits. This featured a box-section chassis with a set of fibreglass panels that could be easily assembled to form a Willys Jeep lookalike. The majority of the Anglia's rolling parts would bolt in with a minimum of alteration apart from shortening the propshaft. Even the wiring harness could be reused. It was not long before a variety of other kit cars began to appear, also aimed at this segment of the market.

As the years passed, the availability of cars in general increased and with it came a lowering of prices, especially for the rough, bottom end of the range car. It became clear that there was a substantial untapped market waiting for kits that could be based on these cars and that could be assembled without recourse to expensive or specialised tools and equipment. Some of the kits of this period still required a fair amount of fabrication as well as a reasonably sound knowledge of automotive engineering and it was apparent that there was a ready market for kit cars that could be assembled quickly and simply with a minimum of knowledge and tools. There was an often-quoted remark, from the late 1950s stating that it was possible to build a kit car "with 50 bobs worth of tools" and whereas this may have been true where this merely involved the rebodying of a Ford 8 chassis, it was sometimes not as straightforward with other types.

Gradually, kit manufacturers took note and simplified the assembly procedures. In addition, kits became more comprehensive, often including many of the small fittings and accessories that previously had to be obtained independently. Other problem areas, such as specially shortened propshafts or lengthened steering columns began to be supplied as part of the kit. The same became true of interior trim, instrumentation and seating. Gradually, kits became easier to build and more fully equipped.

Several interesting developments occurred during 1987, which only goes to prove that some kit cars refuse to lie down even when they are dead. One involved the long-defunct Falcon Shells. Anthony Taylor of Autotune, came upon an old, but still remarkably contemporary looking, original Falcon Shells body, designed to fit the Ford 10 chassis. The carefully restored body was adapted to a new chassis, intended to make use of, mainly Escort running-gear. The front suspension was built around Cortina uprights. The Escort rear axle was located by means of four trailing-arms and a Fiesta Panhard rod. The engine of the prototype car was not the standard, but a two-litre twin-cam unit. The little reborn Falcon is destined to emerge in two forms. The "Gemini" has been designed with the 750 MC racing in mind and will use a diminutive aero screen. The "Roadster", based along similar lines, is destined for road use and uses a full screen.

A second, equally interesting development concerns the long-departed Fairthorpe company. Fairthorpe originally produced a number of cars such as the Coventry Climax-powered Electron Sports, the BSA-powered Atom and, perhaps the best known, the Standard-powered Electron Minor. A number of the latter also used the 105E Anglia engine.

Two active members of the Fairthorpe Sports Car Club are the father and son team of Frank and Martin Collins. They have recently moved into the old Fairthorpe factory at Watford, bought up remaining stocks of spares and are currently rebuilding seven Fairthorpes. Several others have already been completed in race-ready condition, for competing in Post-Historic Racing activities. The new company is known as Motorville (Watford) Ltd and is now preparing to produce an Escort-based Fairthorpe kit, using the original body styles. The final body shells will be very similar in design to the originals, however, will benefit from the addition of slightly wider rear arches and a small front spoiler.

It is gratifying to see what, in retrospect, was an important stage in the development of the kit car industry, being given something of the recognition that has for so long been denied to it.

Stability of the industry

Ever since its first appearance, in line with motoring manufacturer in general, the kit car industry has been in a continual state of change. Since the 1950s, there have been numerous kit car manufacturers appearing on the scene that, just as quickly, have disappeared. Some have flourished, while others have vanished almost overnight, leaving customers with lost deposits or half-completed and near-worthless cars.

These problems were less in the early days of the replacement bodyshell/Ford rolling chassis concept. Once the body had been bought, the supplier was no longer strictly necessary for further specialised parts, Ford providing most of the necessary mechanical pieces. As kits progressed and became more sophisticated, more ancillaries, body and mechanical parts came to be produced "in house" by the kit manufacturer. This obviously avoided certain design compromises, but equally, it sometimes led to problems when a manufacturer went out of business, leaving car builders unable to complete or maintain their cars through a lack of such parts. Generally speaking, the smaller the company, the greater were the problems encountered.

The estate car body shell of Conversion Car Bodies used Ford mechanical components, even retaining the standard 17 inch wheels. The car made use of much of the trim from the Ford Popular, the finished result bearing some resemblance to both the later 100E estates and the Austin A40 Farina. This was one of the comparatively few options available to sports bodies.

One kit car that was destined to have a huge impact on the scene was the Jago Geep, originally intended to make use of the 105E Anglia mechanical parts. This was followed by later Escort-based versions. The Geep on the left, is a fairly early one, the styling differences between this and its later stablemate being clearly obvious.

With the passage of time and the gradual move away from the replacement body shell towards the complete body/chassis configuration, came further problems. During this period of change, comparatively few cars were available, many of the major manufacturers from the 1950s going out of business during the early part of the 1960s. Into this void stepped a number of "companies" offering cars that were often not fully developed or lacking in respect of styling, reliability and workmanship. As there was so little competition during this period, some managed to survive longer than they should have done. Eventually, most faded in the face of opposition from the more professionally organised companies that came to supersede them.

The 1970s saw a number of companies appear supplying what can only be described as fairly eccentric cars. These

were kits that sold largely on their novelty value, often being impractical for normal use. The "fun" aspect of motoring was their main claim to fame. Although their appeal was clearly limited, they did form a solid base of experience from which some of the more practical and sophisticated kit cars of later years were to spring.

Times were, once again, changing in the kit car industry and public demand altered substantially over the ensuing years. Gradually the emphasis shifted away from the fun cars to those that were more practical, more thoroughly equipped and designed, and easier to assemble. Many smaller companies fell by the wayside during this period, simply because they failed to appreciate the significance of the change in buying requirements, their orders dwindling until they were finally forced to cease trading. At the time, as each company disappeared, it seemed to be replaced just as quickly by yet another hopeful. Companies were set up, often consisting of no more than one or two optimistic individuals. Frequently they failed to appreciate just what was involved in designing, manufacturing and marketing an acceptable kit car in an increasingly sophisticated market. Thorough development of a kit car requires either a great deal of time or money, something that was often lacking. As a result, kits were marketed, that were poorly designed, underdeveloped or just plain ugly! These situations frequently found the customer having to complete the development and detailing of the car, things that should have been carried out by the manufacturer in the first place. Consequently, the kit car industry in general came to be regarded by many who were not directly involved in it, as a supplier of cars that were sorely lacking in many areas. It took the industry a long time to shake off this, often incorrect, image and to compete as a viable alternative to established motor manufacturers.

The current situation is much healthier, the industry now having a backbone of professional and well run suppliers and manufacturers such as Marcos, Ginetta, Eagle, Dutton, Jago, GP Developments and DJ Sports Cars. New kit cars still appear on the market from time to time and just as quickly disappear if their public appeal is lacking. Anyone wishing to break into the market should consider a few basic points if they hope to meet with success. Clearly, an appropriate

The Gemini, based on an updated Falcon Shells body, now designed to use mainly Escort running-gear. This re-creation was built by Anthony Taylor of Autotune, the car using Cortina front uprights, Escort rear axle, Fiesta Panhard rod and a Lotus twin-cam engine. The prototype car was built with kit car racing in mind.

compromise must be reached with regards to price and quality, these two tending to go hand in hand. The line obviously has to be drawn somewhere, however, blatantly cutting corners will guarantee the project's failure under the critical gaze of the buying public.

Ideally the car should be based on a single, easily obtainable donor. It is futile to produce a budget-priced car that requires the drive-train from a Ferrari or a Maserati. Although a single, mass-produced, donor car is the ideal source, it is sometimes necessary to use parts from a variety of vehicles. In this case, all of the donors should be equally easily available. This avoids the frustrating situation of the builder, with his car virtually complete, scouring the countryside in search of a 1947 Hupmobile steering column! The designer must take such things into consideration at an early stage and ensure that, say, a Cortina unit would do the job instead.

Apart from its quality, one of the most important and obvious points is that the vehicle must look "right" in its styling and proportions. Whereas peculiar-looking cars were acceptable in the industry's infancy, they are no longer. There have been a remarkable number of cars that have burst onto the scene in a blaze of publicity, that have lacked basic proportions or displayed the designer's obviously peculiar tastes. The hopeful manufacturer has quickly found that his idea of a good-looking car did not correspond with that of the general public. The result is inevitable, the company mysteriously vanishing.

The market today is in a fairly healthy state, the tardy image that the industry had for so long having finally been replaced. There are now a large number of both large and small firms turning out products that defy criticism. The large ones now have research and testing facilities and personnel and can thoroughly develop a new product before launching it onto the market. They are also financially stable enough to carry stocks of spare parts, an important point and one that may not be considered until the car is off the road awaiting a replacement. It is now not uncommon for manufacturers to have agencies in both the UK and overseas, as well as links with other specialist companies who are authorised to carry out the build up of their kits for an individual. With the increasing professionalism to be found within the industry, the future looks assured for steady, if not even dramatic, rise in the popularity of kit cars.

2
Why build a kit car?

It might be expected that cost would be a major factor in the decision to build a kit car, although this no longer seems to be such an important consideration. During the 1950s when the kit car industry was in its infancy, there was a whole generation of young men who wanted fast, nippy, little sports cars. Unfortunately, Britain was to some extent, still in its post-war austerity period. Low wages, coupled with a scarcity of such cars, meant that a whole segment of the market was not being catered for. Car manufacturers were not in the business to produce sports cars for youngsters who were in no position to pay for them! Clearly there was a place for a cheap sports-type car and it was this that led to the rash of little, fibreglass-bodied kits, designed to fit onto the early Ford chassis. Some of these were built with an eye to performance but many more were put together merely as cheap, daily transport for the man who wanted no frills and somewhat better performance than the run-of-the-mill saloon that had supplied the mechanical parts. For the modest price of an un-trimmed shell, plus the rolling parts from an old Ford, it was possible to build a "sports" car for less than £100.

For comparison, in 1958, the new Austin-Healey Sprite would set you back around £700. Secondhand cars of this type were not always cheap as might be expected. A 1938 MG T-type would still fetch in the region of £230 and a 1947 Y-type, around £355, both well out of fiscal reach of many. In comparison, a 1938 Ford Anglia in good condition could be bought for around £80 with rough examples being available for as little as £5–£10. With one of the latter, it became a very cost-effective exercise to build a "kit" car as a daily runabout. The problems of maintenance of the bodywork, trim and many of the fittings, immediately disappeared with the replacement of the rusty steel body with a fibreglass shell.

Unless professional help was enlisted during the build-up, it was possible to avoid the dreaded Purchase Tax unless, of course, a van chassis had been used. In this case, the builder could face problems, as the van had now legally become a car.

With the passing years, the increasing availability of cars in general, removed some of the incentive for building such a car, solely on the ground of cost alone, and later builders tended to be more influenced by several other factors.

The introduction of a compulsory vehicle testing during the 1960s, resulted in many thousands of cars becoming illegal. Many were as a result of excessively corroded bodywork. Since the 1950s, the Police had the powers to stop a vehicle for such defects as bald tyres, defective brakes and so on, however they tended to concentrate their efforts largely on commercial vehicles. Sections 64 and 65 of The Road Traffic Act 1960, gave powers for vehicle testing, and as a result,

Marcos.

the Motor Vehicle (Tests) Regulations 1960 came into being with a statutory requirement to test brakes, steering and lighting. This was initially for cars over ten years old, however this situation gradually changed, and by 1969, had been altered to three years old. By 1977, testing was much more rigorous, now including such things as exhaust and suspension. This testing effectively removed large numbers of old cars from the roads. Where a car had separate chassis, bodywork problems were of much less significance than for cars that were unit-constructed. For instance, 105E Anglias, and later, Mk I Escorts and Cortinas, apart from general body rust, were particularly prone to corrosion around the mounting points for the McPherson struts and in the region of the rear axle mounts. Sometimes repairs could be effected, but with older cars the costs were often greater than their value. Mechanically, the cars may have been in excellent

condition, nevertheless they were still unusable.

Fords in particular, have always been easy to repair. Compared with many other makes, spare parts for Fords have usually been easily obtainable and relatively inexpensive. They have always had a good reputation for reliability and when properly maintained, will outlast similar cars from other manufacturers. Like any steel-bodied car however, the British winters, complete with heavy doses of salt on the roads, ultimately began to take its toll. The result was that by the early 1970s, a large number of Anglias, Escorts and Cortinas, that were in good mechanical condition, but well-rusted in the bodywork, became available. As they were in no condition to pass the MOT test, the prices that they would fetch were often little more than their scrap value. There were several options open to the owner. He could spend a lot of money on expensive bodywork repairs, he could sell the car for scrap, or he could do what an increasing number of people began to, use it as the basis of a kit car.

It's quite peculiar how people became so attached to such apparently "ordinary" cars, and in many people's eyes, transferring all the mechanical parts into a new kit car body seemed a sensible way of prolonging the life of their favourite runabout. In reality, disposing of the rusty body and worn-out interior, probably removed 90% of the areas of problem maintenance.

Although there are a number of logical reasons, perhaps based on specific requirements or purely on economics, for building a kit car, equally, there are a number of others that cannot so easily be explained. This category includes building a car based on its visual appeal, the owner's desire to be different from the average mass-produced offerings, or just the sheer thrill of being able to say "I built it myself!", a claim that few people can make.

Where visual appeal is of paramount importance, the modern kit car builder is faced with a much wider choice than his contemporaries of earlier decades. The 1950s tended to concentrate on small sports cars, with a number of sports

Ford based kit cars
2
Why build
a kit car?

saloons and a few other options joining the ranks during the 1960s. The 1970s and 1980s however, have seen something of an explosion in the kit car industry, with re-creations of early racers and sports cars, off-road vehicles, saloons, estates, as well as copies of exotic upmarket cars appearing. The "looks" have been the deciding factor in most of these cases.

Obviously tastes differ, different types of vehicles appealing to different segments of the market. For example, in many people's eyes, the most stylish and desirable cars were the sports cars of the 1930s. It is clearly not a practical proposition to use such a car on a regular basis for daily driving. Often, such cars are both rare and expensive to acquire in the first place. In addition, mechanical and body spares are now virtually unobtainable. It may be practical to use such a car on a few fine weekends during the summer, but throughout the year, through the ravages of the winter, is not feasible. The obvious answer lies in a number of kit cars, currently in production, that have been designed in the styles and proportions of the 1930s, but make use of modern, easily obtainable running-gear. The Merlin range of cars, for instance, are good examples. Although they are not based directly on any particular 1930s sports car, their sweeping lines are somewhat reminiscent of a number of cars of this period (such as the 1932 NAG 212 Cabriolet). They have taken the lines and styles of the period and successfully married them to modern Ford components. Using substantial steel chassis, the Merlin cars will accept the drive-train and much of the running-gear from the ubiquitous Cortina. The results are both stylish and, with the modern mechanical parts, practical for daily use.

In addition, recent years have seen a huge increase in interest in various forms

JBA Javelin.

of off-road and Jeep-type vehicles. Often, these are sold on their looks alone, very little actual off-road use being made of them. The genuine article is clearly expensive, and a substantial market has built up for kits that emulate the rugged looks of these vehicles but utilise more conventional, two-wheel drive components. Eagle are something of an exception in this respect as they have recently introduced a four-wheel drive option for their RV. The trend-setting Jago Geep was the first of the breed to arrive on the scene, during the early 1970s. This used a steel box-section chassis with a set of fibreglass mouldings that, when assembled, produced a very acceptable Willys Jeep lookalike. These were originally intended to take the mechanical parts from the, then plentiful, 105E Anglia, however as supplies dried up, it was

redesigned to take those of the newer Escort range.

This serves to illustrate the flexibility of the kit car industry and its ability to swiftly respond and shift emphasis with changes in market requirements, something the conventional manufacturers are often unable to do.

It is an undisputed fact that manufacturing industry of any type likes uniformity. This means that they can tool-up and equip themselves to produce identical units in vast numbers, using as many automated stages as possible. At the end of the day, the main consideration is almost always the economics of production. The more of a particular item that can be produced, the cheaper it becomes. This clearly applies to motor car production as much as in any other sphere.

The greatest market for cars lies in the "average" saloon car bracket. Admittedly, there are many variations on the theme, some clearly more sophisticated than others, however the vast majority consist of multipurpose two or four-door family saloons and hatchbacks. Clearly this is the most popular segment of the market and motor manufacturers understandably target much of their production at this substantial and lucrative area. The

results are very obvious, the roads being full of the products of a few major manufacturers. There is no disputing that many of these are very good cars but they do have a certain uniformity about them, a legacy of their mass-produced heritage. They also often carry a high price tag.

The main aim of major motor manufacturers is obviously to operate under profitable conditions and one sure way *not* to achieve this, is to produce a diverse range of vehicles aimed at relatively small, specialised sections of the market. Such procedures do not warrant the huge tooling costs that are necessary, costs that can easily be amortised during the production of vast numbers of family saloons.

Over the years, the net result has been a great reduction in the number and variety of models and styles available to the public. For instance, one only has to compare the number of independent motor manufacturers that were operating during the 1930s, 40s and 50s, with those of the 1980s. A major part of manufacturing is now carried out by a handful of multinational companies.

Because of the specialised and comparatively small market segments occupied by such groups as sports car and "off-road" fraternities, major manu-

JBA Falcon.

facturers have gradually moved away from them. When produced in small numbers, such cars tend to be labour intensive and consequently expensive. The result has been that such vehicles have become highly desirable but as a result of their scarcity and cost, have been outside the fiscal reach of most people.

The kit car market now partially plugs this gap. By its very nature, of small companies producing specialised vehicles, it provides a wide and varied choice of products. For comparatively small outlays, it is now possible to assemble a whole host of practical and stylish vehicles, the cost of which would be prohibitive if produced by a major manufacturer. In short, the kit car manufacturers now provide a much wider range of choices. Almost inevitably, there will be something to appeal to most enthusiasts.

Of the few smaller concerns who still produce individually-built cars, such as Panther, the waiting list is often very lengthy, a situation that is not acceptable to many. A similarly-styled kit car can often be produced for considerably less outlay and in a much shorter time, the buyer replacing the manufacturer's labour with his own.

There is also a network of smaller companies producing, perhaps, more specialised cars, whose products are equally as good. They are sometimes more vulnerable to the whims of the public, however most seem to have successfully carved themselves a niche in the market place. Some have not been so lucky, for despite good products, the economic climate managed to get the better of them. For instance, Seraph Cars, of Temple Cloud near Bristol, produced beautifully built, sleek, stylish sports cars (such as the 115, 215 and the Bonito) but were eventually forced to cease trading.

Other companies such as Carlton Mouldings and Merlin also submerged late in 1986, only to resurface later in different forms.

Half-baked schemes still appear from time to time, but under the critical eye of both the motoring press as well as the public's, these seem to be getting scarcer and shorter-lived. There have been occasions in the past where unscrupulous individuals have advertised cars that didn't actually exist, collected various deposits and disappeared! In other cases, the customers' deposits were used for the development work. The size of the market is now such that it is able to support a number of national magazines solely devoted to the kit car industry, who because of their independent nature, are in a position to safeguard the public to a certain extent. A number of other national magazines, who generally cover more diverse aspects of motoring, regularly carry articles relating to kit cars, this extra interest also helping to keep the industry on its toes.

As a result of this, new kit car companies are going to find it increasingly difficult to break into the "volume" markets, as their products will come under close scrutiny and comparison with those of the well-established concerns, some of whom may have been in business for two to three decades. Despite this, there are still openings for the right vehicles at the right prices. Designers and manufacturers of new products will have to ensure that their cars are "right" from the start, if they hope to succeed. This currently appears to be the case and is a sign of a maturing kit car industry, surely a good omen for the future.

Registration

This, to many people, seems to be a more daunting task than the actual build-up of the car! There is no reason for this to be the case, as the procedures, once acquainted with, are fairly straightforward. There are a number of different procedures which can apply, this largely depending on how the car has been built.

The most expensive way encountered

is where the car has been entirely built using new components supplied from the kit manufacturer. In this case, the manufacturers are required to supply a Certificate of Newness covering all of the parts that were used in the car. This is followed by a Customs and Excise inspection and the payment of the dreaded Car Tax. When this route has been taken, the completed vehicle would normally be issued with a registration bearing the current year's prefix letter.

An alternative procedure can be applied where a single donor car has been used to supply all of the necessary parts for the kit. Clearly, certain parts may have needed replacement or rebuilding for reasons of safety or to comply with legal requirements, however, in this case the finished kit car can usually retain the original registration of the donor.

The most common method applied, is where the major mechanical parts have been taken from one (or possibly more) donor vehicles and transplanted into a new body/chassis assembly from a kit manufacturer. In this case, it is not possible to retain the registration from the donor vehicle(s). Up to August 1983, kit cars were either given a new registration or allowed to keep that of the donor car. If the authorities decided that sufficient old parts had been retained, it was possible to keep the donor's registration. If, on the other hand, the proportion of new parts was greater, then a new registration was given. Many completed cars fell somewhere between these two areas and as a result, the "Q" plate became applicable for kit cars. The majority of kit cars now receive a "Q" plate, one that can never be transferred to another vehicle.

The registration procedures can sometimes turn out to be a lengthy business, depending upon which area of the country is involved. The appropriate forms (currently V627 and V55) require submission well in advance of the vehicles planned completion date, this helping to avoid any undue delays in getting the car "legalised". The V627 form requires information (and receipts) relating to the origin of the major components, as well as any registration documents from the donor car(s). Following submission of the documents, a Police inspection is carried out on the completed car, the normal procedures for obtaining road fund licence, MOT certificate and insurance then being followed. In certain cases the insurance company may require a Motor Engineer's report before accepting the car.

Assuming that any money is left, it's now a simple case of filling the petrol tank and taking to the road! Remember, its worth taking the initial road trials fairly carefully, for despite an MOT certificate and/or an engineers report, its not unknown for various bits to come adrift in the first few miles!

The Society of Motor Manufacturers and Traders Ltd.

When looking through the magazines at all of the kit car advertisements, it is not unusual to come across the circular emblem of the Society of Motor Manufacturers and Traders (SMMT). Companies displaying this are members of The Specialist Car Manufacturers Group of the SMMT. The Society was set up for companies who manufacture self-build kits, and who are aware of their responsibilities to provide customers with kits of a high standard (for construction and assembly) and that perform as described in their advertisements. The Society has a code to combine sound engineering principles with high standards of business integrity (an important subject in today's uncertain financial climate) and customer care before, during and after purchase. The code sets out minimum standards for the design of a kit car and its assembly instructions. The Society then inspects products to make sure that the minimum standards are complied with and if this is so (after an inspection and a test drive) the company is issued with a certificate of conformity. Once this has been issued, the manufacturer is obliged to inform the inspector, and the SMMT, of any changes to the tested specification. It has to be remembered that the test certificate is normally issued after inspection of a single vehicle and

**Ford based kit cars
2
Why build
a kit car?**

that the SMMT relies on the company's integrity, that the car is representative.

The absence of Type Approval requirements for kit cars, initiated the formation of the Specialist Car Manufacturers Group. As far as engineering standards are concerned, the inspector appointed by the SMMT will inspect member companies' kit cars against some of the following recognised automotive quality standards. Door hinges and latches have to be of recognised automotive quality and if hinged doors are fitted, they have to be burst-proof. If a Q registration is granted, or the donor vehicle has dual-circuit brakes, then the kit itself must also have them. The chassis is examined, together with any attachments, to consider its crash worthiness. The fuel lines used, or recommended, should be of recognised automotive quality with mechanical connections. Any side screens, if they are not constructed from safety glass, have to be designed or constructed so as not to splinter on impact. Seat belt anchorages have to be designed and tested to Type Approval Standards and there should be no internal projections that could injure the occupants. Any modifications that are required to the chassis or any suspension or steering item, have to be notified to the inspector. A vehicle identification number is stamped onto a plate and placed discretely on the chassis or body. The wheel size and offset, together with tyre sizes, recommended speed and load ratings, have to be quoted. The wheel studs have to be of a one-piece construction and loose spacers of over 25 mm per wheel are not permitted. Mirrors and lighting are also important safety features. Lighting obviously has to be adequate, and mirrors, if supplied, have to be "E" or "e" marked and are subject to an assessment of satisfactory

field of view. One very important item and one not to skimp on, is brake pipes, which member manufacturers have to be able to offer as new items. To conform to the SMMT, the assembly instructions have to be comprehensive and to be made available to prospective customers. They should include a statement on the importance of using new brake pipes and advice on all the aspects involved on registration. As far as wiring is concerned, the instructions should include a complete wiring diagram, if the kit includes a harness, and very comprehensive instructions in every other case. Details of lighting regulations have to be supplied together with a detailed specification of all fixings. The recommended engine, wheels, tyres (load and speed rating), brakes etc must be specified. The manufacturer also has to be in the position to supply all of the parts necessary that cannot be obtained from the donor vehicle. As previously mentioned, after a certificate has been issued, the manufacturer has to notify the inspector of any changes. As a back-up to this, the Society's regulations include a clause that any members products can be checked at random to ensure that they still comply.

With the occurrence of firms going out of business, and then reappearing weeks later, the section of the code dealing with business integrity is perhaps just as important as some of its other features. The code states that no member should initiate another SMMT member's kit car without express permission, or adversely mention a fellow member in advertisements. The company's staff also have to be available, during normal working hours, for verbal instruction and advice to customers during the construction of their kit. The manufacturer is also obliged, according to the code, to offer a full engineers report on a customer's vehicle returned to the factory within the first 1000 miles.

Members have to comply with the Code of Practice on Action Concerning Vehicle Safety Defects, agreed between the SMMT and The Department of Transport. The Vehicle Manufacturer's Code, determined by the SMMT, The

Caterham Seven.

Jago Samuri.

Motor Agents Association, The Scottish Motor Trade Association and the Office of Fair Trading has to be adhered to. The manufacturers also have to give a twelve month warranty and keep in force product liability insurance, for a minimum of £1 million, for any one occurrence, with a reputable insurer, in respect of any legal responsibility for injury to their customers and any third parties.

In conclusion, the Code of Practice for Specialist Car Manufacturers, covers many important safety issues which should be a minimum for *all* kit cars. Not all manufacturers are members of this association but many companies who are not, often have Type Approval for such things as seat belt mountings, and in many cases, the kits are just as safe as member's products. At the end of the day, if prospective buyers require the safeguards set out by the SMMT they should check whether the manufacturer they intend to purchase from is a member, and that the kit car selected carries an SMMT certificate number.

3

Owners' clubs

Owners' clubs exist for many reasons, some of them being of a "practical" nature and others, perhaps more for social contact. Probably the majority fall into the former category.

Clearly, the most obvious reason for owners' clubs, is the mutual interest in a particular marque or type of vehicle. In addition, when build-up problems arise, as they inevitably do, it's remarkable how a chat with a better-informed colleague, can solve even the most apparently insurmountable problem. It is in this field that owners' clubs reign supreme. Kit cars, by their very nature, attract a wide range of enthusiasts of widely differing abilities. Despite their obvious enthusiasm, a number will lack some of the basic skills required, and discussion with more expert members usually results in a solution being found in one way or another. Assembly of the same type of kit car usually follows roughly the same pattern (hopefully reasonably well explained in the manufacturer's literature) hence any unforeseen snags will almost certainly have been encountered before. In most cases, a cure has already been found. It might be something as simple as a wiring problem, or perhaps something more substantial, such as insufficient wheel/suspension clearance, but whatever, another member of the club will almost certainly have already encountered it and found a way round it! A good example was recently to be found in the pages of the *Carltonian*, the magazine of the Carlton Owners Club. The issue contained a useful and comprehensive article on appropriate rear axle ratios as well as information regarding springs and shock absorbers for the Commando models, all invaluable stuff! All of this useful information was gained as a result of the efforts of the club's membership themselves.

Another useful function of many

Part of the impressive line-up of the Carlton Owners Club, here shown at a major kit car show at Newark. The club is steadily growing, and caters for both Carlton models, namely the Commando and the Carrera.

owners' clubs, is the production of their own workshop manuals. Clubs such as the Marcos OC, produce manuals that include test reports, service data and technical tips. Even in situations where no official manuals are published, a letter to the Technical Secretary or Advisor, will usually produce the required result.

As well as assisting with verbal and written advice, many of the clubs operate a spare parts section. For instance, the Fairthorpe Sports Car Club caters for some of the older kit cars, namely Fairthorpe, Rochdale, Turner, Ashley, Falcon and Tornado. Because of the various types of cars covered, and the obvious differences between them, there is an individual Marque Registrar for each type, who supplies technical advice and spare parts numbers, where possible. A limited number of spares are held by the Registrars, however, if they do not have the appropriate component, they can often assist in locating it. Most of the clubs catering for cars currently in production, also have Technical Secretaries. In the case of the Marlin club, they have no less than four!

Where spares are no longer available, it is not unknown for owners' clubs to go to the extent of arranging for the remanufacture of parts. For instance, in the case of the long-departed Turner marque, the club organised the production of wind-

The Spartan Owners Club is now over a decade old, and has a membership of over 300. The club caters for both the earlier Triumph-based cars as well as the multitude of newer Ford-based versions. The club has members throughout the UK and Europe.

Ford based kit cars

3
Owners' clubs

screens, an item not available for many years. Likewise, such items as Fairthorpe scripts and Turner badges have also been produced.

Even where a car is still in production, such as the Marcos, it is sometimes possible to obtain spare parts, quickly and at competitive prices, through the owners' club. Amongst its many functions, the Marcos club can supply such things as new front and rear road springs, rod-end bearings, suspension overhaul kits, wheel bearings and accessories, a fairly lengthy, but not untypical, list. In addition, a number of clubs have successfully negotiated preferential insurance rates, the resultant discounts being, in some cases, quite sizeable.

Virtually every club publishes regular newsletters or magazines, and although these vary enormously in quality, they can be an invaluable source of technical and related information. Apart from build-up tips, they often contain items of more general interest, reports on individual's cars and their construction, modifications, spares section and cars for sale. Often, as a result of this written contact between members, it is not unusual for local groups to be formed in different parts of the country, and many good friendships have been forged at these semi-social functions.

Most clubs turn out in force for the national shows, and it is at such events that the professional organisation of some of them becomes apparent. Neatly laid out and well-prepared vehicles, club assembly points, banners, and officials on hand, are often to be found, even with the smaller and more specialised clubs.

Events of a competitive nature are often arranged, such as standing quarter mile, sprints and driving tests. This gives member a chance to test their car's performance against one another, in conditions of safety. On occasions, the event may be against a "rival" club, the good-natured competition that follows, being tremendous fun for all concerned! On a less competitive front, clubs frequently organise various forms of car shows around the country. For instance, the ever-active Marcos Owners Club, organise an Annual International Rally, frequently with over 250 examples of the marque attending. As they say, "a genuine mind-blowing experience for all true Marcos enthusiasts". The Marlin Owners Club, as do many others, hosts an annual gathering, now in its fifth year, that includes their Annual General Meeting, followed by various social events. In some cases, where clubs are smaller and members more widely scattered, such as the 45–strong Karma Owners Club, meetings tend to be held at major kit car shows, these acting as a focal point for the membership.

The larger clubs, such as the Dutton Owners Club, not surprisingly, have members in most parts of the country. As a result of their great numbers, it is a practical proposition for them to hold local area meetings, their main venues being as far apart as Westerham, East Grinstead, Billericay, Bristol, as well as groups in the Southwest Midlands (operating in the Leicester/Nottingham area) and a group in the Southampton area. Likewise, the Spartan Owners Club, which is now in its tenth year, has over 300 members in its national club, plus a thriving branch in the Nottingham area.

Another of the large clubs is the Jago Owners Club, which was founded in 1984 and has been increasing its membership ever since. They publish a club magazine *Transmission*, bi-monthly, which includes build-up features, a letters page, events diary and a small ads section. They also market (as do most clubs) the usual range of sweatshirts, T-shirts, hats, "I love my Jago" stickers and so on. The membership spreads country-wide and there are regular monthly meetings at pubs, or at the National shows, held throughout the year, where they always put on a good display.

The club, in only its second year, won the "Best Club-Par excellence" at

Right: The Jago Owners Club was founded in 1984, covering all types of Jago's products. Membership is well into the hundreds, with large turnouts being seen at most major events. This particular olive-green Geep, was built in World War II-style by Paul Burr of Woldingham, Surrey, and is powered by a 1600 ohc engine. It is typical of the variety and general high standards to be found amongst the club's cars.

Right: An indication of the obviously close links that exist between the factory and the owners club. This 2 litre ohc powered Rico Shuttle was bought by the factory and formed part of the Club Dutton display at Mallory Park in 1987. Examples of all of the Dutton range made up the remainder of the impressive display. Although the club was originally founded by Tim Dutton himself, he has now taken a back seat, handing over the running of the club to its enthusiastic membership.

Newark, quite an achievement for such a young organisation. For builders and prospective buyers there is plenty of advice from the magazine, or from the individual members who have already built Jagos. The newsletter contains a list of all of the membership together with their kit type, engine choice and registration. This means it is possible to contact someone who has the same "odd" engine that you are contemplating and hopefully advice is just a phone call away. The club is now four years old and is going from strength to strength.

Membership is by no means limited to the UK, as overseas members are often encountered. For instance, the Spartan OC has members in Holland, Germany and Spain, the Dutton OC, in the USA and Holland, the Marlin OC, in Canada, Saudi Arabia, Sweden and Germany, and the Fairthorpe SCC, in the USA and Australia. The Marcos club is truly international in this respect, with members in fourteen countries, including Switzerland, Australia, the USA, and Denmark, as well as members throughout Europe. So the list goes on, the popularity of the clubs spreading far beyond the shores of the UK. For overseas members, this is the most sensible and, often, the only practical way to stay in touch with like-minded individuals.

In most cases, a good working relationship exists between the kit car manu-

facturer and the appropriate owners' club. This interaction, where it exists, can be both useful and beneficial to both parties. In the case of the Marlin OC, Paul Moorhouse, the founder of Marlin Engineering, is Honorary President. Even where a car has been long out of production, as is the case of the Tornado company, the company founder, Bill Woodhouse, remains actively involved, as the Vice-President of the Fairthorpe SCC, which encompasses the Tornado register. Frequently, when a customer takes delivery of his new project, he is furnished with details of the owners club, as a matter of course, by the manufacturer. This is not always the case, however, and several instances of the manufacturer and the club failing to see eye to eye have occurred, open hostility being the end result! Fortunately these seem to be rare occurrences, the majority being content to work hand in hand.

In a few cases, manufacturers have founded the clubs themselves. Such is the case with Club Dutton. Dutton owners now have the choice of two clubs and, in fact, many are members of both. Club Dutton was formed by Tim Dutton himself, and in its first year of operation attracted over 400 members! Clearly, many owners welcome the close links with the factory. The club magazine is now edited by one of its enthusiastic members, Tim having taken a back seat. The members' enthusiasm clearly shines through in the club magazine, this being packed with interesting and useful feedback from the membership. Club Dutton are probably unique in as much as the factory will either take members cars into their showrooms for resale, or hold details on computer for prospective buyers.

In conclusion, once the project car reaches home, one of the best moves that the new owner can make, is to join the appropriate owners' club. Not only will he or she make a lot of new friends, they will also be in direct contact with people who have gone through the same learning experience that they are also about to embark on. People, who for the most part, will be more than happy to steer them in the right direction.

One of the smaller, but nonetheless, very active clubs, is the Merlin Owners Club, here shown at a major kit car show. The club usually has a number of their high quality cars on display at most events. This well made example is the 2 litre powered car of Mark Dean.

The JBA Owners Club is a relative newcomer, having been formed in February 1987. The members is already around the 100 mark, the majority of the club's cars consisting of Falcons plus a lesser number of Javelins. The standard of workmanship of the club's vehicles is always very high.

4

Traditionally styled sports cars

It is perhaps in the field of traditionally styled sports cars, that the kit buyer currently has the widest choice. The 1930s and early 1940s saw the appearance of a number of vehicles that, in later years, were to become regarded as the archetypal British sports car. Although the following decades saw new ideas, new styles and a multitude of mechanical refinements, these early, and often quite primitive, performance cars, were the only ones that really mattered. For many years, these were the only *real* cars as far as "wind-in-the-hair" performance buffs were concerned.

This period saw classic sports cars produced by most of the major manufacturers as well as many of the smaller ones.

For those with the money, the choice seemed almost limitless. The opening years of the decade saw sporting classics produced from such manufacturers as Bentley, Invicta, Lagonda, MG, Humber, Daimler, SS and Riley. These were later joined by open-top sports and touring cars from the likes of Frazer-Nash, Lea Francis, Wolsely, AC, Alvis, Railton, Singer and Talbot. Other famous marques of the era included Hillman, Alta, Morgan, British Salmson and later, Allard.

The variety to emerge during this formative period was endless. At one extreme were the eight-litre sports/tourers from Bentley and the huge Daimler Double Six (of 7136 cc) and at the other end, such diminutive cars as the

1931 Aston Martin 1.5 litre Sports, the 1089 cc Riley Brooklands and the little MG Magna. A whole host of others fell somewhere in between these two extremes.

The majority had a number of styling and design features that were common to one another. For instance, they were either devoid of a roof or only had fairly rudimentary weather protection. The wings were generally of the sweeping, graceful variety, very characteristic of the time, or in some cases, cycle wings. The front end almost invariably consisted of a vertical, or near vertical, radiator grille, coupled with a comparatively long bonnet. The latter was usually filled with louvres and the headlights generally quite large and freestanding.

These styling characteristics were to have a great influence on the looks of the sports cars that were to follow in later years, and even in the face of new ideas and influences, never fell entirely from favour. There has always been a sizeable band of motorists to whom the looks of a pre-war sports car came second to none, and even today, such cars are still regarded with a certain reverence. A number of cars still in production look as if they had stepped straight out of the pages of the history books. Morgan, for instance, still sell pre-war styled cars as fast as they can produce them. A look at the incredibly long waiting list for such a car adds further proof to the fact that they have never really gone out of fashion.

In later years, kit car manufacturers were able to "attack" this section of the market with relative ease. Although such cars had always been desirable, they were also difficult and expensive to obtain. Kit designers and manufacturers were now able to work along similar lines to the originals and produce cars at a fraction of the price of the real thing.

This type of car was comparatively easy to make, from a manufacturing point of view. The bodywork was often not extensive and of a fairly simple design. In addition, it was made from a number of separate panels, unlike most modern cars, this allowing the use of a number of dissimilar materials for different parts. A choice could be made between, for instance, wood, aluminium, steel or fibreglass, often dependent on economy. As a result, kit car bodies could be made in separate parts, often in keeping with original practice.

Perhaps of equal importance, when it comes to marketing, was the fact that these cars evoke such a sense of nostalgia for the simple, carefree "good old days", a feeling that many wanted to recapture. It was only with the advent of kit-based replicas that this dream could become something of a reality for most.

Not surprisingly the market blossomed, with many traditionally-styled kit cars

appearing. Unfortunately for some, "good" styling and correct proportions were always to be elusive things, and amongst the well designed and nicely proportioned cars were the inevitable collection that clearly showed the designer/manufacturer's lack of flair or experience. Inevitably, in most cases, sales were poor or non-existent and the projects rapidly faded.

Designers have adopted several approaches when it comes to designing 1930s-styled kit cars. Firstly there is the direct copy. In this case, reproduction bodywork is produced, accurate at least, in most major aspects. These are sometimes the most difficult and expensive cars to produce and assemble, often because of the difficulty of obtaining appropriate period accessories, wheels and tyres. When taken to extremes, this approach tends to defeat the object of building a kit car, as the problems of maintenance and running an "old" car are still to some extent present.

The approach more often encountered was a sensible compromise of adopting the main styling features of the period, such as long bonnets, open tops, vertical grilles and sweeping wings, and modifying them so that they will comfortably clothe a reproduction chassis, modern drive-train and suspension. The overall

The Wyvern of JC Composites was one of the many kit cars, initially offered with non-Ford power, that was redesigned to make use of the many advantages offered by the range of Ford engines. The Wyvern was originally designed to take much of its running-gear from the 1300 cc Vauxhall Viva, with the later option of the Ford ohv units.

Initially using the mechanical parts from either the Vauxhall Viva or HC or Magnum, the Imperial Specialist Vehicles Jackal was later redesigned to accept much of the running-gear from the Ford Cortina. The car will take any of the range of ohv and ohc engines, these making a powerful and cost effective alternative to the Vauxhall parts.

illusion is thus maintained but the car is driveable, reliable, easily maintained and considerably cheaper than the original. An example of "compromise" styling is where 1930s cars had, for instance, 18, 19, 20 or 21 inch diameter wheels. Clearly these sizes are no longer easily obtainable, so a designer must therefore take this into account and design his wings, running-boards and wheel openings so that they will successfully accommodate for instance, 15 or 16 inch wheels. The rest of the car must also remain in proportion. Many such re-stylings and modifications to the design can ultimately lead to a kit car that only vaguely resembles the original that inspired it, nevertheless, it is often these very re-stylings that give the car its own individual appeal and characteristics. These are important factors when it comes to selling into an already heavily populated market place.

Another way of tackling the design of such a car is to take various visual aspects from a number of different cars and combine them in a new way. Marlin's Berlinetta is perhaps a good example of this. Although the car's design was not based on any one particular example, it took the shapes, lines and styling features common to many cars of the period and successfully drew them together into a vehicle that has the looks and aura of the 1930s era, but is undeniably a car of the 1980s. Another good example was the Gentry (Ford-based in its later years), a popular kit which unfortunately is no longer manufactured.

In some cases, a designer has focused his attention on one particular feature and has used this as the focal point for his design. One such example is GP's Madison Roadster, conceived and designed by Neville Trickett. Although not based on any one car, the grille shell and bonnet area are undoubtedly based on

**Ford based kit cars
4
Traditionally
styled sports cars**

Spartan

One of the first companies to seriously capitalise on this part of the market was Spartan. Founded by James Alistair McIntyre, they were one of the first companies to offer a traditional 1930s styled sports car in kit form, being introduced in 1973. McIntyre had worked on and rebuilt virtually every type of production sports car available and drawing on his great experience, decided to design and build his own. Since then, the kit has undergone many alterations and refinements in order to further improve its design as well as aiming to make construction easier. The Spartan originally came into being as a result of a great deal of "in house" motor body repair and manufacturing expertise and was designed to provide an alternative to the modern sports cars available at the time.

The Spartan is a 2+2, the rear seating however, is really only adequate for carrying children or extra luggage, although the front seat area is quite comfortable.

The backbone for the Spartan is a steel chassis which will accept the full front and

the mid 1930s Packard 120 range. Even the small styling lines along the bonnet tops and sides are clearly recognisable. In this case, the original deep Packard grille has been reduced in height by about 50% and this, along with the bonnet tops and sides and headlight pods have been used as the focal point for a stylish, 1930s style boat-tail roadster, that Packard themselves would have been justifiably proud of.

Another interesting car of this type is the Vincent Brooklands. Although not an exact copy, it has the same grille, bonnet and front end treatment of the little 1931 Riley Brooklands. Once again, this has been used to great effect as the basis for a very neat and practical two-seater sports car. In a similar vein, the Beribo Replica Automobiles "P" type is styled in the fashion of its MG namesake.

The stylish Beribo Replica Automobiles (BRA) P-type was named after its 1930s MG namesake, and was intended to make use of the MGB as its main donor car. This supplied engine, gearbox and much of the suspension system. A further option that came hot on its heels, was the use of any of the 4–cylinder Ford ohv and ohc engines. The completed car is very classy!

Above and below: **Spartan were one of the first companies to produce an economically priced traditionally-styled sports car. Early examples were Triumph-based and although this option is still available, the majority of new cars are now Ford-based. The Mk III, IV and V Cortina supplies the drive-train and suspension systems, the majority fitting without modification. The easy to build Spartan features a combination of aluminium and fibreglass body panels and has been systematically refined over the years. Notice the well fitting hood that does not detract from the car's overall appearance.**

rear suspension systems from a Cortina. The completed car weighs in at a relatively nimble 18 cwt, considerably less than the standard Cortina. As a result of the weight reduction and the lower centre of gravity, the ride and handling of the car are greatly improved over the donor. The Spartan can be based on the mechanical components from any of the Mk III, IV or Cortina 80 (Mk V) range and can be powered by any of the usual Ford engines up to the 2.3 litre V6. The Cortina normally supplies engine, gearbox, suspension and steering, as well as the multitude of ancillary and small parts such as wiring harness, exhaust system, linkages and hoses.

As well as the chassis, the Spartan kit

Ford based kit cars
&
**Traditionally
styled sports cars**

includes a body package consisting of a combination of aluminium and fibreglass panels. Also included are a cast aluminium windscreen surround, that comes ready polished and fitted with safety glass, an aluminium radiator grille and a roll-over bar. The optional "weather protection pack" includes aluminium side-screens and a black hood that is both functional and stylish.

The Spartan is one of the easier kit cars to assemble, requiring little fabrication and no specialised equipment such as welding facilities. The very comprehensive kit is supplied with virtually all of the necessary fasteners, fittings and accessories and these, when combined with the Cortina's mechanical components, add up to a very successful package. A great deal of thought has clearly been put into the kit, which now includes a special lower steering column (which avoids the need to weld in an extension piece), patterned aluminium grille mesh, wing piping, a wooden dashboard and a set of door-capping strips.

The company claim that as a result of their policy of continually improving the car, it "cannot be made better". Their thoroughness has paid off and the success of their strategy can clearly be seen from the fact that sales of the car have now passed the 3000 mark.

JBA Falcon Plus 2

A newer, but equally stylish arrival on the scene in recent years has been the Falcon Plus 2, produced by JBA Engineering of Standish, near Wigan. JBA are members of The Specialist Car Manufacturers Group (of the SMMT) this being an indication of their professionalism.

As with the Spartan, the Falcon's body is made up of a combination of aluminium and fibreglass panels, the car being the culmination of several years development on the original two-seater Falcon.

A substantial steel chassis, which combines both backbone and ladder elements in it, is used to carry the project. Further strength is supplied by a steel bulkhead and a deep tunnel section as well as the use of steel body framing. The chassis accepts the main mechanical components from the Mk III or IV Cortina range, this obviously giving a choice of engines, gearboxes and rear axles. The Cortina also supplies the suspension, braking and steering systems, all of which will bolt in with only a few alterations. Modifications are required to the steering shaft, pedal assembly and propshaft. In addition, the front springs are slightly shortened in order to stiffen them up.

The kit can be supplied in two stages. Stage One consists of the well-engineered chassis, a pair of door aperture mouldings, the scuttle panel, rear floor, rear body moulding and fastener pack. In addition, a pair of doors, complete with hinges and anti-burst locks, and a steering shaft extension are

The stylish and well engineered JBA Falcon, a car that is universally admired. The running-gear, suspension and braking systems are all pirated from the Mk III/IV Cortina range. This 2 litre powered car sports the new hard top, introduced in 1987. This is interchangeable with the conventional soft top.

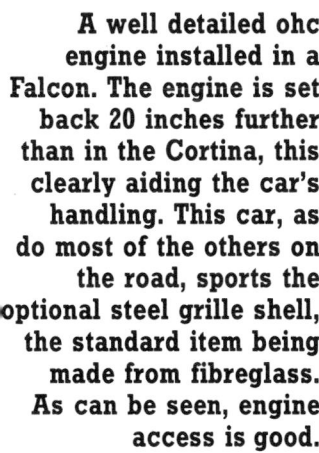

A well detailed ohc engine installed in a Falcon. The engine is set back 20 inches further than in the Cortina, this clearly aiding the car's handling. This car, as do most of the others on the road, sports the optional steel grille shell, the standard item being made from fibreglass. As can be seen, engine access is good.

Looking good, with or without the top on, the Falcon oozes workmanship and quality. JBA are members of the SMMT Specialist Car Group, and the Falcon has been fully tested to TUV standards. The car uses a combination of aluminium and fibreglass panels to make up its stylish body.

supplied. The Stage Two kit supplies the front and rear wings, boot lid, boot, aluminium bonnet, remaining body panels and windscreen. A fibreglass radiator shell is also included although a steel version is available as an option. Obviously Stage One and Two kits can be purchased together. Other options listed by JBA include a Double Duck or Mohair

hood, sliding window kits and bumpers.

The performance of the car depends upon the drive-train selected. With the great reduction in body weight (the Falcon weighs about 18 cwt), lower centre of gravity and engine set 20 inches further back than in the Cortina, the handling and road holding are very good. The car is capable of showing a clean pair of heels to many so-called sports cars.

The finish of the whole car is excellent, good design and workmanship oozing from every nut and bolt. JBA's attention to detail has resulted in a very comprehensively equipped and well styled addition to the ranks of the traditionally-styled sports cars. Although it is one of the more expensive kits of this type, general opinion is that it undoubtedly provides good value for money. Its high standard of workmanship, excellently styled and proportioned bodywork, coupled with is practicality, make it a very desirable sports car and one which is finding favour with a growing band of enthusiasts. JBA actively encourage prospective buyers to visit their premises and test drive a Falcon, a pleasure not to be missed. An addition (in 1987) was a new hard top which could be permanently fitted, or interchangeable with the normal soft top. This hard top, with a black gel-coat finish is a definite advantage for all that winter driving.

Vincent Brooklands Roadster

The first seeds from which the Vincent Roadster was to grow were sown in 1982, when Martin and Robin Vincent started manufacture of their first Triumph Spitfire-based kit car. This was fairly successful, however it was decided that the next one should appeal to a greater section of the populous. Following a period of development, this emerged as the Brooklands, largely based on cheap and easily available Ford components.

Although the car is not a direct copy, many of its styling elements are derived from the Riley models of the era, in particular, the Brooklands which provided the inspiration for the project.

The chassis is of fairly simple ladder design, with additional cross-bracing, that accepts most of the mechanical components from either the Mk I or MK II Escort range. The one main assembly that is not of Ford origin is the complete front suspension, steering and brakes that come from the Triumph Herald/Vitesse/Spitfire range. The chassis is MIG welded and comes fully drilled for quick and easy assembly. A steel framework extends from the chassis up into the scuttle area, this providing support for both the windscreen and the steering column.

The main body structure consists of a single fibreglass unit of excellent quality, the same material being used for the cycle wings, front and rear valance and radiator grille shell. The beautifully louvered bonnet and side panels are made from aluminium, this combination of materials also being encountered in a number of other kit cars.

The drive-train can consist of either the

1300 or 1600 cc cross-flow engine and gearbox (or pre cross-flow units) these providing more than adequate performance for the lightweight car. The larger 2.0 litre ohc engine can also be fitted but a number of modifications are required. The Escort rear axle is used, although this does require certain alterations. The standard leaf springs and shock absorbers are removed and axle conversion brackets fitted. These allow the use of coil-over units, and are bolted or welded to the original spring pads. All of the necessary parts are included in the kit. Once complete, the rear suspension consists of a coil sprung, five-link system with a Panhard rod.

The Escort also supplies numerous smaller parts such as pedal box, steering column, radiator, petrol tank, wiring and handbrake mechanism. The kit includes all of the other necessary parts such as windscreen, brackets, dash panel and fasteners.

Building the Brooklands is a speedy and painless operation despite the rear axle modifications, the result being an agile and rapid little road car with room

An early version of the Vincent Brooklands, now marketed by Swindon Sports Cars. The car's styling is based on that of the 1930s Riley of the same name, this providing the inspiration for the project. The front suspension is Triumph-based, the Escort supplying engine, gearbox, rear axle, steering column, radiator and many other parts. The quality of both the body and chassis are excellent.

A rare surviving Cheetah, produced by Watford Sports Cars. The fibreglass body, that came complete with floor, bulkhead, doors, and wheel arches, was designed to use Ford 8/10 mechanical parts. The chassis was a specially made tubular steel unit that came complete. The Company claimed that the car could be completely finished for around £300.

A 1962 Tornado Talisman GT, as discovered by its new owner Dudley Guest after a decade in storage. The only major problem encountered after its storage was a very thick layer of dust! (D. Malins)

A typically impressive line up of the Jago Owners Club, shown here at a major car event. The club now boasts a membership well into the hundreds and was first formed in 1984.

Main inset:
The JC Composites Wyvern was originally designed to make use of the main mechanical parts of the Vauxhall Viva. Although it retained the Vauxhall suspension system, Ford engine/gearbox options were later offered. Sadly, the Wyvern is no longer available.

Opposite page left inset:
The Spartan has been around in various forms for many years. Initially, the car used Triumph running-gear although a later redesign allowed the use of the main mechanical assemblies from the Cortina range. Visually, there is little difference between the two versions, the majority of cars built during recent years opting for the Ford route.

Opposite page middle inset:
The stylish Vincent MPH is virtually identical, with the exception of the full wings, to its stablemate, the Brooklands. Both cars use mainly Ford Escort mechanical parts, with the exception of the Triumph-based front suspension. The cross-flow Ford engines form a popular and cost effective choice.

Opposite page right inset:
The superbly built Marlin Berlinetta of Don Collins of Gloucester. The immaculate car runs a 2.8 litre V6, complete with autobox, this giving the car a top speed somewhere in excess of 115 mph. The car makes use of stainless steel for a number of parts and features numerous owner-made parts. The detailing throughout the car is exceptional.

Opposite bottom inset:
This highly unusual Merlin TF looks as if it belongs on the streets of California. The US-styled car features white-wall tyres and such touches as chromed bonnet portholes. In addition, it has a stylish hard top, complete with dummy irons. Once again, it serves to illustrate how individual modifications and refinements can completely alter a car's character.

One of the first, and still one of the best, Berlinettas to be built in the UK. This particular car was skilfully assembled by Derek Grimes, using a 1600 Cortina as the donor car. The paint scheme is particularly eye-catching, featuring a two-tone pearlescent finish. Remarkably, the immaculate car is in constant use throughout the year and has now covered well over 100,000 miles.

This well built two-tone Merlin TF runs on steel spoke wheels, suitably modified by the addition of chrome wire baskets. It's difficult to believe that such a stylish 1930s inspired 2+2 houses the mechanical parts from the everyday Cortina.

Neville Trickett was also responsible for the design of the Madison Coupe, a follow up to the successful Roadster. Mechanically, the cars are identical, the Coupe differing in its rear end styling treatment. Surprisingly, there is a fair amount of room in the Coupe's apparently small interior.

The 1950s GP-styled Monaco, based its design on the track cars of the period. The one piece fibreglass body-shell increases its authenticity by the use of such styling features as dummy rivet heads moulded into the fibreglass. With even a Ford 2 litre ohc in place, the ultra-lightweight car has shattering performance.

The beautiful red GP Madison Roadster of David Schofield, from Barnsley. He used a Mk III Cortina as the donor car, this supplying the running-gear and suspension etc. The 2 litre ohc power-plant endows the lightweight car with a top speed well in excess of 115 mph. Remarkably, the car is regularly used throughout the year. The Cortina mechanical parts fit with only few alterations, the build-up being straightforward and trouble free. The Roadster's design came from the pen of Neville Trickett.

Nick Durow based the design of his remarkable cars on the looks and styles of the expensive, upmarket American cars of the 1930s. It is one of the few kits to make use of the main body shell from another car. In this case, a Midget shell (suitably modified) is used as the basis for the car's central body section and supplies doors and a number of other components. This is fitted to an immensely long box-section steel chassis that accepts the running-gear from the Ford Granada. This supplies both the front and rear suspension as well as the complete drive-train. Durow offers his cars in various forms, such as two or four-door, in kit form, or as fully completed vehicles. The elegant cars make use of a great deal of stainless steel in their construction.

The Gazelle of Roger Kernan, was unusually, imported directly from the USA, where it was available in either VW Beetle or Ford Pinto-based forms. This particular car was converted to make use of much of the running-gear, from the Cortina, an option that was available, when the car was offered by several manufacturers in the UK. The Mercedes SSK lookalike is currently out of production.

The remarkable Beauford makes use of a Mini shell for the central body section and passenger compartment. This is disguised by the use of additional panels and a rear trunk. The body mounts on a steel box-section chassis which makes use of much of the running-gear from the Cortina range. Virtually any of the Ford range of engines can be accommodated, although at least a 2 litre ohc engine is really necessary for adequate performance. The cars are available, built to any stage of completion.

The immaculate black Karma of Trevor Semark. This is one of the few to use the front-mounted Ford engine layout. As a result of a number of problems, the manufacturers, RW kit cars, withdrew this option, concentrating on either VW or mid-mounted Ford layouts. This car is powered by a well set back Ford 1600 ohv engine.

One of the first Countach replicas to appear, was the Prova Designs Countach. The impressive chassis came as a result of the racing experience of Kit Deal, a name often associated with automotive competition. This consists of a 16 gauge steel tube space-frame, that comes equipped with special wishbones, rear hub carriers and Spax coil-over units. A Ford V6 or V8 unit can be mid-mounted, driving through a Renault 30 transaxle, courtesy of an adaptor plate. The kit is available in various degrees of completion.

The remarkably authentic E-Type lookalike, the Wildcat, made by JPR Cars. Styled on the lines of the Mk I E-Type, only minor alterations have been made to the styling to allow use of the running-gear from either the Mk III or IV Cortina or the Taunus. The kit comes supplied as a fully assembled body/chassis unit, complete with bonnet, boot lid, doors and various pieces of hardware installed.

A fine example of a fairly early DAX Cobra, built by garage owner Malcolm Griffith of Cheltenham. The power-plant is a 302 ci Ford V8 from an Australian Fairmont. The autobox was changed for a four-speed manual unit, the majority of the suspension system being composed of Jaguar and DAX parts. The completed car manages to look very authentic as a result of the use of the various accessories and replica pieces supplied by DJS. The fibreglass body shell was painted Ford Royal Blue, and the interior trimmed in Conolly hide. The wheels are Solar 10s fitted with imitation knock-offs. Despite the fact that the car was professionally built, the construction period turned out to be quite lengthy, however the end result was clearly worth the effort.

The V8 powered DAX Tojeiro of Street Machine Magazine. Having decided that the Tojeiro was one of the best Cobra kits available, they catalogued the assembly over a number of months. Although this particular example is not Ford powered, it is visually identical to those using the Ford option. The immaculate interior, seats and instruments were supplied by Speedograph and Colin Biott applied the Talbot Rouge Valalunga red paint. The immaculately prepared car is a credit to the magazine. (Street Machine Magazine)

At first glance, this remarkable car is often mistaken for an early Porsche 911. It is, in fact, the much modified Rochdale Olympic of Barney Concannon. He has systematically modified virtually every part and panel of the car, the final result now looking more like a Porsche than a Rochdale. The 1977 car now features a 1600 GT Ford engine, Corsair rear axle and Triumph Vitesse-based front suspension. The car was re-worked over a four year period.

The red GT40 lookalike of Peter Harding also uses a combination of a GTD chassis with a KVA body shell. The workmanship, as with all of the GT40s, is of the highest standard.

Rob Side's GT40 is based on an early KVA kit. The immaculate and beautifully detailed car is powered by a potent, tuned 3.1 RS V6 unit. Virtually all of the GT40s, both completed and under construction, belong to members of the GT40 Replicas Club.

The Vincent MPH is, in effect, a fully-winged version of the Brooklands, the cars using identical chassis and drive-train arrangements. Both can be powered by any of the pre-X flow, X flow or ohc engines. The most popular choice currently seems to be the 1600cc X flow.

for two adults and their luggage. The road holding and handling are generally renowned as being "excellent" and overall opinion is that the kit provides good value for money.

The interesting little car is now produced by Swindon Sports Cars (Martin Vincent now needing more time to concentrate on his position as editor of *Which Kit* magazine) who also market a mechanically similar, full winged version of the Brooklands known as The MPH. This is based on the 1934 Riley MPH which was a very expensive sports car of its time (only 15 were produced). The kit is based on Mk I Escort parts with a 1.6/ 2.0 litre ohc Cortina/Capri/RS2000 engine options. Most buyers opt for the 1.6 although there are a number of cars which are Lotus twin-cam and Rover V8 powered.

Beauford

Perhaps one of the most interesting 1930s styled newcomers of recent years has been the Beauford. It is an attempt by designer Gorden Geskell to recreate the classic sweeping lines of the large luxury cars of the era, but at an affordable price.

Geskell has a long pedigree working on and restoring such cars such as Rolls-Royces and Bentleys and with this background he set about laying plans for this innovative car. Perhaps the most unusual feature is the use of a Mini body shell as the centre section of the project. Although this concept is not common, at least one other manufacturer has recently adopted a similar approach. The use of the Mini shell (any post 1968 saloon) makes sense for a number of reasons. It supplies many of the modern day comforts that are sometimes lacking in kit cars, such as lockable doors, draught-free, wind-up windows and a fully equipped and trimmed interior.

Supporting the project is a rectangular-section steel chassis of 4 x 2 x ⅛ inch dimensions. The modified Mini shell is bolted amidships to the chassis and cunningly disguised by the addition of the various other panels, both back and front. These include the long bonnet, sweeping wings, sun visor, wide running boards and rear trunk, so typical of the 1930s.

The remainder of the running gear comes from the Mk III or Mk IV Cortina range. This supplies engine, gearbox, propshaft, handbrake, exhaust system, radiator and heater, as well as the complete front and rear suspensions. The chassis comes jig-built and MIG welded and is supplied primed and pre-drilled, ready to take the Mini and Cortina components. The performance of the 100 kg car clearly depends upon the engine chosen which can be anything from the 1300 cc up to the 2.3 litre V6. Beauford recommend the 2.0 litre ohc engine as the best bet. The majority of the mechanical components can be bolted in without modification, however the Mini steering column requires an extension piece to mate with the Cortina rack. The car utilises virtually all of the mechanical parts of the Cortina with the exception of the 13 inch wheels which are replaced with 15 inch units, more in proportion with the rest of the car.

It is impossible not to notice the Beauford when on the move, complete with its Duesenberg-styled exhaust system and side-mounted spare wheel retained by stainless bands. A few have

Above: **The amazing Beauford cunningly uses a Mini bodyshell for its passenger compartment. This unusual approach means that a fully-trimmed and well appointed interior is economically provided. The box-section steel chassis accepts much of the running-gear from the Mk III and IV Cortina, this also supplying such diverse items as the propshaft, radiator and heater.**

Right: **This beautifully finished example is resplendent in 1930s styled two-tone, white-wall tyres, and twin side-mounted spares, as well as many period accessories. This car is one of the manufacturer's demonstrators. The cars cause a great deal of interest wherever they go!**

even found their way to Spain where they have been used as wedding cars.

Opinion is divided on its styling, people either love it or hate it, but whatever, it is

Right: This V6 powered version has the optional Duesenberg-styled side exhaust system. Although non-functional, it looks superb and helps to enhance the 1930s illusion. Notice the chequered alloy bulkhead and genuine vintage headlights used on this example.

Far Right: The Beauford's impressive frontal styling, showing the side-mounted spare wheels, louvers and twin-bar bumpers.

certainly an interesting car and not one to be ignored!

The Malvern 2+2

The Malvern 2+2 is descended from a Triumph-based kit car developed by John Cowperthwaite. He originally designed and produced a two-seater sports car known simply as the Roadster and based on the, then plentiful, Triumph Herald range. It utilised the complete Triumph chassis and running gear, fitting of the new body being a quick and simple operation. As sound supplies became scarcer, it became clear that a replace-

ment chassis would prove popular and as a result, a chassis of 80 x 40 x 3 mm steel box-section was produced. The Triumph mechanical parts fitted without modification.

Triumph components have some limitations and it became obvious that a larger market could be reached if the kit was redesigned to accept the ubiquitous Ford parts. The fact that a replacement chassis was now available made this alternative much easier and the Ford-based Malvern was the result.

The new kit made use of the Mk I and II Escort range and the wisdom of offering this Ford-based option was clearly re-

The Mini body shell is clearly visible, although well disguised by the use of additional panels and rear trunk. The Beauford can be powered by any of the Ford range of engines, up to the V6 units. The Cortina front and rear suspension systems are used almost in their entirety although the 13 inch wheels are switched for 15 inch items, more in proportion with the rest of the car.

flected in the increased sales. Around 60% of the kits currently produced are Ford-based.

The chassis comes primed and jig-drilled, ready to accept the mechanical parts from the Escort. Any of the Ford range of engines up to the 3.0 litre V6 can be fitted although the latter requires the use of the rear axle from a 3.0 litre Capri. The standard Escort axle is satisfactory for engines up to about 2.0 litres. An interesting front suspension system is used, consisting of modified McPherson struts, fabricated upper wishbones and the standard Escort lower arms and anti-roll bar. Short coil-over units complete the set-up. The modified struts are supplied on an exchange basis. At the back, the rear axle is located with trailing arms, lateral movement being checked by means of a Panhard rod. The rear coil-over units can be Imp or Triumph based. The standard Escort braking system is retained although no servo is used as this tends to overbrake the 11 cwt car. Several other components are modified on an

exchange basis including the shortening of the one-piece propshaft (from early Mk I Escorts) and the lengthening of the Escort steering column.

The main body tub is produced in fibreglass and comes complete with a bonded in fibreglass/plywood/fibreglass floor. The comprehensive kit also includes front and rear wings, bonnet sides and tops, dash panel, running boards,

One of the first Marlin Berlinettas to hit the streets. This particular car was built by Derek Grimes and is powered by a 1600 ohc engine. The stylish car is composed of aluminium and fibre-glass panels, in this case, beautifully painted in two-tone pearl paint. The car has now covered over 100,000 miles!

Above and below: **The remarkably detailed Berlinetta of Don Collins. The immaculate two-tone car is powered by a 2.8 litre Granada V6, complete with its autobox. It abounds with detailed and individual** touches and makes extensive use of stainless steel for such parts as exhaust system, step plates and fasteners. The wheels are 15 inch Compomotives, the rear lights are Volvo P1800 items, and the twin-lift sun roof, of American origin. The car gives around 27 mpg and the top speed, in the region of 115 mph. The limiting factor is the aerodynamics!

doors and nose cone. The quality of the fibreglass is generally considered to be very good. Finishing off the front, is a polished aluminium radiator shell. Other components in the kit include an anodised screen surround, complete with a toughened glass screen, as well as all the necessary fasteners. The Escort wiring harness can be used, however a custom-made harness is also available specifically for the Malvern.

The general opinion is that the car is one of the easier kits to build, the assembly being quite straightforward. The usual procedure adopted is to assemble the panels onto the main body tub and then lower this onto the completed chassis. Trimming, wiring and detailing then follow.

Weather equipment can include a nicely proportioned and well-fitting hood and side screens, as well as the tonneau cover.

Clearly performance depends upon the engine option, however even with a 1300 engine, a top speed in excess of 90 mph with a 0-60 time of around 10 seconds can be expected. Most people are more than happy with the way that the car handles.

John Couperwaite's cars were originally marketed under the Moss banner, however in 1985, following a move to larger and newer premises, the Moss

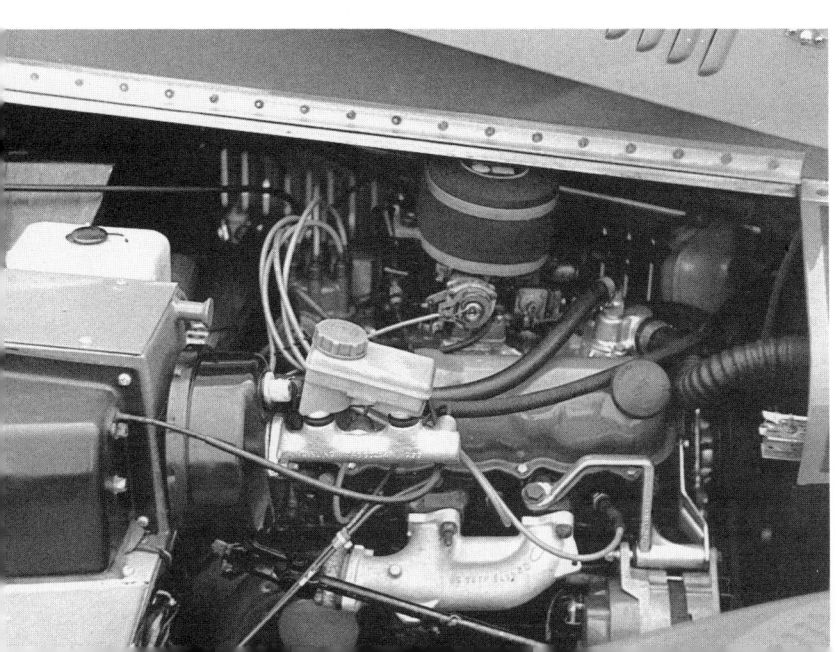

factory was gutted by fire. The losses included the moulds for the car. As a result, it was 1986 before production resumed, the operation eventually being taken over by Jim Day of Hampshire Classics who now market the range.

Marlin Berlinetta

The stylish 2+2 Berlinetta is a product of the active and successful kit car manufacturing company of Marlin. Marlin Engineering first opened their doors in 1979, having been founded by Paul Moorhouse and their first product was known simply as the "Marlin". It was based on the main components taken from the Triumph Herald range. This sold reasonably well, however the decision to opt for the cheap and plentiful supply of Marina parts was soon taken, the Mk II being the result. This version was an instant hit and was soon finding favour with a wide range of enthusiasts. Its one real limitation was that it was strictly a two-seater, which clearly limited its appeal to the family man. After listening to a great deal of customer feedback, it became clear that there was a gap in the market for a 2+2, styled along similar lines to the successful little Marlin. The result was unveiled in 1984 as the bigger, roomier Berlinetta.

Apart from the increase in size, the decision had been taken to switch from Marina mechanical components to those of the tried and trusted Ford Cortina. A new chassis was designed to accept the main mechanical assemblies from either

Yet another tastefully finished Berlinetta, featuring Compomotive wheels. The Berlinetta is notably bigger than its diminutive predecessor, being 21 inches longer and 5 inches wider. The attractions for the family man are obvious. The majority of Berlinettas seem to have been built to a very high standard.

the Mk III saloon or estate (1970–1976) or the Mk IV or V saloon or estate (1976 to 1983). The resultant chassis was both strong, well designed and used perimeter rails of 80 x 80 x 3 mm steel box-section as well as a very strong scuttle framework and screen surround. The latter is strong enough to double as a roll-over bar if necessary! The resultant unit was very tough and very safe.

Virtually all of the mechanical parts can be transferred without modification. The Cortina supplies the engine, gearbox, radiator, heater, wiring, servo and braking system. Special pedals and pedal-box are supplied with the kit, these allowing the use of the Cortina servo and dual-circuit master cylinder.

The body consists of a combination of fibreglass and aluminium panels, the latter featuring heavily in the car's con-struction. The door frames and skins are fabricated from aluminium, as are the front bulkhead, bonnet, transmission tunnel and inner wheel arches. The remaining panels such as the hard top and wings are manufactured from fibreglass of excellent quality.

As supplied, the kit is very comprehensive and includes dash panel, full glass set with all the necessary seals, rear seat panels, fasteners and side and rear lights. The buyer needs to supply a few additional items such as an Escort fuel tank (Estate or Van) and Mini window winder mechanisms.

The choice of engine is clearly at the discretion of the buyer, however Marlin suggest that at least a 2.0 litre ohc engine is fitted in order to provide adequate performance. There is also an option for V6 or V8 engine mounts to be fitted.

The Berlinetta weighs around 700 kg less than a Cortina, so that even with one of the smaller engines, it is no slouch. The weight reduction coupled with a low centre of gravity means that the handling of the car is well up to expectations. There seems to be few complaints about its good firm ride, handling and cornering abilities.

The car has proved to be a great success, not only because of its impressive, well proportioned lines and stance, but because of its overall quality. The whole package has been thoroughly designed with the added bonus of being "exceptionally easy" to assemble. A major factor in its success story is that the car is practical for a small family. It is 21 inches longer and 5 inches wider than the original Marlin and will comfortably seat two adults and two children.

There are examples now on the road, regularly driven, that have clocked up in excess of 100,000 virtually trouble free miles, a testament to the car's thorough development.

The Merlin TF and Plus 2

The Merlin is another of those cars that seems to have developed and improved with the passage of time, its graceful lines now having found a place in the hearts of many open-top enthusiasts.

This immaculate Merlin TF's engine bay houses a heavily chromed and meticulously detailed 2 litre ohc Cortina engine. With Merlins, such attention to detail seems to be the rule rather than the exception. The engine cooling is handled by the standard Cortina radiator.

The Merlin TF is strictly a two-seater car and is based on the Mk III or IV Cortina range. The chassis is a simple twin rail affair and although some doubts were originally voiced concerning its suitability for "hard" driving, there seem to be plenty of well satisfied owners who are quite content with its performance. The chassis is jig-built and MIG welded and accepts the complete Cortina front suspension assembly. This is unmodified, apart from a change to softer springs that are supplied with the kit. Apart from the front suspension, the Cortina donates its engine, gearbox, rear axle, pedal assembly, steering column and propshaft. The original radiator is also used as are most of the electrical components and wiring harness. Only a few non-Ford items are required, such as the VW Beetle rear light assemblies.

Clothing the mechanical components is a very graceful body shell that is well designed and proportioned and was originally based on the American Witton, which was either VW or Pinto powered. The bodywork exhibits a high standard of workmanship and the fibreglass work throughout the car is of a very good quality. It certainly gives the impression that a great deal of attention to detail was lavished at the manufacturing stage. The body is somewhat different from most cars of this type, in that it consists of a single component, the wings and running boards being bonded onto the body tub forming a complete unit.

The cockpit area has been carefully designed, attention to detail once again being obvious. Although there is very little excess room, the driving position is comfortable with everything easily to hand.

Apart from the body and chassis, the kit includes bumpers, grille shell and head-lights as well as a special steering column extension with two universal joints. This ensures that the steering wheel is placed in the ideal position. Numerous small parts and accessories are included in the

This US-inspired Merlin TF features numerous styling features more commonly found across the Atlantic. Apart from white-wall tyres, it also sports chromed tubular bumpers, bonnet port-holes and a hard top, complete with dummy irons. The Merlin cars are becoming very popular throughout Europe, particularly in Germany, having gained TUV Type Approval in 1986. The Merlins are based on an earlier American version known as the Witton, but have been greatly improved and refined with the passage of time.

kit, with other options including exhaust systems and weather equipment.

The general opinion amongst owners, seems to indicate that the kit is fairly easy to assemble, the majority of components bolting straight into place.

The quality and looks of the TF meant that it soon found many admirers and satisfied owners however, like Marlin, it was apparent that sales were being lost as there was no provision for carrying more than two people. In Marlin's case, the 2+2 Berlinetta was the result. In Merlin's the Plus 2 came into being.

The Plus 2 was not merely a TF with two extra seats squeezed in, as some fairly substantial improvements were engineered into the chassis at the same time. The rear suspension came in for a fair degree of redesign, the result being a system of leading and trailing arms with a Panhard rod to control lateral movement. Lotus were called in to assist with the redesign of the rear end. At the end of the day, the chassis featured some fairly substantial alterations, the result being a well equipped set-up that was more than adequate for even the hardest of driving conditions.

The new body was still clearly from the Merlin stable but featured a number of restyled features. Apart from alterations to the rear section, it featured a new nose cone, with a redesigned grille, as well as side-mounted spare wheel. The wings were all widened by an inch and the interior of the cockpit, by two inches. The new body was by now obviously of a 2+2 configuration.

Once again, a successful compromise between practicality and style had been reached, the new Plus 2, like its brother the TF, soon finding many admirers. Like a number of other companies, Thoroughbred Cars who were producing the Merlin ceased trading in 1984. By 1985, a new company known as Paris Cars had been formed and production restarted. To date the new company looks stable and with such good products a secure future now seems assured.

The Buckland B3

Perhaps one of the most unusual arrivals on the kit car scene in recent years has been the diminutive three-wheeled Buckland B3, designed and built by Dick Buckland. As a result of his life-long interest in Morgan three-wheelers, he

Ford based kit cars 4 Traditionally styled sports cars

decided to construct an updated version based on one of the 1930s examples. The B3 has its origins in the F-type Morgan, the only one to be powered by a fully enclosed Ford engine. The majority featured front mounted, exposed V-twin engines such as the fabled JAP and Anzani units.

The interesting little car features innumerable innovative and superbly constructed features, starting with the chassis which is based on a pair of 5 x 1.5 inch steel channel sections with two-inch diameter removable cross-members. At the front, additional steel framing provides the suspension mounting points and necessary mounts for the Ford engine used. This can be either the 1100 or 1300 Escort unit, complete with its ancillaries and gearbox. The engine/gearbox is mounted solidly onto the frame, forming a load-bearing, integral part of the whole structure. The gearbox bell-housing bolts through the steel front bulkhead. Although it is unusual to find the engine being used as a stressed component in a road-going vehicle, perhaps even more unusual is the remainder of the drive train. The power is taken from the Escort gearbox and transmitted via a short drive shaft to a second box mounted on the chassis. This contains Reliant gears which then pass on the power through a chain drive to a sprocket on the rear driving wheel! Hardly the usual modus operandi for a contemporary car, but nonetheless very successful.

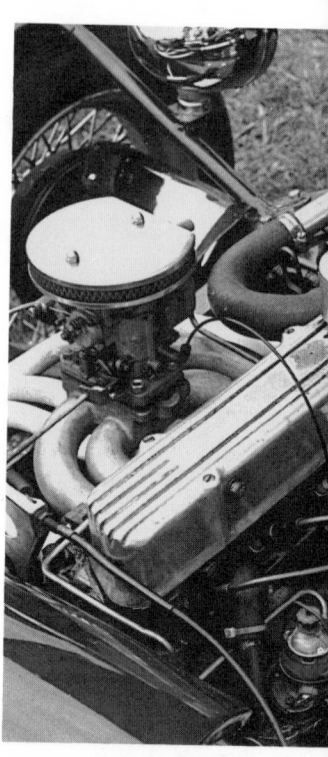

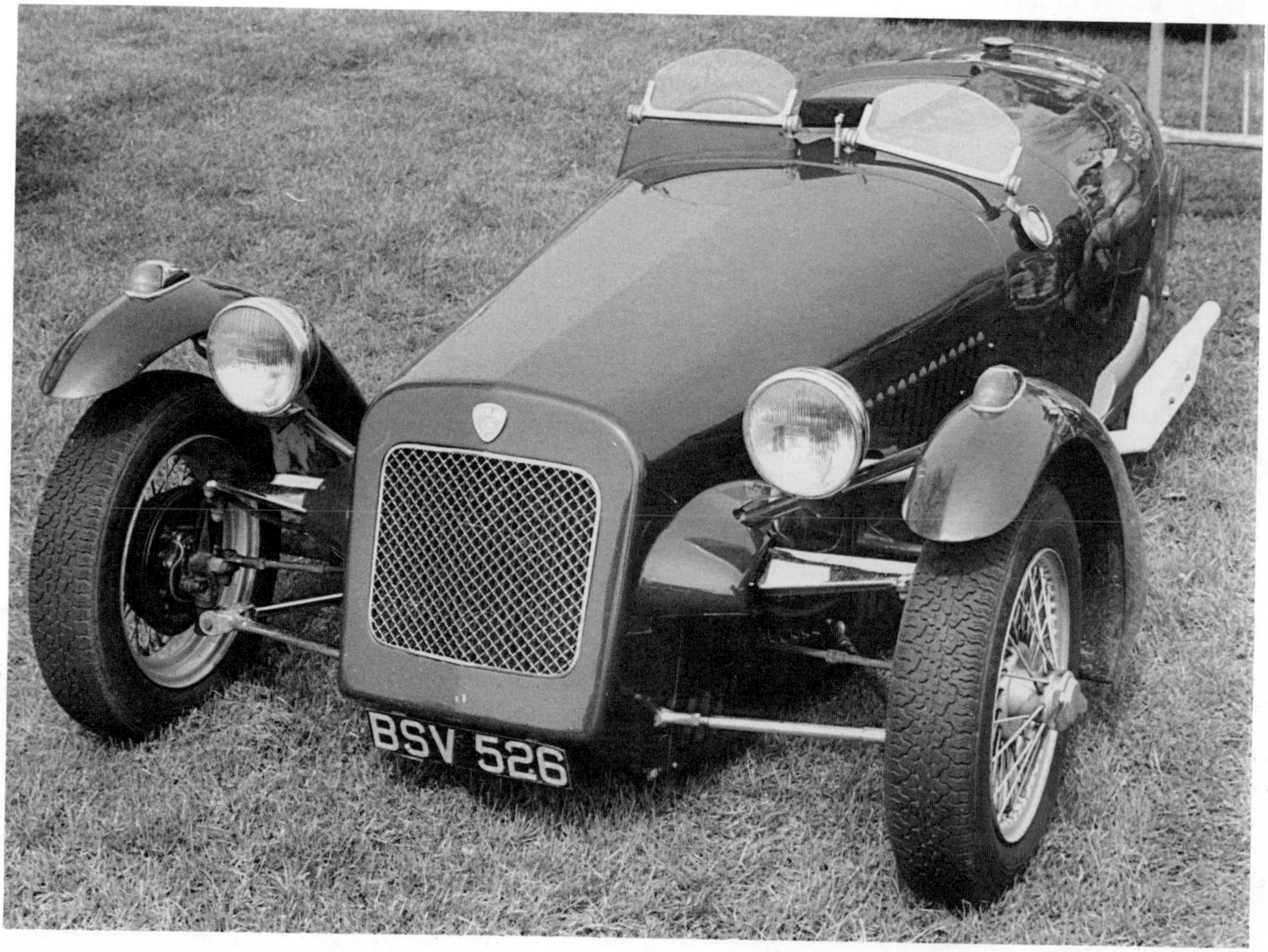

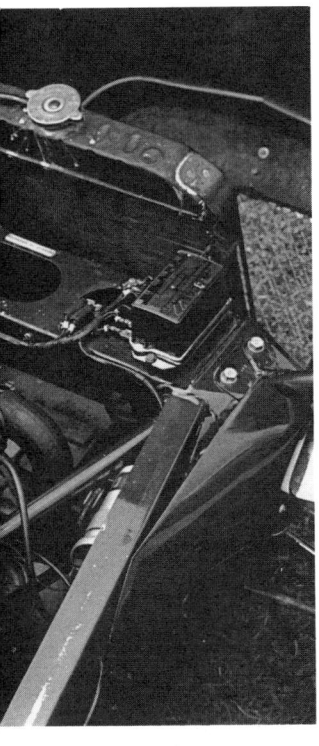

Left and photographs above: **The unusual little Buckland B3, designed and built by Dick Buckland. The innovative 3-wheeler features a special chassis which carries a solidly mounted pre-X flow Escort engine and gearbox. This forms a load-bearing, integral part of the overall structure. Power is passed via a bevel gearbox, through a chain drive to the rear wheel. The quality of the fibreglass components and body shell is exceptional. The performance, even with a 1300 cc engine is electrifying, with the top speed well in excess of 100 mph!**

The deceptively simple-looking front suspension is equally innovative and would look very much at home in many circuit racers. Spax coil-over units are mounted inboard and operated through rocker arm top links. Rose-jointed unequal length wishbones complete the lower end of the package. The steering rack is a modified Mini unit and the drum brakes composed of Ford back plates and Triumph drums, and heavily modified uprights also being of Triumph origin. An even more sophisticated rising rate front end set-up is currently in the pipeline.

As would be expected for a car of this type, wire wheels are used all around. The front are 4.5 x 15 knock-offs and the rear, a heavy duty 14 inch item. The rear suspension is as unusual as the rest of the car, making use of a modified Mini rubber cone and a very short adjustable Spax unit.

The bodywork and the cycle guards are made from fibreglass, the quality of which is exceptionally good. The moulds, like practically everything else connected with the car, were made by Dick Buckland himself. Access to the engine is via the hinged front body section with entry to the rear end being gained by lifting the entire body which hinges at the base of the cowl area. The rear section houses the aluminium petrol tank.

The handling and performance of the B3 is not remotely like any other three-wheeler currently in production. These, at best, have only mediocre performance, and at worst, unstable and unpredictable handling. Dick Buckland's creation is the complete opposite in both respects. Even with a 1300 cc X-flow engine in place, the performance of the 8 cwt car is quite remarkable. Its rate of acceleration puts it well into the sports car bracket, and its claimed top speed is somewhere in the 130 mph region! Likewise, the car manages to handle in a most non three-wheeler fashion, being quite capable of out-cornering many of its four-wheeled counterparts. As a result of its sophisticated (and unusual) layout and suspension system, it corners as if it were on the proverbial rails! All credit to Dick Buckland's ingenuity and workmanship. By mid 1987 there were six B3s under construction and a further two in use on the road. Although the little flier does not come cheaply, it does offer the chance of incredible performance, low road fund licence, petrol economy, and a vehicle that is guaranteed to cause a stir wherever it goes. It really is a remarkable little vehicle in so many respects, and is a tangible display of the many talents of its creator.

GP Madison Roadster and Coupe

The GP Madison Roadster was the brainchild of the prolific specialist car designer, Neville Tricket, and was originally intended to make use of the VW Beetle as the donor car. Although the car met with a good deal of success, VW components are not to everyone's liking and it became apparent that a wider market could be reached if a more conventional layout was adopted. As with a number of other kit cars, the Madison was redesigned to accept the mechanical parts from the Cortina, an increasingly popular base car for very obvious reasons. The use of the Cortina resulted in the more traditional, and in many people's

eyes, the more desirable, front-mounted, water-cooled engine and rear-wheel-drive. With the swap came all of the obvious advantages of availability, easy maintainance and realistic parts pricing.

The GP kit is very comprehensive and includes amongst other things, a full set of well-made body mouldings (that come in self-coloured fibreglass), scuttle, grille, bonnet halves, boat tail boot section and headlight shells. Doors are also listed as optional extras. The quality and detailing of the fibreglass is very good, as is the way that all the panels fit together.

Carrying the stylish body is a substantial box-section steel chassis that comes fully drilled so that, to quote GP "everything will fit first time". This is a claim that a number of other manufacturers also make, not always with complete accuracy! General opinion seems to confirm that GP's claim is reasonably accurate, few reporting any real problems with the build-up.

To this package must be added one Mk III, IV or V Cortina, preferably a 2 litre. Virtually all of the mechanical parts such as the engine and ancillaries, gearbox, steering and braking systems can be pirated from the Cortina and, after any refurbishing, bolted straight into place. A few modifications are necessary, such as

The Trickett-designed Madison Roadster of GP Developments uses much of the running-gear and suspension from the Cortina range. The daring styling features a Packard-inspired front end, with a boat-tail rear section. A steel chassis accepts virtually all of the Ford components without modification, the body consisting of high quality fibreglass panels. The car was originally VW-based but was redesigned to accept the Ford mechanical parts. (GP Developments)

Photographs on this page: **The Madison Roadster of David Schofield of Barnsley. This car was based on a Mk III Cortina, this supplying the 2 litre ohc engine and running-gear. The top speed of the 14 cwt car is in excess of 115 mph, and the 0–60 time, around 7 seconds. The car, which rides on 14 inch Mangel wheels, is in daily use as a work-horse and yet still manages to retain the "as new" look. The rear boat-tail section lifts upwards on Morris 1000 hinges to reveal the spare wheel and the Escort estate petrol tank. The exhaust system consists of a Janspeed manifold connected directly to a single side-pipe.**

lengthening the steering column and shortening the propshaft, both commonly encountered modifications hence presenting no real problems.

There are a number of options available as well as the aforementioned doors, these including full weather equipment, such as hood and side screens, as well as Madison "leisure clothing". This includes T-shirts and umbrellas and could be useful if the weather equipment is not included on the shopping list!

The front end of the car is carried by the normal Cortina suspension assembly, complete with disc brakes and steering rack, whilst the Cortina axle, complete with coil springs, resides at the back.

The car tips the scales at a meagre 14 cwt and not surprisingly, the performance reflects this. Top speed with a standard untuned 2 litre ohc engine will generally give a top speed somewhere around 115 mph with a 0–60 time in the region of seven seconds. The lightweight car is fairly economical with owners frequently reporting figures in excess of 40–45 mpg.

The interior of the two-seater Roadster body will take seats that can be supplied by GP, whereas the instrumentation and gauges, usually come courtesy of the Cortina. At the rear, the elegant boat-tail lid hinges upwards on Morris 1000 hinges to reveal a fairly spacious boot that holds an Escort Estate, or van, petrol tank.

A number of kit cars have appeared on

Photographs left: **The mechanically similar Madison Coupe, also designed by Neville Tricket. The boat-tail has been replaced by a sweeping back section, this clearly providing greater weather protection. This car, rather mysteriously named the Frazer-Griffith, appears to be a much modified Coupe, featuring a single rear window (as opposed to the usual two), chromed grille surround, and vintage headlights. A most interesting machine and one that shows how individual touches can completely transform a car.**

the market at different times, looking as if the designer ran out of ideas half way through the project. Happily the Madison does not suffer from such maladies, for despite fairly daring lines, the car manages to look more than acceptable from every angle. It clearly owes much of its frontal styling to the 1930s Packhard range, a period when Packhard arguably produced their best looking cars. This was a very clever concept adopted by Trickett and one that he managed to make work perfectly.

GP claim that the build-up time should be around 130 hours and this would not appear to be excessively over optimistic. The Madison Roadster is described by GP as "a successful blend of rakish 30s styling and realistic 80s running gear". It seems that most people would agree whole heartedly with that statement! The kit also showed its credibility by appearing in a nationally televised Cadbury's commercial.

Following the Roadster's great success, Trickett once again put pen to paper and came up with the equally radical Coupe version. Mechanically, the Coupe is identical, the obvious difference being the fully enclosed passenger compartment. Although the car looks rather cramped due to the low roof line, there is still adequate room for even tall drivers, mainly due to the low seating position.

The styling is once again, distinctly daring, the car looking quite amazing on the move. Clearly, the boat tail has now gone, this being replaced by the sweeping back and the small, split rear screen. The Coupe clearly provides an acceptable alternative for those who like the looks of the Roadster but prefer to have a roof over their heads!

The Monaco

The Monaco is yet another product of the fertile imagination of John Cowperthwaite and owes much of its looks and stance to the early 1950s Grand Prix racers of that period. It bears a striking resemblance (minus lights) to Ferraris experimental GP racer from 1951, (with a 2.5 litre V12) and to the Ferrari 375, of the same year. This later model was powered by a 4.5 litre

V12. Originally, the kit was offered, based on the Herald, Spitfire, Vitesse range, the cars creating a tremendous amount of interest wherever they went. Cowperthwaite's concept was of an easy-to-build, affordable, performance car, and this is what he undoubtedly created. On the heels of the successful Triumph-based range, came the development of the Ford-based version, with it, coming all of the obvious benefits associated with Ford mechanical parts.

The donor car selected was the Mk I and II Escort, this supplying much of the running-gear. The chassis adopted is basically the same as that used for Cowperthwaite's other cars (the Malvern and Mamba) and is a ladder frame configuration built from 80 x 40 x 3 mm rectangular steel tubing. A great deal of expertise and development went into the chassis design and this is clearly reflected in the standard of workmanship.

The front suspension is based around that of the Mk III, IV or V Cortina, and uses the wishbones, bottom arms, shock absorbers and hub assemblies complete. The anti-roll bar is no longer necessary and is therefore discarded. A Mk II Escort steering rack completes the front end.

At the back, the Escort axle is used in conjunction with trailing arms, a Panhard rod and a pair of Armstrong coil-overs. The standard Escort/Cortina braking system is used, although the servo is discarded as this tends to over-brake the lightweight car.

The choice of wheels is clearly up to the buyer, however, even skinny, standard 13 inch rims do not look completely out of place. Clearly, there are a vast range of aftermarket wheels that will also fit the bill.

A number of the Escort's parts need modifying, however, these can be supplied on an exchange basis. The single-piece propshaft required (from either an Escort Van or Estate, or Mk II Cortina) needs shortening, and the steering-column, lengthening, both services being available. The only other modification sometimes necessary, is alteration of the pedals, however this is only in the case of particularly tall drivers.

The Grand Prix-styled body is made,

The 1950s GP-styled Moss Monaco, looking as if it had just escaped from the race track! Originally offered in Triumph-based form, this remarkable car, like many others, was modified to accept Ford mechanical parts. The Mk I and II Escort supplies the running-gear, instruments, pedals, steering column and handbrake mechanism. The Cortina provides much of the front suspension, the steering rack coming from the Mk II Escort. Visually, both types of car are virtually identical. The one-piece fibreglass body will house any of the Ford range of engines, up to the 3 litre V6. Performance, even with a 2 litre ohc unit aboard, is not for the faint-hearted!

not surprisingly, from fibreglass, as are the four cycle wings. The body comes complete with front and rear bulkheads and with a wood/fibreglass floor bonded in place. The lay-up is quite light but more than adequate for the body's unstressed role. The racing illusion is carried further by the addition of rivet heads moulded into the bodywork, a styling touch fashioned after the early racers that inspired this unusual project.

Although primarily designed to accept the Escort and Cortina parts, the car will also handle any of the range of Ford engines, up the the 3 litre V6. Where larger engines are selected (2 litre or above) the use of the slightly wider and much stronger 3 litre Capri rear axle is recommended.

The kit contains, in addition to the body tub and chassis, a bonnet, four wings,

cockpit cowl, headlamp shells, gearbox cover, badges, twenty feet of steel strip, plus all of the necessary brackets, catches, stays and bolts. Optional extras include seats, carpets, lights and a tonneau cover.

As can be well imagined, the performance of the 8 cwt car when fitted with the V6, is shattering! Even with a 2 litre ohc unit, a 0–60 time in the region of five seconds is achieved.

In conclusion, the Monaco, currently marketed by Hampshire Classics Ltd, is a fascinating project and quite unlike anything else currently available. It can hardly be described as a "sensible" car, being more akin to a four-wheeled motor cycle. It has virtually no luggage space, little weather protection and a firm ride. Somehow this does not seem to matter, for the car has excellent performance and a uniqueness all of its own. For the sheer thrill and exhilaration that comes of driving, what appears to be a vintage racing car on the road, there is nothing to touch it!

Durow Deluge

The Durow Deluge is the product of the gifted and imaginative Nick Durow, who drew inspiration for his elegant creation from the looks and styles of the upmarket American cars of the 1930s. It emulates these, with its sweeping, graceful wings, long bonnet and its overall length. The clever use of period-styled options and accessories, such as sidepipes (a la Deusenberg) and side-mounted spare wheel, help to complete the illusion.

Nick's first car, the one that inspired the Durow range, was constructed using a Midget body tub and a combination of Triumph 2000 and Vitesse running-gear. The car used fibreglass wings and a steel bonnet and caused quite a stir wherever it went. Out of this initial design, the Deluge was ultimately born, having been re-designed to accept the running-gear from the Mk I and II Ford Granada.

A new chassis was designed and constructed from 60 x 60 x 4 mm box section steel, this taking the Granada front and rear sub-frames complete. The concept of using the Midget body tub was

retained, this, less its front end, providing a number of essential parts, as well as supplying the central body section. The Midget provides the doors, screen, quarter lights and part of the floor. Not surprisingly, the Midget body requires a number of alterations, including the removal of the transmission tunnel and the outer skin of the rear body section, this being replaced with a fibreglass panel combining the boot opening and the rear wheel arches.

The craftsman-built body features fibreglass wings and rear section, as well as the aforementioned Midget tub, the remainder normally being constructed from stainless steel. This includes the immensely long bonnet, the side-panels, valances, grille shell and bumpers. Clearly longevity was at the back of Nick Durow's mind!

The car will accommodate any of the range of Ford engines in its roomy engine compartment, however, at least a 2 litre ohc unit is suggested for adequate performance. Probably the best bet is the Granada's V6.

The car is available in kit form, this including the chassis, body panels, dashboard, interior package and hood. From there on, a wide range of options and accessories are available to the customer. Such options include side-pipes, bonnet louvers, spare wheel carrier, and so on. Nick Durow prefers to offer as comprehensive a service as possible, even down to the final spraying and trimming stages. He will take the project to whatever stage of completion is required, the customer completing the package. There is even the option of having the Midget tub fully prepared, this simplifying the build up even further.

What is it like driving such a behemoth? Once allowance has been made for its enormous length, it does not present any real problems, the handling being surprisingly good for such a long car. With Granada coil springs all round and the possibility of using the Granada's p.a.s. system, the car can be made to handle in a most acceptable fashion. With the V6 on board, a 0–60 time in the region of 10 seconds is attainable, quite respectable for a car of its proportions.

The Deluge is both a daring venture and an interesting one. It is clearly daring in its styling and proportions, however it seems to be finding itself a small band of owners and a growing band of admirers. To date, seven examples have been constructed. It is particularly interesting in its reuse of the major body section from another vehicle, the only other car to do something similar, being the Beauford.

The company offer enough options to ensure that no two cars are ever likely to be exactly the same. They have even produced a four-door version, of even greater length! Although the Deluge will only find a home in a comparatively few hands, its styling and workmanship will hopefully ensure that is has a long and active career.

The Gazelle

The Gazelle has something of a curious and chequered career and even now, its future seems unsure. Originally, the car hailed from the United States, where it was being produced by the Classic Motor Carriage Company of Florida. Although by no means an exact replica, its styling

was broadly based on that of the classic 1929 Le Baron-bodied Mercedes Roadster. The car was available to fit either the ubiquitous VW floor-pan, or in a chassised form, to accept the running-gear from the Ford Pinto. Although the car clearly lacked the detail and accessories

Above and left: **The Gazelle was originally produced in the USA, making use of either the running-gear from the VW Beetle or the Ford Pinto. Its styling is loosely based on that of the 1929 Mercedes SSK, the car being available in the UK using a box-section chassis designed to accept the main assemblies from the Mk III/IV Cortina. The car shown here, was imported directly from the USA by Roger Kernan (shown polishing) who carried out his own conversion to allow the use of Cortina parts. The Gazelle has been marketed under a number of different banners in the UK, but is currently out of production.**

Photographs below: **This Gazelle features Ford power and, unusually, a Jaguar independent rear suspension set-up. Apart from its two-tone paint and wire wheels, it also, rather cheekily, carries a Mercedes grille emblem.**

to turn it into a Mercedes replica, it managed to adopt some of the main styling features, the resultant fibreglass body being of very good quality.

The project was eventually brought to the UK in the hope that its uniqueness would endow it with success. This was not to be the case however, and the project passed through a succession of different hands, for various reasons, failing to achieve many sales.

Some criticisms were levelled at its looks and proportions although, with the appropriate accessories added, it could be made to look reasonably authentic and quite presentable.

The Gazelle was available in the UK, using a 3 x 1.5 inch box section chassis, designed to accept the running-gear from the Mk III and IV Cortina. This supplied the majority of the major components including the drive-train and much of the front and rear suspension. The commonly-encountered modifications such as the lengthening of the steering column and the shortening of the propshaft were met but apart from these, construction was fairly straightforward. Virtually all of the Ford engine range could be accommodated, although the ohc units were considered to be the most suitable.

A deluxe kit was also available, this including upholstery, instruments, lights, exhaust system and stainless steel bumpers and spare carrier. What eventually became of the project is still unclear, however few cars were sold.

Despite the UK connections, the odd kit found its way to our shores by other means. For instance, Roger Kernan imported one directly, carrying out his own conversion to allow the car to take Cortina parts. The car was by no means cheap to complete, costing in the region of £5,500, some years ago. On current prices, it would probably cost nearer £8,000! This was probably the main reason behind the car's poor sales.

Although not currently in production in the UK, rumours concerning its future still circulate. With its looks and quality, it always had the potential to become a winner. If the price could be reduced to a more realistic level, it still could.

AF Sports

The AF Sports Car (made by Auto-Forge Automobiles) made its debut at Mallory Park (The Kit Cars and Specials Action Day) at the end of June 1987. It was parked well away from the main con-

The well proportioned AF Sports, designed by David Pepper. The prototype made use of Triumph parts, although production models will feature predominantly Ford components. This will include Escort rear axle (located by four Fiesta links and a Panhard rod), brakes, propshaft, pedal box, handbrake, and any of the Ford 1100–1600 X flow engines. The front suspension will continue to use the Triumph assembly. Excellent quality and workmanship is exhibited in the 1930s-styled 2-seater.

glomeration of manufacturers but soon managed to draw the crowds.

It is the brainchild of David Pepper who for many years has been working in the forefront of the kit car industry, on a number of traditionally styled sports cars. He started his career with Burlington, as a laminator, and became heavily involved with the styling of the Burlington SS, later to become the Dorian SS. His later work included helping to design the excellent Berretta SS, a car that was on show at the Stoneleigh meeting of 1987. His own project has taken almost three years (or will have, when the first Ford-based production models are on the road) of planning and building (he started full-time in 1984) with the ultimate aim of producing a well designed and engineered traditional-styled sports car. David wanted his car to be completely Ford-based but initially, due to lack of funds, he put his elegantly styled body onto a Triumph-based tubular chassis, fitted with a 1275 cc Spitfire engine. The product of this combination was the car on show at Mallory, not as yet Ford-based, but a demonstrator to give the public an idea of what was to come, with the final production version using Ford components.

Nick Durow, of Durow Cars fame, was given a body tub and designed a tubular steel chassis for Auto-Forge, to form the basis of the Ford-based production model. The chassis will have all of the necessary mounting points for the Ford components as well as inertia reel seat belt mounting points and front uprights to support the chromed grille surround.

As far as the body is concerned, the finish is excellent. The paintwork, on the demonstrator, being the work of Auto-spray, of Coventry, who also incidently, supply the 1930s styled front and rear bumpers (somewhat reminiscent of Ford Model A items, less the number plate). The front chromed bumper houses the number plate with its own chrome surround. The sweeping front lines (not unlike the Squire) and running boards, together with the wire wheels, and rear boot-mounted spare, give it that definite 1930s look. The body is constructed from a combination of glassfibre and plywood which is all skinned in aluminium sheet by Auto-Forge. All of the louvers in the alloy front panel, bonnet top and sides are punched at the factory, if required. The wings are also supplied, a few customer-drilled holes being necessary and they are then ready for fitting. The unusual bench-type seat (supplied with the kit together with carpets) folds forward to reveal a small luggage area, but do not expect to fit in large cases. This is definitely a two-seater, with a minimal load carrying area.

The final production model will retain the Triumph front suspension but will have a Ford rear. This will consist of an Escort (Mk I or II) rear axle (plus brakes and handbrake), with four Fiesta links and Panhard rod. This means a Triumph donor is required as well as at least one Escort and a few Fiesta parts. The wiring loom can be obtained from the same source as the front suspension or alternatively AF can supply a new one. Ford also supply the pedal box and master cylinder, radiator, fan and of course the engine and gearbox. The engine selected can be any Escort crossflow unit from the 1100 cc up to the 1600, the latter becoming recommended. The walnut dash adds to the 30s look, especially when fitted out with Jaguar instruments.

The driving position of the demonstrator is a little cramped however production models with the Durrow-designed chassis will have extra room so the driving position will be more comfortable.

David Pepper has selected perhaps one of the more difficult areas of the kit car market to enter as there are already a number of excellent traditionally-styled cars on the market, the Madison and Falcon to name just two. Despite this, he has come up with a unique design that is both well engineered and with a styling of just the right proportions. This is one kit that is a match for any of the others and will undoubtedly do well in the future.

The Invader and Predator

A pair of graceful newcomers set to join the ranks of traditionally-styled sports cars, are the Invader and Predator from Pike Automotive, a company founded by Arnold Pearce and originally known as PYK Autotech Ltd. Later, he was joined by Micky Finn and Tony Brown, and Pike was born. (The company's cars now sport a pike as part of their logos!) The design of their cars has been likened by some to that of the early Jaguars, and was no less than four years in the making. These are two of the few kits currently available, to make use of the mechanical parts from the Sierra.

It is sometimes difficult to categorise whether a car is truly a kit or a component car as there is often a certain amount of overlap, however, in this case, the cars

are available in a fully-assembled form (plus, of course, Car Tax), or as a comprehensive kit of all new parts. Alternatively, for those with smaller wallets, Pike also has a budget system, supplying the kit in various stages.

For power, the Invader uses the 2 litre ohc Sierra engine, with electronic ignition and Ford EEC IV engine management system, while the Predator relies on the 2.8 litre V6, complete with fuel injection. There is a choice of gearboxes, namely the standard Ford five-speed manual, or the four-speed Automatic box.

The suspension is a combination of Sierra and Cortina, the rear set-up consisting of the independent, semi-trailing arm, coil-spring set-up from the Sierra. This uses adjustable gas shock absorbers and is mounted on a fully-insulated sub-frame. The front comes courtesy of the Cortina (Mk V) and uses double wishbones with coil-over gas shock absorbers, mounted in a detachable sub-frame.

The braking system is Sierra, and uses

Invader and Predator are two newcomers from Pike Automotive, the former using a 2 litre engine, and the latter, the 2.8 i V6. These can be used with either the 4- or 5-speed Ford gearboxes, the final performance depending on the options chosen. The rear suspension uses the independent, semi-trailing set-up from the Sierra. The traditionally styled pair are some of the first kit cars to make use of the Sierra parts, a sure sign of things to come. (Photo courtesy of Pike)

disc brakes all round (9" front, 8" rear) with a dual-circuit system. The steering uses a Cortina rack, topped with a safety column and steering link, with a Rally Sport 3- or 4-spoke steering wheel.

The chassis is certainly sturdy (and heavy!) and is largely constructed from 100 x 50, 50 x 50, and 40 x 40 mm box-section steel tube. It is MIG welded and fully treated against corrosion. With longevity also in mind, the exhaust system is of stainless steel construction, as is the 50 litre petrol tank.

The bodies of both, are made from very good quality fibreglass of 9.5 ounce lay-up, and are of very good fit and finish. The panels bolt together, aiding repair in the event of accident damage, and are reinforced with steel inserts in stressed areas.

The wheels suggested are 6J cast aluminium items although the choice is clearly wide open.

The interior is given a classy 1930s feel, as a result of the walnut burr dashpanel and the tasteful trimming options available. A choice of instrumentation is also listed. The wiper assembly is another Sierra part.

Driving the cars is a real pleasure, the handling being very safe and predictable as a consequence of their strong chassis and full independent suspension. The performance depends on the model and hence, engine choice, but clearly, both can be driven very rapidly. Not surprisingly, their styling draws the looks of the passers by, the cars receiving a good deal of compliments and positive comment.

In this already saturated section of the market, the Invader and Predator are going to have to fight hard for a place. The cars are certainly very strong and well made, and their style and proportions puts them in the class of, for instance, the JBA Falcon, the Merlin, and the AF Sports. These relative newcomers are showing a good deal of styling refinement over some of their predecessors, and although they are more expensive, are finding an appreciative band of enthusiasts who are prepared to find the extra money. Such cars are likely to appreciate in value with the passage of time, and it seems likely that the Pike products are set to join them. The Invader and Predator are some of the first càrs to make use of the increasingly available Sierra components, a sure sign of things to come!

5

Clone cars

This definition covers a whole spectrum of kit cars, manufactured with the intention of emulating a car that is, or was, originally produced at some time by another manufacturer. The majority of cars that fall into this category are either exotic, expensive or scarce.

Their lack of numbers is usually directly reflected in the prices paid for original versions, this factor alone putting many cars in this bracket out of the reach of most people. For instance, although the much-loved E-type Jaguar has been out of production for some years, they are still greatly sought after and, not surprisingly, their prices reflect this. In good condition, a V12 roadster will fetch around £18–19,000 and its 4.2 litre brethren, in the £14–15,000 range. A 1967 4.2 roadster in concours condition was recently sold, at auction, for the sum of £27,500.

The reasons for the relative scarcity of such cars are often complex and varied. It may simply have been a very expensive car to produce in the first place, requiring a great deal of labour-intensive operations with all of the costs that go with it. Any craftsman-built vehicle has always been expensive, this being one of the main motivations behind the adoption of automated and mass-production systems. In some situations, it may also have been a deliberate marketing tactic of the manufacturer in order to keep up the selling price.

In some cases, the lookalike may have been based on a car that has long been out of production. In this case, the numbers will have dwindled as a result of the natural ravages of time. The inevitable result is, that as well as the difficulty in getting hold of such a car in the first place, such a vehicle is going to be very difficult to run and maintain owing to the virtual non-existence of spare parts. This will clearly limit its usefulness as a reliable and practical means of transport. Although this situation applies to any old or specialised car, the older or more specialised that it is, the greater the problems.

Most of the aforementioned points generally refer to cars that were originally produced with road use as the main object. A number of kits however, owe their heritage to competition cars that were only intended for the race track. The result may be that few, if any, were ever offered for public sale.

The situation can clearly be a complex one and the availability, or lack of, a particular car is often as a result of a combination of circumstances. For instance, it is quite possible that future years will see a reproduction De Lorean appear (the headlights already have appeared in the Mk I Dutton Rico!). The bizarre circumstances behind the failure of the company are still fresh in most people's minds so will not be examined further, however it serves to illustrate the fact that a car's scarcity may be due to a number of complex factors. Whatever the reasons, it inevitably means that there are many people who would like to own such cars, but that are never going to do so! The best and most sensible solution, apart from selling the house and all the worldly possessions, is a kit car replica.

A further complication in this area is defining what is truly "Ford-based'. Many of these pseudo-exotic cars only make use of Ford components for motive power, the engine, gearbox and associated ancillaries making up the sum total of Ford origin. In other cases there may be a minimal use of Ford parts. Many replicas use a large number of specially made components and accessories in order to increase their authenticity and attention to detail. A good example of this can be found in many of the Cobra kits currently available. Perhaps one of the best designed, well produced and thoroughly detailed is the DAX Cobra (later Tojeiro) of DJ Sports Cars (DJS). A "typical" example may make use of a Ford V8 engine and gearbox, however much of the front and rear suspension systems are composed of Jaguar parts. Additionally, very little use is made of Ford materials for the body, chassis or even instrumentation and interior, much of this being specially produced by DJS with the commendable aim of making their cars as authentic as possible.

Most cars in this bracket fall somewhere between these two extremes. In the following pages, a number of them are examined in more detail.

Ferrari replicas

Ferraris, both old and new, have always been highly desirable motor cars. They have also been very expensive and difficult to obtain, these factors limiting their availability to only those with large wallets! The mere name conjures up images of wealth, power and of course, some of the most sleek and stylish cars ever to hit the highways and race tracks. The looks and charisma of Ferrari, coupled with their scarcity, has ensured that there would be a ready market in the unlikely event that an "affordable" Ferrari should ever appear on the scene.

One of the most desirable Ferraris must be the legendary Dino, the Pininfarina-designed beauty being introduced as the Dino 206 in 1965, and going on general sale in 1967. Within two years, the engine capacity was increased from 2 litres, to 2.4 litres, the car now being designated the 246 GT. With nearly 200 bhp from its mid-mounted V6, a top speed of around 150 mph, coupled with exceptionally good handling and road holding, was possible. The 250LM series of Ferraris were also very popular, the LM standing for Le Mans and the 250 representing the cubic capacity of each cylinder.

The mere mention of the word "affordable" and "Ferrari" in the same sentence seem to be something of a contradiction however, once again, the kit car industry managed to come up with suitable compromises.

The 164LM

Classic Replicars was set up by Mike Lemon and Bruce Swale who developed their Ferrari lookalike on the famous 250LM model. Basing their design on an earlier 2+2 VW-based version, they set out to produce a visually exciting car with Ferrari styling, but using Ford components for many of the main mechanical assemblies. As well as looking the part, the car was intended to perform and handle as similarly as possible to the original, this being accomplished by the use of all-round independent suspension and a mid-engined configuration.

Holding everything together is a square-section tube chassis with 3-inch square main rails doing much of the work. Extra strength is supplied by the use of triangulated sections in appropriate places and a galvanised steel floor. The chassis was designed and developed by none other than the ubiquitous firm of Jago, who are also responsible for its manufacture.

There is a choice when it comes to powerplants as the 164LM can provide a home for either the Ford 1300, 1600, 1600i or 1600 Turbo CVH units. This can be backed up by either the four-or five-speed standard Ford gearbox and transaxle. The engine is mounted in true mid-engine position, in front of the rear wheels and behind the passenger compartment, and is cooled by means of the Escort radiator. Naturally, the layout has involved some clever engineering in the transmission area. The independent rear suspension system is derived from the Mk II Granada and uses modified trailing-arms as well as special drive shafts, produced by Classic Replicars.

The front suspension is also largely Granada-based and makes use of the Granada uprights, wishbones, hubs and discs. Spax adjustable shock absorbers are used (as well as at the rear) and a modified anti-roll bar is supplied with the kit. The steering rack comes from a Vauxhall HC Viva fitted with Saab track rod ends. A number of non-Ford com-

ponents are of Alfa Romeo origin. These include the master cylinders, pedal box and adjustable steering column, the latter requiring the use of an extension piece.

A considerable amount of time was spent on the design of both the chassis and the body in order to make a safe and overall, very strong unit. This is reflected in the high quality of workmanship that is in evidence. The comprehensive chassis comes fully equipped with welded steel bulkheads. The graceful, swoopy body consists of a single piece moulding, with internal box-sections in the inner wing and sill regions providing extra strength. Rawlinsons of Dover supply the body, the overall quality and finish of the fibreglass being very good.

The steering geometry and suspension has been "race designed to ensure that the handling matches the performance" and few seem to doubt this claim. The road holding, ride and general handling characteristics of the lightweight (13 cwt) car are excellent.

Performance is clearly dependent upon the engine option chosen, however when powered by the RS1600i Turbo unit, a top speed in excess of 135 mph and a

The 164 LM Ferrari clone of Classic Replicars can be powered by either a mid-mounted Ford 1300, 1600, 1600I or 1600 turbo cvh engine. The rear suspension is derived from the Mk II Granada, and the front, from the same source. The chassis is constructed from 3″ square-section steel, with triangulated sections, and was built by Jago. The prototype car, shown here in final stages of completion, is powered by an RS 1600 engine. The car features some excellent engineering and fibreglass work.

0–60 time of around 7 seconds is claimed. Even when fitted with the standard 1300 CVH engine, the top speed is expected to be around 105 mph.

Shortly after the launch of the LM164, the company found itself in difficulties and as a result, Alan Frener and Lynn Mayoh of Western Classics, took control of Classic Replicars, Bruce Swale, however, remaining involved. Western Classics have been active for many years, specialising in restoration and kit build-up work these activities now carrying on alongside the 164 LM project.

The kit is being offered in three different forms. Stage I contains the bodyshell (complete with inner panels and dashboard bonded in), boot lid, engine cover, boot box, and rear under-panel, as well as the fully bracketed chassis, sub-frame, steel floor, and engine mount set. Modifications are needed to the customer's Granada rear swinging arms and the Cortina anti-roll bar, these being carried out by the factory. The Stage II kit includes all of the above list, plus a full hardware package, containing such things as side-windows, hinges, door rubbers, latches and locks. The Stage III kit comes as the Stage II, but with the body fully assembled and all of the necessary hardware fitted.

Virtually all of the other parts needed are available, including lighting kit, exhaust system, instruments, fuel tank, trim package, gear linkage, shock absorbers, springs, and numerous smaller parts.

A further option is that of a fully-assembled car, complete with new Ford RS turbo engine, leather interior, and sprayed to the colour of your choice. Further engine options include the possibility of a 1600 cc XR3i fuel injected engine in a Stage III state of tune, or even with a Sprintex supercharger.

The prototype car is shortly to undergo testing, with Ford, at MIRA, one of the few kit cars that has been in such a situation. Hopefully the very thorough development of the 164LM by Classic Replicars, and latterly by Western Classics, will ensure its well-deserved success.

Classic Replicars, latterly with the involvement of Western Classics, set out to produce a car that had "Ferrari panache at Ford prices". It appears that they succeeded!

The Karma

The Dino clearly provided the inspiration for the Karma, a car that now owes much of its success to the efforts of Roger Wooley of RW Kit Cars. With a long history of Specials, sports cars and kit cars behind him, in 1982, he set up RW with the aim of offering a build-up service for other manufacturer's cars. Feeling that he would like a product of his own, he began to look around, the end-result being the appearance of the Karma.

The Karma had something of a torturous journey before coming into Roger Wooley's hands, and was originally being produced by the American firm of Custom Classics in California. At the time, it went under the name of the Kelmark. The project was brought to the UK by another concern, but eventually ended up being marketed under the RW banner who, in 1983, became the sole UK distributors.

Over the years, the Karma, not surprisingly, has sold well, the mechanical base being the ubiquitous VW Beetle floorpan. Realising that VW components have certain limitations and are consequently not to everyone's liking, a number of different options were made available to take alternative running-gear. One such option was the introduction of a mid-engined chassis, in keeping with the original Ferrari concept. Over the years a number of these have been sold and fitted out with various engines such as the Ford four-cylinder, V6 and ohc units.

The mid-engined layout is a very flexible one, leading to a wide possible choice of components. The RW chassis, when fitted with a Ford engine, usually drives through a VW transaxle, although Renault 30 or Citroen units are also possibilities. Ford components also find their way into the front end, in the form of the Granada front suspension/cross-member, used almost in its entirety. The Granada also supplies hubs and drive

shafts. Cortina parts encountered, include the steering column and pedal assembly.

A further alternative was available in the form of a front-mounted Ford engine configuration. This suffered from a number of drawbacks, mainly associated with clearance of the very low bonnet line. The limited space available was sufficient to take Ford X-flow engines but not the taller ohc units. A number of these kits were sold, the builders facing a number of problems during the build-up, as well as limited engine access in the completed car. Nonetheless, those individuals who perservered, ended up with very acceptable cars. As a result of these drawbacks, the front-engined configuration was eventually withdrawn.

Since its introduction in 1982, the kit has been the recipient of numerous refinements and improvements, some of them minor, others fairly substantial. Perhaps the most noticeable was the enlargement of the rear screen, this increasing the space and making the car into an, albeit cramped, 2+2. In addition,

side air intakes were added, front indicators blended in, and the door and screen pillars slimmed down.

The kit is available in both Basic and Deluxe form. The Basic kit includes the body which comes complete with doors and locks, tinted windows, screen, rear window, and bonnet and boot lid, ready fitted. Clearly, if the mid-engined option is selected, the RW chassis is also included. The Deluxe kit contains, in addition to the above, a full set of lights, instrumentation pack, interior trim kit, wiring harness, seats and runners, weather trim, and wheels and tyres. The wheel sizes suggested are 8 x 15 at the front or and either 8 or 10 x 15 at the rear.

Whichever route is adopted and whichever donor vehicle supplies the mechanical parts, the final result is a superb looking car. The end performance is clearly dependent on the drive-train and chassis, however, opinion on handling and general practicality is generally very favourable.

The success of the car can be judged by the fact that RW have now set up a

Photographs above and right: **This is one of the few front engined versions of the Karma, the layout being withdrawn following a number of problems. This Karma was built by Trevor Semark and is powered by a 1600 ohv Ford engine and gearbox. The problems associated with the limited access to the well set-back engine can clearly be seen. The tastefully finished car is of a very high standard and features flawless black paint, well finished interior and rolls on Compomotive wheels.**

overall, the car still retained its own special looks and characteristics. Motoring writers of the time quipped that the car had the ability to look as if it was doing 150 mph when it was standing still! It was this sort of response that helped to establish the car as a much sought after piece of Britain's performance motoring heritage.

As a consequence, there has always been a tendency to look back on E-Types through rose-coloured glasses and although they were undoubtedly fine cars in many respects, the passing years did show up a number of problem areas. The main body structure was composed of a steel monocoque and one of the major problems to emerge was the tendency for this to rust. What made matters worse was the fact that this often occurred from the inside, making treatment even more difficult. Many mechanically sound E-Types bit the dust as a result of excessively corroded bodywork. Not surprisingly, this helped to reduce their overall numbers quite substantially. Another problem area was the front sub-frame, this also being prone to rust.

As their numbers diminished over the years, so the prices being paid for good examples rose accordingly. Clearly the dream car of many was still an E-Type, however the survivors were either showing their age or far too expensive. Anyone who has ever completely restored a Jaguar will undoubtedly have something to say on the subject of the exorbitant cost of parts and as a result, the cost of restoring an E-Type often ended up exceeding the capacity of the hopeful individual's purse.

network of dealers throughout Europe and as far a way as Australia and Canada. It looks like the Karma is here to stay, but if it doesn't fit the bill exactly, there is always the Dino to consider!

E-Type Jaguar Replicas

The E-Type Jaguar has become a piece of British motoring history, something of a legend. Production started in 1961 and finally ended in 1975. During those fourteen years, a number of different versions and engines appeared, but

The Triple C Challenger

Once again, it was left up to kit manufacturers to provide an alternative to purchasing the real thing, this time in the shape of Derek Robinson's Company.

After expending a considerable amount of effort and a great deal of development time, he eventually produced the Triple C (Car Care Clinic) Challenger, a car that was virtually identical in appearance to the E-Type.

There are minor differences but it really takes an E-Type aficionado to spot them. The main visual difference is the fact that the rear wheel arches are, of necessity, slightly wider than the original although it certainly isn't apparent at first glance.

Derek Robinson had very definite ideas when it came to a chassis and was determined that his car would have a full space-frame. The final design was arrived at after consultation with a number of professional designers and was largely constructed from one-inch square steel tubing with a steel fireproof bulkhead between the driver's compartment and the engine. The advantages of a space-frame are obvious. It is both stiff and strong, as well as being comparatively light, but on the other hand, it is expensive and complicated to construct. The Challenger's frame is a well designed and well made unit and shows some similarities to that of the Lotus Seven.

The front end is part Ford and part Triple C. Ford components include Cortina uprights, Mk III/IV Cortina disc assemblies and stub axles, and a modified steering rack from the same source. Triple C manufacture the special wishbones needed, with Spax coil-over units completing the picture.

At the rear, a Capri axle, suitably modified, is used, this being located by trailing arms and a Panhard rod. Once again, Spax coil-over units are used.

Motive power can be provided by a number of sources including the Ford ohc and V6 engines. Triple C suggest the use of the rear axle from a 3 litre Capri where larger engines are selected.

The lines and style of the body obviously need little description, however the quality of the fibreglass work is excellent. Unlike many other bodies, the Challenger's is made up of a number of separate pieces that a jigged and bonded into place. Once complete, the body is bonded to the chassis, the overall structure being exceedingly strong, as well as light, the one-piece bonnet section hinges forward, as on the E-Type, giving good access to the engine bay.

The lines of the classic E-Type Jaguar have here been re-created by Derek Robinson of the Triple C company. His clone uses a full space-frame chassis with a Cortina-based front suspension set-up that uses specially made wishbones. A modified Capri axle is used at the back, the power coming from virtually any of the Ford four-cylinder or V6 engines. The quality and strength of the Challenger's body, which is assembled from separate panels, is most impressive. Triple C can provide virtually every piece necessary to complete their stylish imitation.

A comprehensive range of electrical equipment, wiring harness, lights and instrumentation is available from Triple C, as well as the modified Marina steering column and pedal assembly needed. Also available is a well fitting hood and a multitude of other parts and accessories such as bumpers, handles, catches, trim parts, wheels, exhaust system and fuel tank.

The very rigid chassis/body structure and thoroughly engineered suspension and steering systems means that the Challenger handles likes the true high-performance sports car that it undoubtedly is. The performance is clearly dependent on the drive train selected, however by way of example, with a 3 litre Ford V6 on board, the top speed is in excess of 120 mph and the 0-60 time around seven seconds. With a 2 litre ohc in its place, top speed is around 108 mph and a 0-60 time, around 9 seconds. Certainly not shabby performance by any standards. The Challenger has one other advantage, for, like the E-Type, this very desirable car also has the ability to look as if it is doing 150 mph whilst standing still!

The Wildcat

The UK is currently in the fortunate position of having not one, but two, Jaguar E-Type replicas. The Triple C Challenger has a rival in the form of the JPR Wildcat, a car that is also of excellent design, quality and finish.

The Wildcat, like the Challenger, is visually very similar to the original Mk I E-Type, with the exception of a few minor details. Perhaps the most noticeable, although not very obvious, is the slightly wider rear end and the different front and rear light units. Overall, however, it would take a Jaguar enthusiast to spot these points, its well made and very strong fibreglass body looking every bit as good as the original.

JPR used a multi-tubular space-frame, incorporating a backbone section, for the Wildcat, the resultant chassis being very strong and rigid. This is designed to accept the majority of the mechanical parts from either the Mk III or IV Cortina, or the European Taunus, only a few modifications being necessary. Naturally, the chassis comes fully bracketed and jig-drilled, ensuring that assembly of the main components is a straightforward operation. At the front, the Cortina suspension and steering assembly is used, unmodified with the exception of the replacement of the standard springs and shock absorbers with a pair of specially made coil-over units. The Cortina also donates its engine and gearbox, as well as the complete rear suspension set-up.

A few modifications are needed to the Cortina's steering column and servo mounting bracket, these parts being supplied off the shelf by JPR, on an exchange basis

The Wildcat is available in both Basic and Deluxe kit form. The Basic kit consists of the chassis, complete with the body ready fitted. The body comes complete with the bonnet, doors and boot lid, already in place. New hinges, locking mechanisms and door handles are already fitted, as is the laminated windscreen. A comprehensive selection of additional parts are also included in the Basic kit including, the dashboard, bumpers, headlight surrounds, rear lights, front indicators, and inner trim panels.

In addition to the components supplied in the Basic kit, the deluxe version contains various parts such as a carpet and trim set, brake pipe set, a pair of Jaguar tail pipes, coil-spring shocks, reclining seats and runners, head rests, wind-up windows, all included to finish off the interior and trim. The suggested wheels for the car are 14 x 6 GB Alloys, a set of four being included. Further pieces of the kit are a pair of inner wings, a brake pipe and flexi hose kit, and shock absorber sets. Final authentic touches that JPR can supply, are a set of Jaguar tail pipes and a walnut facia panel.

This Wildcat is running on a set of 14 x 6 GB alloy wheels, as recommended by the company. The body comes ready fitted with its bonnet, doors, boot lid and with many other smaller parts in place, thus easing assembly. Several dozen Wildcats have already been built, the majority making use of the running-gear from the 2 litre Cortina.

There are a number of options when it comes to keeping the elements at bay, namely a soft top, a hard top, or a tonneau cover.

The Wildcat, like the Challenger and the original E-Type, is a very nimble, agile and beautifully-handling car. JPR claim that the car's handling capabilities have proved to be one of the main reasons for the rapid public acceptance, and driving impressions would seem to confirm this. Ultimate performance is clearly dependent on the drive-train selected, however, even with a 2 litre unit in place, the car's comparatively light weight, coupled with its excellent aerodynamics, should ensure that acceleration and top speed are more than acceptable. By late 1987 over 22 had been sold, mostly 2 litre Cortina powered and a hard top version of the kit was launched, the roof section being moulded from an early E-Type.

The Wildcat, like the Challenger, provides an economically viable route to owning what appears to be one of the all-time favourites of UK performance motoring. With its Ford drive-train, it is now possible to combine classic styling with sensible costs and regular, reliable driving, a combination that is hard to beat.

Lamborghini replicas

Ferruccio Lamborghini started his famous company in 1960 which was, after his first production car was released, to become one of the most distinguished, exotic sports car companies. This was a considerable achievement considering the age of his company.

He rapidly became known for his wedge-shaped cars, which could be seen evolving from the 350 GTV (with 360 bhp V12 and five-speed box) in 1963 through to the Miura in 1966 and the Countach in the 1970s.

Bertone was the originator of the Miura. It was launched in 1967 and was a low, road-going racing car, powered by an uprated 4 litre V12 positioned directly behind the driver's seat. Unlike the Lotus 25s and the GT40s of that period, this was one car which didn't go racing. Full credit

for the design is uncertain but it was probably a combination of Bertone and Giugiara (later of Ghia and Tomaso fame). With a few minor body changes (including alloy wheels) the Miura S was born. 1967 came along and brought with it the Marzel, a four-seater sports with the engine in the rear. This was an interestingly designed car with a gull-wing doors glazed from roof to floor. Later, a similar model came onto the scene, the Espada, very much like the Marzel but with conventional doors. The Jarama followed, and by the mid 1970s, Lamborghini's "wedge" culminated in one of the most popular exotic sports cars, the Lamborghini Countach. The Nuccio Bertone designed-Countach, as with all of the other Lamborghinis, was built for performance and handling. The Countach was originally planned to take a 5 litre V12 (producing 440 bhp) but finished up with a mid-engined 4 litre V12 unit, producing 370 bhp. The engine had four overhead cams and six dual cross-draught carburettors (40DCDE Webers) giving a very respectable top speed of 190 mph, and a 0–100 time around eight seconds (although fuel consumption did suffer slightly at only 12 mpg).

One of the Lamborghinis more recent products (and certainly different) is a type of Jeep. It was specially built for Arabs. It has enormous wheels, no doors and is powered by a Chrysler 5.9 litre V8 (with a turbo option).

Prova Countach

The Prova Designs Countach replica is a superb example of "cloning". The body dimensions are very close to the original and on the road, it definitely has the Lamborghini look and style about it. The chassis has a good pedigree, originating from Kit Deal, whose chassis have been proved time and time again by the "Ultima" on the race track. It is of 16 gauge 1.5 inch box-section construction and is a three-dimensional space-frame. The engine, as with the original, is mid-mounted. It uses a Renault 30 transaxle and can be driven, via. adaptors, by the Ford 2.8 and 3.0 V6 or the 289 and 302 ci

V8s. Stopping power is provided by disc brakes all round. These have twin master cylinders with a dual-circuit system operating from a Prova pedal assembly.

For steering and front suspension, Mk III Cortina or Granada parts are used. The chassis is supplied with four purpose-built wishbones ready to accept the Ford uprights, discs and callipers. Spax concentric spring/gas damper units are utilised, as are Cortina rack and steering column. Cortina track rods are used, but need lengthening, this being a service that Prova offer. The rear suspension comes courtesy of a Renault 30, this supplying drive-shafts, hubs and wheel bearings. The uprights and wishbones are supplied by Prova who will also undertake the necessary machining of the Renault hub flanges. For driving, forward vision is excellent, if a little low, and the rest, well, what do you expect for a Countach!

It is very difficult to tell the replica and the original apart, the main difference being the rear tail spoiler (only present on some later originals) and the rear wings, which, on the original, blend more into the body. On the other, these are touches which Ferruccio himself may approve of, certainly with production in 1987 at 2 kits per week many satisfied customers do!

The BBL Primo

As with the Prova Countach, the Broadbest (BBL) Primo is both a beautifully made and very accurate copy of the original. The Primo came about as a result of the combined efforts of Broadbest, who have been in the business of producing chassis and high quality body mouldings for many years, in conjunction with GTD. Broadbest purchased the full manufacturing and sales rights to what was the old GTD Countach, GTD deciding to concentrate on their GT40 business. Broadbest was involved with the GTD Countach on a 50/50 basis from birth (Broadbest producing all of the fibreglass and fine tuning the chassis) and hence they were the idea company to take over the production. Venom initially had dealings with GTD, with the aim of producing the Venom Countach, but unfortunately they went out of business. Broadbest, once in control of the Countach, renamed it the Primo.

The fibreglass body is a very accurate reproduction and comes with its doors fitted and inner skin fully moulded in. Additional panels include engine cover, boot lid, bonnet, rear wings and pedestal mounting, air boxes, headlamp covers, and dashboard.

The chassis for this sleek beauty, is a full space-frame, that comes pre-drilled ready to accept all of the necessary parts, the bottom plane of the chassis being identical to that of the GTD40 chassis. Engine mounts are supplied, a good choice of power-plant being either the Ford 289 or 302ci V8s. Various options are available for the chassis, this being available in a number of forms, right up to a complete rolling-chassis.

The front suspension consists of an independent, unequal length wishbone system of BBL's manufacture, with an anti-

roll bar. The steering rack is a Granada item. At the rear, independent, unequal length wishbones are to be found, once again, with trailing arms and a rear anti-roll bar. Adjustable Spax coil-over units are used all round. The transmission used is the increasingly popular Renault 30, this coupling to the Ford V8 via an adapter plate.

The space-frame chassis is available in both left and right-hand drive versions, and can be bought in four separate packages, each one being successively more complete than the last one. For instance, Kit 1 consists of the basic chassis with brackets and engine mounts, whereas Kit 4 is the rolling-chassis option, coming complete with wishbones, hub carriers, Spax shock absorbers, spindles, ball joints, hubs, brakes, and so on. All it lacks is wheels!

Likewise, the body is available in four different packages. Kit 1 includes the main body moulding with inner and outer skins, engine cover, bonnet, boot lid, and air intakes. Further options include such panels as spoiler, inner wings, and seat moulding. Yet another package contains a full set of inner panels.

BBL have a huge list of parts which includes virtually every conceivable part needed to assemble the Primo. Complete

wiring looms, exhaust systems, and stainless steel water pipe kits are all available, as are such necessary items as pedal box, windscreen, grille set, and wiper assembly. A flywheel and clutch conversion set is available, allowing the Ford V8 engine to be mated to the Renault 30 gearbox, and suitable gear-linkages listed. BBL even carry the necessary Ford parts needed, such as steering rack, and can even supply reconditioned Ford V8 engines. The chassis comes with a normal drum/disc brake configuration, although BBL offer a conversion, to add disc brakes to the rear. Needless to say, all of the necessary pipes, discs, servo, etc. are available for both systems.

Such cars as the Primo are not the easiest or cheapest of vehicles to assemble, however, for those with determination and finance to carry the project through, the results will be well worth it. As with the original, the car looks stunning, whether static or on the move. In action, the vision is as for the Prova. Forward vision is fine however anything else is restricted, but then so was the original. The Primo's quality is obvious, and helps to ensure that the car looks every bit as good as the original. The body is a faithful replica, and this, combined with a rather more "sensible" drive-train, makes the "Countach" a distinct possibility for a lot more people.

The Miura

The Miura clone, produced by Cheetah Cars, is fairly close to the Lamborghini original. This is perhaps not so surprising considering that their car was produced from a set of moulds taken off the real thing! Clearly this is a very satisfactory way of producing a clone car, however,

depending on the reaction of the original manufacturer, it can also be a tricky route to take in terms of such aspects as copyright. Quite a large proportion of clone cars have been produced by this means and in some cases the response of the original manufacturer has been decidedly hostile! Presumably, in the case of the Miura (and also the Countach) replicas, Lamborghini did not voice any objections, hence the Cheetah Miura was born.

Despite the fact that the main body mouldings were taken from an original, Cheetah were still faced with innumerable problems when it came to producing the many smaller parts needed to complete the package. Ultimately they succeeded in producing what is considered to be a very passable, at least visually, replica of the Miura. A few differences are apparent between the two, but it would take someone with a reasonably good knowledge of Lamborghinis to immediately spot them. For instance, unlike the original, the rear panel is not hinged, now being a permanently bonded part of the bodywork. Perhaps more noticeable are the differences around the headlights, Cheetah having opted for the simpler surrounds of the later SV model. These are only minor points as the overall looks and styling of the car are still quite convincing.

Unlike the Lamborghini, which used a pressed steel monocoque, the backbone for the Cheetah consists of a steel chassis, designed to accept much of the running

A recent addition to the ranks of the Countach clones is the Conan Countach. The body is available in either fibreglass or as a Kevlar composite, and mounts on a full space-frame chassis that uses Conan-designed front and rear suspension. As with the other Countach clones, a Renault transaxle is used, the power being provided by either a Ford V6 or V8 engine.
(Photo courtesy of Conan)

gear from the Ford XR3i, the one major exception being the front suspension which comes, largely unmodified, from the Cortina.

The most innovative part of the car is to be found nearer the rear! The XR3i engine and five-speed gearbox is mounted in a mid-engined layout although remains largely unmodified. Various linkages such as the gearchange, clutch and throttle clearly require some alteration although surprisingly little.

As well as the drive-train, the Escort inner wings are utilised, this supplying the necessary mounting points for the McPherson struts. The standard Escort drive-shafts, hubs and disc brakes are also retained. The standard radiator and electric fan are also used. The car will accept any of the Escort range of engines and clearly the performance will be dependent on this choice.

The interior was largely modelled, as with the body, on an original Miura, many of the interior panels having been moulded from the interior panels of the same car. Some doubts as to the future of Cheetah's Miura have recently been voiced however there is some possibility that the Ford option may be complemented with that of the Lancia Beta.

Cobra Clones

In automotive terms, the period immediately following the Second World War can hardly be described as an exciting time, with many pre-war models simply being put back into production. The year 1953 was hardly any different, except for the almost-unnoticed appearance of a diminutive sports/racing car, designed by John Tojeiro. The successful little car caught the eye of AC, and before long, Tojeiro had been commisssioned to design a new car. This featured a ladder-type chassis of three-inch diameter tubes, and was powered by a triple SU-fed, aluminium 6-cylinder AC engine. It was simply christened the "Ace".

Other options followed, including the 118 mph Bristol D2-powered version, and in 1961, one with the 2.6 litre Ford Zephyr engine. Not surprisingly, the Ace was raced with a good deal of success throughout Europe and, perhaps more significantly, in the USA. Here, an ex-road racing Texan, Carroll Shelby, first became involved with the car. The rest is history! Following negotiations with AC, an uprated version featuring a 221 ci Ford V8, soon appeared. This was to be the first of the Cobras!

A host of chassis refinements followed, as well as the fitting of the 289 ci Mustang engine. The Cobras were having a ball on the race tracks, winning races everywhere, including the ISC Championship.

Despite the excellent power to weight ratio of the 289 package, 1966 saw the emergence of what was, perhaps the ultimate road-going performance car to ever hit the streets. The legendary 427 Cobra, named after the 7 litre Ford V8 that now resided under its sleek hood, had arrived.

The chassis tubes were increased to four-inch diameter, Girling disc brakes added, and a Salisbury LSD fitted. For less than $10,000, Shelby would now sell you a low-slung rocket that was capable of hitting 160 mph. With the appropriate gearing, 180 mph was not unknown. With 425 bhp on tap, the performance of the 2500lb car was staggering! 0-60 took around 4 seconds and 0-100, around 14. It all depended how well the wheel-spin could be controlled.

When the last car rolled out of Shelby American in 1968, it really was the end of an era, however, in the following years it became apparent that although the Cobra was dead, it would not lie down. As genuine models soared in price, to become inaccessible to all but the wealthiest, a whole new chapter in its history opened up with the appearance of the repli-Cobra.

Over the last decade or so, a remarkable number of Cobra replicas have appeared. Quite a few did not survive, however those that did have now matured into very impressive machines. The Cobra is one of the most copied cars, some examples using a fairly high Ford content and others, merely the engine and gearbox. There are also a number of others that are neither Ford-based or

This is an example of the Gravetti 427 Cobra from Gravetti Engineering. They are one of the few kit car companies to remain a family business (being run by Nigel Gravetti, his wife and his father). The company has been in business for over five years and have, so far, over 90 satisfied customers, a large percentage of these being overseas. Gravetti follow a "Cob in a box" policy, meaning that only the engine and gearbox is necessary to complete the car. The power can come courtesy of a Chevrolet or Rover V8, or Ford 289 and 427 V8s. There are several options including the choice of the body in aluminium or Kevlar.

powered. If the market for Cobras has not yet been saturated, it must surely be close to it! The Cobra is dead, long live the Cobra!

Dax Tojeiro

The DAX Tojeiro (formerly Cobra) is the product of one of the best-known kit car manufacturers in the UK, DJ Sportscars. The company came into being in 1968, initially producing reproduction panels for traditional British sportscars, such as TRs, MGs and Healeys. Eventually acquiring a genuine 427 Cobra, DJS produced a set of moulds from it, and with the help of a computer-aided designed chassis, produced in 1982, the first of their immensely successful Cobras. The DAX is one of the best established quality Cobra replicas currently on the market and has always had a good reputation for both the quality of its fibreglass as well as its authenticity. Since its introduction, it has met with great success, sales world-

This is the interior of the Gravetti 427, showing great attention to detail. Everything required for the kit is supplied, including the body, chassis, suspension set-up, brake pipes, steering and braking components, dashboard, instruments, lights, Revolution wheels, "Cobra" steering wheel and windscreen. In addition, the very comprehensive kit also includes heating system, all locks, radiator, header tank, electric fans, carpets, seats, nudge bars and over-riders. What many other manufacturers consider to be optional extras, Gravetti include as a matter of course.

This is a fine example of a DAX Cobra built by Malcolm Griffiths, with assistance from Ken Britten and Tom Jurgens. The power is supplied by a Ford 302 ci V8 that originated from an Australian Fairmont. This was rebuilt, and a hotter cam and electronic ignition installed. The original autobox was replaced with a four-speed manual unit. The suspension consists largely of the recommended Jaguar parts, the steering being handled by a Triumph Dolomite column with Triumph 2000 splined shaft. The car is resplendent in Ford Royal Blue, the interior being trimmed in Midnight Blue Connolly hide. The wheels on this beast are solar 10s with P60 Pirelli-shod 7 x 15s up front, and 8 x 15s at the back.

wide, now having climbed well into the hundreds.

As would be expected from a company as professionally run as DJS, the product has been continually refined and improved as a result of the company's experiences. Recent years have seen the arrival of an alternative body style, in the shape of the 289 model, this being produced alongside the more macho 427. Not surprisingly, the fit and finish of the 289 body is every bit as good as the its stablemate. The bodies come supplied with all internal panels, bulkheads and arches bonded in place, and complete with double-skinned doors, boot lid and bonnet.

There is now even a choice of chassis, for as well as the well-established platform chssis that has seen service under most of the Cobras/Tojeiros, DJS have recently introduced a new "Supertube" unit. This consists of a backbone-type chassis, which is not only stronger and stiffer, but also 40% lighter than the standard unit. The Supertube is constructed from seamless steel tubing of various diameters, and is notable for both its complexity, as well as the quality of workmanship in evidence. It comes complete with an integral pedal box and aluminium floorpan, and is, as with the standard chassis, fully drilled and bracketed.

Both chassis are designed to take much of their running-gear from the

Jaguar XJ6 or 12, DJS suggesting the use of a post-1974 model in order to make use of the better braking system (namely 4-pot ventilated units). The front-end uses Jaguar wishbones, in conjunction with special DAX adjustable coil-over units. The steering gear consists of a rack and pinion set-up, topped with a Triumph Dolomite steering column.

At the rear, more Jaguar components are to be found in the shape of centre-section, drive-shafts and wishbones. Both of the latter require modification, DJS carrying this out on an exchange basis.

As with a number of other companies, DJS offer a number of options when it comes to the build-up. For instance, their "Starter Pack" consists of the chassis, body, steering rack, anti-roll bar, tie bars, and set of six special coil-over units. In addition, the modifications to the rear suspension parts are carried out. At the other end of the spectrum is the option of a complete rolling-chassis, complete with suspension, brakes, steering, radiator, and so on. All non-DJS parts are completely overhauled prior to use. In addition, DJS will also build the Tojeiro to any stage of completion requested, right up to complete "turn-key" cars.

The list of additional parts available is very impressive, and includes not only necessary components, such as wind-screen, petrol tank and dashboard, but also a huge list of reproduction Cobra parts, enabling the completed car to resemble the original, right down to the smallest detail. Such items as wind-wings, front and rear over-riders, nudge bars, bonnet locks and handles, side-vents, badges, filler caps, and seats are listed.

For all year round driving, there is the option of a soft top, in various choices of materials, tonneauxs, or hard tops, for

Above: **This is the rather full engine compartment of a 427-powered DAX Cobra. This was caught momentarily with the bonnet up, after a few laps of the Mallory Park circuit. Notice the detailing and the stainless parts that abound. By late 1987 DJ Sports Cars had sold hundreds of cars, both here and overseas.**

both the 289 and 427 versions. A vast array of other parts including wiring harness, instruments, lights, and trim parts, enables the builder to obtain virtually every necessary part from one source.

When it comes to the power-plant, there are a number of alternatives. The Tojeiro will take the Jaguar V12, and Chevrolet and Rover V8s. In addition, it will also house virtually all of the Ford range of engines, including the small-block V8, the V6 range, and any of the ohc four-cylinder units. The American V8s seem to be the most popular units opted for.

An interesting postscript to the story, involves John Tojeiro himself. Since 1985, he has been involved with DJ Sportscars, in the role of Technical Director. The current DJS cars now bear his name, perhaps the most fitting honour for the man who effectively set the ball rolling with his Ace.

Python Roadster

The Python Roadster is a Cobra 427 replica produced by Unique Autocraft. They have been in business now for around seven years. The firm was started by Peter Gottlieb, Robert Whitwell and Christopher Brown (ex-Jaguar and Panther). Initially they started a 'Rod shop', with the Python as an additional side line. As time went on, the Python became the major product, mainly due to a fall off in interest in rods and customs in the late 1970s (a situation which

Left: **This is the DAX Tojeiro which now has the option of the standard platform or the competition-inspired "Supertube" chassis, the latter offering a 40% weight saving. The donor for most of the mechanical parts is the Jaguar XJ6 or XJ12. If the engine choice is not a Jaguar V12, American or Rover V8s, as well as Ford V6 or V8 engines can be accommodated. The current DJS products carry John Tojeiro's 'seal of approval'.**

fortunately has now reversed in the 1980s).

Unique Autocraft were one of the first UK companies on the Cobra replica scene, the Python's life starting back in 1981. It was designed from the outset to take the 427 ci big block Ford. Due to Autocraft's desire for "excellence in engineering", they have been criticised by the press, on a number of occasions for "over engineering". This is somewhat unfair, as the Python, at the end of the day, is a credit to the company and the considerable amount of time spent at the design and engineering stage has paid off in producing one of the finest Cobra replicas that money can buy. This emphasis on fine engineering shows up in a very strong and well designed jig and MIG welded chassis. The chassis has mounts for Jaguar front suspension and a narrowed Jaguar rear end. Mounts are also in place for fuel lines, handbrake, seat belts, door locking mounting plates and all of the necessary brake lines. There is also a rear body hoop with roll bar spigots and a split front body hoop with steering column mounts, front screen and scuttle supports. This comprehensive chassis also includes door hinges/ locating points, door beams, radiator points (and radiator), anti-roll bar and petrol tank mounts, the whole unit being supplied in red primer.

The engine and gearbox mounts are not included in the kit and can be purchased from Unique Autocraft depending upon the engine option chosen; Ford, Rover or Chevrolet. The body is of a one-piece construction (based on a Mk III C Cobra) with a boot, bonnet and doors. All the internal mouldings are supplied together with wheel wells, boot, bulkhead and floor. The under panels are pre-drilled for mounting onto the chassis and located by over 56 mounting points. The steering rack is a modified Ford unit, manufactured by Unique Autocraft, and ready to bolt directly onto chassis mountings. All of the fibreglass panels are drilled on a body mounting jig, fitted to the chassis jig, so all of the mounting holes line up correctly during kit assembly.

Unique Autocraft can supply a complete front suspension package including two Spax adjustable coil-overs, to allow for adjustment of suspension ride, height and damper rates. There are two bottom wishbone tie plates, an anti-roll

The Unique Autocraft Python Roadster uses an all-Jaguar based suspension set-up, with the power coming courtesy of a Ford V8. The backbone of the car is a substantial twin-rail chassis that comes complete with all of the necessary mounting brackets in place. The authentic fibreglass body shell is of good quality and comes in a white gel coat finish. The engineering and attention to detail of the Python is most impressive.

bar with all of the necessary links, rose-joints, rubbers and chassis plates. The layout uses the standard Jaguar XJ6 Series One upper wishbones and rubber bush arrangement. The rear suspension package includes top shock mounting shafts, spacers and nuts, bottom differential and pinion support plate, front and rear tie straps as well as the narrowing the XJ drive shafts and lower wishbones. Compomotive HB series or Tru-Spoke wheels are recommended, 8 x 15 at the front and 10 x 15 taking up the rear. Recommended tyres are BF Goodrich P 265/50 R15 and P295/50 R15's.

Many accessories are available, including such items as a chrome roll bar, side grilles (in stainless), headlights, wiring loom, nudge bars, soft top, tonneau cover, hard top and many others to tempt the wallet.

In the driver's seat, and with a big block Ford under the bonnet, acceleration is impressive (to say the least!) and the 0–60 dash forces the driver back firmly into the seat. Many of the Pythons on the road have a top speed well in excess of 120 mph. The overall driving and cornering characteristics are excellent and a credit to the designers, particularly for the chassis, its strength and integrity becoming obvious as the car is put through it paces. This is one replica, that along with such quality kits as the DAX, will undoubtedly remain on the streets for many years to come.

Magnum 427

The Cobra has always been a ferocious-looking car, but of the current crop of Cobra clones, the prize for the most ferocious looking must go to the Magnum 427. The Magnum is the product of Auto Power Services (APS) in Daventry, and manages to shout "power" from every angle. The design of the car was based on that of the Mk III Cobra and was designed with both fast road and track use in mind.

The chassis is of the space-frame variety, with full triangulation, and is constructed from 1.5 inch 16 gauge seamless steel tubing. A lightweight competition version is identical, except that lighter 18 gauge steel is used in the chassis construction. It comes fully bracketed to take specially fabricated APS wishbones and Jaguar uprights, front and rear. Engine mounts are available for a number of different choices, such as Ford 289, 302, 351, and 427 ci V8s. The space-frame features a central tubular backbone that extends to the full width of the chassis, with full triangulation in the door areas, this increasing the side-impact resistance. A single roll-over bar is used, with mountings for either 4- or 6-point harnesses.

The shape of the bodyshell is virtually identical to that of the 427 Mk III Cobra, and as a result of its carbon fibre and Kevlar content, is immensely strong. The only slight variation from the original shape is the front panel, beneath the grille, this having been altered to increase the ground clearance and create a small spoiler. The front-hinged bonnet has a NCA duct, feeding air into the cold airbox built into the bonnet bulge, and is held in place with quick-release fasteners. The boot lid is attached in a similar fashion. The customer has a choice of either functional or non-functional doors, and where doors are selected, these are fully double-skinned. There is also a choice of a full width screen, or a half width Brooklands unit. The bodyshell is available in two forms, namely Stage I, which has a Kevlar content of 27–30%, and Stage II, which uses 48–52%. The latter is normally selected where a full race car is being constructed. Internally, the car is panelled in aluminium, as is both the dash panel and the under side of the body.

The front suspension consists of Jaguar XJ6 uprights, with special APS wishbones, adjustable coil-over units, Rose-jointed anti-roll bar, and Ford Rally Sport steering

The Libre Cobras are some of the least expensive Cobra replicas currently available, and will accept any Ford engine from the 1300 cc four-cylinder, up to the American Ford V8s. This particular car is the Libre 289, its stablemate being the 427. For economy, Cortina front suspension is used in its entirety, with the option of the Capri or Cortina axle at the back. In addition, the entire braking system can also be Ford-based. For performance in keeping with its image, Libre suggest the use of the Essex V6 as a suitable compromise between performance and economy.

rack. At the rear, more XJ6 components are found in the shape of a Salisbury 4HA limited-slip differential, lightweight wishbones, and one coil-over unit each side, as opposed to the normal two. An anti-roll bar is also used.

A choice of either 4, 8 or 12 gallon steel tanks is available, these being available with aluminium foam filling, and mounted in the boot area of the chassis.

A full range of ancillary parts for the trimming of the interior is available, such as carpet sets, door trim panels, specially designed seats, plus a full range of instruments. Weather protection, where road use is anticipated, is available in the form of a soft top and side-screens, or alternatively, a hard top can be supplied. All of the necessary parts and accessories needed to add authenticity, are also listed by APS. This includes such things as over-riders, side louvre panels, bonnet handles, and wind wings. In fact, virtually every part needed to complete the Magnum is available from APS.

Amongst repli-Cobras, and even the

genuine article, the Magnum 427 is one hell of a beast. Needless to say, the quality of the car is excellent, and excellence does not come cheaply. The car can be ordered in various stages of completion, depending upon the customer's choice, however, at 1987 prices, a completed car will cost from £12,000 plus VAT. The final price depends on the individual specification. The Magnum would make either the ultimate road car, or alternatively, a very competitive competition car. It is eligible for such sporting events as hill climbs, sprints, and drag racing, as well as Mod Sports, Inter Marque, Formula Libra, as well as the Kit Cars Challenge series, on the race track. The car has been meticulously designed and fabricated, with a dual role in mind, and with a Ford 427 V8 on board, would certainly be a hard act to follow!

The Libra Cobras

Libra Cars produce two Cobra replicas, both Ford-based, the KC427 and the KC289, which have been developed over the last five years. The 427 was the first, called the King Cobra and is based on Cortina Mk III, IV and V mechanicals (with a V6 power plant recommended) and the 289 on a combination of Capri (rear-end set-up, including axle) and Cortina (front set-up) with the V6 Capri engine, or with up to a V12 power-plant.

The chassis is jig assembled, with all of the location points pre-drilled for easy assembly. It is constructed from ⅛" wall (3 x 2 and 3 x 1.5 inch) box-section steel in a ladder frame arrangement. The front suspension is taken from a Cortina, virtually complete, and includes steering rack (requiring only a minor modification), shock absorbers, wishbones and springs, the latter being re-rated to allow for the reduced weight. These parts bolt directly to the chassis, using solid fixing, to give what Libra Cars describe as a "true sports car feel". They do supply, as an option, their own "quick rack" system for those who require it. The rear axle for the 427 comes from a Cortina and a Capri supplies the 289s. The rear axles use fully adjustable coil-overs which fix directly to the chassis, using pre-drilled mounting points. The engine selected, can be from any model of the Cortina or Capri. The Essex V6 is recommended for normal road use. If the engine choice is a Ford four-cylinder or V6, then the propshaft can be used without modification, however, if a non-Ford power plant is to be installed, then a specially made shaft is required. Libra claim that the Ford axle and suspension set-up can easily handle a Rover V8, but for engines larger than this, such as the big block Fords, their chassis based on Jaguar components is suggested.

Inside the scuttle, is a detachable sub-frame, which carries the windscreen mounts, steering column and door hinges. The hinges are fully adjustable and are supplied with the kit.

The floors, boot, bulkhead and inner wheel arches are held in a jig while they are bonded to the bodyshell, whilst still in its mould. This helps to ensure correct alignment during assembly as well as increasing torsional rigidity and producing a very good seal for weather protection. For further protection, hard and soft tops are available as optional extras.

The Ford donor will also supply all of the braking system, the disc and drum combination depending upon the trim level of the donor (ventilated discs are available as options). The wiring loom can also be used largely intact, although if the thought of that is too daunting, then this can also be bought from Libra.

The kit comprises the chassis, scuttle frame with door hinges, bodyshell, doors, boot lid, bonnet, dash panel, side panels, door trim panels, back panel and the front grille, all constructed from very good quality fibreglass. Options include side-screens, chrome surrounds for the

screen, over-riders in stainless steel, bonnet and boot locks, 427 Cobra badges, side louvers, seats, escutcheon plates and so on.

Libras are some of the cheapest Cobra kits on the market but depending on the builder, they can look just as good as any other. Libra Cars are also one of the few companies to use such a high Ford content, which allows the "average" kit car builder to enter the replica scene. Many manufacturers tend to list only their large engine options and as a result, consequently put the price out of the reach of many potential builders.

As for driving the Libras, with the Essex V6 on board they are very quick (+110 mph) and the 0-60 dash is exhilarating. The handling, particularly cornering, is as would be expected with so many Ford components being used, very good and definitely helped by the re-rated springs. If the racetrack is the proving ground, then its a different story, but one where Libra still has the edge over many competitors. Obviously, with a V6, it is no match for the DAX V8s and V12s, but with the Jaguar based chassis and the choice of a larger power-plant it can certainly hold its own both in performance and looks!

Brightwheel Viper

Brightwheel originally became involved in the repli-Cobra scene as build-up specialists and agents for Sheldonhurst, who at the time, were producing a Granada-based clone. 1986 saw Sheldonhurst go into liquidation and it was at this point that Brightwheel director, Ken Cook stepped in and eventually took over the project. He revitalised and improved the product, the culmination being the appearance of the Brightwheel Replicas Viper.

Brightwheel had already established themselves as very proficient car builders, and had built up a good reputation for their skills and workmanship. They were particularly proficient with the assembly of the Sheldonhurst Cobra.

Ken Cook already had a good deal of

Below and right: The Brightwheel Cobras arrived on the scene as a result of the collapse of the Sheldonhurst Company, the Brightwheel Viper now using an excellent body and chassis, both produced by Rickmans. Granada running-gear can be used almost in its entirety, this making the car a popular choice throughout Europe. Following their great success with the Viper, the company are currently putting the finishing touches to an equally impressive Countach Replica.

experience in a variety of fields, including sportscar restoration, ski boat and, of course, kit car manufacture. Under his control, the project was revamped, still retaining the concept of a high Ford

content in the shape of the Granada running-gear.

The Viper chassis is now made by Rickmans (of Ranger fame) and takes the form of a beautifully finished, MIG-welded and baked epoxy-coated unit, largely constructed of 3 x 2 inch steel box-section. It comes complete with engine-mounts, brackets, hinges, and special pedal box. Brightwheel describe it as a ladder/space frame unit, the basic design being twin-rail, heavily reinforced with substantial amounts of cross-bracing. This is designed to accept the Granada front suspension, complete with its cross-member, intact. The Granada steering system is also retained, although power-steering is not used. The standard springs and shock absorbers are up to the job, although adjustable Spax coil-overs are available as an option. The rear suspension consists of the independent Granada set-up, complete with semi-trailing arms and wishbone. The coil springs and shock absorbers are mounted in a similar fashion to the donor. All of the Ford parts will fit without modification.

The brakes also come from the Granada, the standard front discs/rear drums, having proved to be more than adequate for the job. Providing the power is of course, the Granada's V6, the resultant performance with even a standard engine, being excellent.

Clothing the mechanical parts is the high quality fibreglass body. When Brightwheel took over the project, new moulds were produced, the actual manufacture now being carried out by Rickmans. The results are impressive, the finish, fit, and strength of the body being one of the best currently available. The boot, bonnet, and doors are double-skinned, and the rear bulkhead, boot liner and inner rear wheel arches, are all in place.

Needless to say, with a company as professional as Brightwheel, virtually all of the non-Granada parts are available from stock. The hardware necessary to complete the car's exterior is available, such as nerf bars, side vents, roll-over bar, hinges and locks, and stone guards. Additional parts such as windscreen, wind-wings, and petrol tank, are also listed.

For the interior, Brightwheel supply dash panel, carpet sets, door panels, seats (or shells), with weather protection coming in the form of a double-duck soft top. For the more hardy, there is the option of a tonneau cover.

Although the modification of the Granada's exhaust system is a possibility, a much better bet is one of Brightwheel's underfloor twin-flow systems, or even a set of side-pipes. Both would be equally beneficial in terms of performance.

Amongst the multitude of other parts stocked, are electric fans, steering wheels, full brake pipe/master cylinder kits, and replica Halibrand wheels. In truth, there is virtually nothing missing!

The Viper is, at present, the only British-made Cobra that has been tested and granted German TUV approval, this clearly aiding its sales appeal throughout Europe.

The chassis can be bought in various stages of completion, from the basic chassis, right up to a driveable, fully-assembled unit. The chassis can be ordered at any stage in between.

The Viper is undoubtedly one of the easiest Cobra kits to assemble, partially because of its high Ford content, and partially because Brightwheel have now assembled so many completed cars, that they have ironed out any problem areas in the build-up. Where Brightwheel supply the engines, they are either new, or totally rebuilt.

To date, a total of thirty five kits have been sold and sixteen in fully-assembled form. Most of the latter have been exported, the easy availability of Ford spare parts, clearly accounting for its popularity throughout Europe.

The verdict? As Cobras clones go, the Viper is by no means the most expensive.

Whether in kit form or as a completed car, it looks tremendous. The quality of the body and chassis are excellent, and this, coupled with its Ford running-gear, means that the car can be made to perform like a true sports/racing car, and yet still remain a practical proposition for daily use. There are clearly plenty of people in both the UK and overseas who agree. Out of the ashes of the Sheldonhurst Cobra, has emerged the Phoenix of the Viper. There is little doubt that this time, and in this form, it is destined to stay!

Porsche clones

In the eyes of the public, Porsche products are probably some of the best known performance cars currently in production. Their characteristic styling and undeniably nippy performance has earned them an enviable reputation, as well as establishing them as many people's firm favourites.

The current phase of Porsche's success story really begins in 1964, with the launch of the 6-cylinder powered 911 series. Over the following two decades, there followed successive boosts in power output, chassis improvements, and cosmetic and aerodynamic refinements. In 1972 the 911S was in action, its 190 bhp giving it a top speed of 143 mph, but it was really the appearance, in 1977, of the Porsche Turbo that reaffirmed Porsche's edge over much of the opposition. The performance of the Turbo is well documented, its 0–60 time being in the region of six seconds and its top speed around 155 mph. 1978 saw a capacity increase to 3.3 litres, with a corresponding increase in power to 300 bph. The 0–60 time fell to five seconds. At this time, the distinctive whale-tail spoiler first appeared, a styling feature that was to become associated with Porsche cars in particular. For many people, the Porsche Turbo remains an unattainable dream, quality and performance, as usual, not coming cheaply.

This period also saw the water-cooled 924 and 928 models make their first appearance, the latter being voted "Car

of the Year" in 1977. Perhaps ironically, the 924 could almost be regarded as a Porsche-assembled "kit", its 2 litre engine and transmission originating from Audi, the front suspension from the VW Golf/ Scirroco, and the rear suspension from the Beetle! Although its performance of 125 mph and 0–60 time of 8.9 seconds, is well below that of the Turbo, the styling remains well and truly in the Porsche mould.

As a result of their reputation, Porsche cars command a good price, even second-hand models selling for substantial sums. This inevitably puts them out of the fiscal reach of many people. Fortunately, there is now an alternative!

Covin Turbo Coupe and Cabriolet

Covin first came into the spotlight in 1984, as a result of the combined efforts of Tim Cook of Americar, and Nick Vincent, formerly of DJ Sportscars. The name "Covin" is an amalgamation of their surnames.

Their first product was the Turbo Coupe. This immediately attracted a tremendous amount of attention, not merely because of its excellent quality, but also because it bore an uncanny resemblance to a car produced by a certain company called Porsche! The Coupe body was intended to fit a suitably shortened version of the VW Beetle floorpan, and to accept most of the running-gear from the same source. The floorpan needed shortening to the tune of seven inches and the suspension lowering by four, in order to give the required fit and stance. Even when using completely unmodified VW suspension, the car handled remarkably well, the overall performance, however, being dependent on the state of tune of the flat four. The Coupe attracted a great deal of acclaim from the motoring press, as well as the public at large, the majority of whom merely assumed that they were looking at yet another Porsche. The superb quality of the Covin body was mainly responsible for this. The majority of the car's mechanical components were taken from

the Beetle, with Covin supplying all of the non-VW parts.

A significant occurrence came hot on the heels of the floor-pan version, in the shape of the new specially made replacement chassis. This was constructed from steel box-section, and was designed to take its main mechanical parts from the VW Type 3 Variant, and retaining the torsion-bar front-end set-up.

Producing replicas such as these, can sometimes lead to the manufacturer falling foul of the complex, and often unclear, patent and copyright laws. Covin were one such company, and as a result of Porsche's intervention, were forced to redesign several body panels, namely the bumpers and the whale-tail spoiler. These relatively minor alterations seemed to solve the problem!

1985 saw the new Covin Cabriolet appear, this, once again, bearing a distinct resemblance to a custom version of the Porsche 911. As with the Coupe, the quality and finish of the Cabriolet body, was excellent.

Both cars offer the option of using either the VW floor-pan or replacement chassis routes, the former providing the most economical one.

Most people tend to assume that the Covin cars are purely based on, and powered by VW components, however, recent events have added a new dimension to things, with the advent of a Ford engine option, this taking the form of the cvh units. This is mounted in the "conventional" VW location, at the extreme rear, the engine driving through a VW transaxle via a special adaptor plate. The cvh engine is used in its entirety, complete with all of its ancillaries, and unlike the air-cooled alternatives, clearly requires the retention of its radiator. Access to the engine is very good, the choice of a Ford power-plant making the cars even more desirable.

The Covin chassis, is a high strength unit, and encompasses both backbone and space-frame elements in its design. In addition, a substantial perimeter rail runs around the outside. The MIG welded unit comes fully drilled, ready for the relatively painless addition of the VW Variant rear suspension, the torsion-bar

front end and, where selected, the cvh engine.

The Covin bodies are renowned for their finish and fit, all of the panels being double-skinned, with extra strength in stressed areas and the doors, being provided by steel reinforcement. Such is the quality, that little preparation of the gel-coat finish needs to be carried out prior to spraying.

Covin themselves, admit that their cars are neither the cheapest or the easiest cars on the market to assemble, requiring a fair amount of patience and attention to detail, in order to do the kit full justice. They certainly give the builder a good start with their body and chassis combination, as well as the impressive list of additional parts that they can supply. The kits enable the buyer to complete a very passable Porsche clone for considerably less money than an original would cost. For instance, the typical price

for a Porsche 911 Turbo, seems to currently be around the £40,000 mark. It would be quite feasible to assemble one of the Covin cars from all new components, and add a multitude of top-of-the-range extras, for a fraction of the cost.

The handling of both the Coupe and the Cabriolet, is remarkably good, the final performance being dependent on the choice of engine. The VW four clearly makes an economical choice, although there is always the option of fitting a genuine (and horrendously expensive!) Porsche unit. Perhaps the most sensible route to performance would be the use of a comparatively cheap, reliable, and easily tuned Ford cvh engine. This, in a suitable state of tune, coupled with the undisputed quality of the Covin kits, would make a car that could give even a genuine Porsche a good run for its money!

The Cabriolet version was introduced in 1985 and is modelled as a custom version of the Porsche 911. Mechanically, the cars are very similar, however the Cabriolet features pop-up headlights, custom wings and side-skirts. Quality is, once again, excellent. (Photo courtesy of Covin)

Right and below: **The unique handmade "Porsche" clone of Barney Concannon, based on a Rochdale Olympic Phase II. Virtually every panel of the car has been completely reworked by the owner, the end result looking uncannily like a 911. The drive-train consists of a 1600 GT Cortina engine and gearbox, and the back axle, a Corsair unit. The distinctive whale-tail spoiler came courtesy of Covin, whilst the rear trailblazer was, like virtually every other part of the car, homemade.**

Rochdale Olympic "Porsche"

The Rochdale Olympic may not normally look like a Porsche 911 but after some clever alterations, a diminutive Porsche clone is a possibility.

This Porsche lookalike (resplendent in Porsche Guard's Red, after spraying with Berger etch and guide coating) is the brainchild of Barney Concannon, who acquired his Olympic Phase Two in 1977 with 34,000 miles on the clock, originally powered by a 1300 pre-crossflow engine. This was replaced with a 1.6 GT Cortina (Mk II) engine and gearbox, the exhaust gases running out via a homemade, twin exhaust system. A shortened propshaft was constructed, this connecting to a 3.45:1 RS 2000 differential. The front suspension is from a Vitesse, and the rear axle from a Corsair. The stopping power is via the Cortina disc and drum layout and cooling, courtesy of a heavily modified Triumph 1500 radiator and header tank. The instruments are also from the Cortina, with the exception of the tachometer. Avenger air vents were also used. One of the few items of the original to be left are the carpets, the interior now housing a pair of Fiat 124 seats. The moulded bumpers were made by Barney, and the tail fin a cast-off from Covin. In addition, the side mouldings were removed. A Humber Sceptre was utilised initially for window frames which were modified by Barney, with Perspex being used for the quarter lights and large rear window. The latter was later replaced by a Fiat 127 frame and glass. By 1982, Barney had removed the roof and had installed a 1.25 square steel tube frame ready to support a new section. At this time he also reconstructed the window

frames from alloy, and painted them matt black, the Perspex side windows being replaced by laminated glass. Cortina handles, matt black, were also fitted to the doors. The rear quarter petrol tanks were removed and replaced with a unit from a Mk II Cortina, mounted below the boot floor. The spare wheel takes the place of one of the old tanks inside the rear wing. The roof and wing panels were then fitted (all home-constructed), the nose line altered, the bonnet converted to a full length, front-hinged unit, and an air dam constructed from an Alfa Sud and the remains of an Avenger grille. The dash front is of alloy construction, in three pieces, and houses the Cortina instruments (except for the tachometer, which is of Japanese origin). The illumination is via Bosch headlights, Skoda indicators and Marina rear lights. Even the OLYMPIC trail blazer is homemade. All in all, quite a unique and superb one-off clone, a real credit to the skills and imagination of Barney Concannon.

The GT40 clones

It has often been commented that perhaps the GT40 only came about as a result of Ford's failure, in 1963, to buy Ferrari. When negotiations fell through, Roy Lunn was put to work on designing a Le Mans winner. He was joined by John Wye, from Aston Martin, and Eric Broadley, an engineer of Lola fame. The first GT40 (a reference to its height of 40 inches), was completed at the beginning of April 1964. The car's subsequent prowess and success on the race track needs no further description!

Unlike many race cars of the period, the GT40 did not use a space frame-chassis, but utilised a semi-monocoque construction, the central tub supporting the unstressed fibreglass body panels.

1966 saw the announcement of a road-going version, this being virtually identical in appearance to the racers. Minor alterations were made, such as the fitting of mesh grilles over the various intakes, softer springs and the use of a de-tuned 289 ci V8 engine. Very few road cars were sold, of the thirty one that

The GT40 replica of Rob Bloom is based on an early KVA. The power is provided by a Granada V6 which drives through a VW transaxle, via an adaptor kit. The front suspension is largely Cortina, the car rolling on Compomotive wheels. Resplendent in accurate Gulf Team colours, the stunning car makes up one of the very exclusive band of GT40 replicas. A car that would not look out of place on the track at Le Mans!

Photographs above: **Doug Blair's impressive machine uses a GT Developments chassis, with a KVA Mk I body. Power for this low-slung beauty comes from a mid-mounted 289 Ford small-block V8.**

eventually found their way onto the roads, twenty went to the United States. In an attempt to improve sales, Ford introduced the Mk III version in 1967. Some body modifications were made, the interior altered, the luggage space in the rear increased, and even softer springs fitted. The strategy failed to work and only seven Mk IIIs were built. In all, a total of 107 GT40s were constructed but from this small number, a legend was born.

Largely because of their price, few found their way into the hands of the general public, and this, perhaps, helped to surround the car with many myths and legends. Whatever the truth of the matter, the GT40 has now become one of the most

sought-after cars in the world, its performance, looks and charisma, ensuring that on the rare occasions that one comes up for sale, the prices fetched are usually astronomical! To this day, it remains the fastest road-going car that Ford ever produced.

The car remained a virtually unattainable dream up to nearly twenty years after its first introduction, when, in 1983, KVA began producing the first replica GT40s. The company's founder was Ken Attwell (whose initials make up the company name), formerly a senior engineer at Ford's Swansea plant. Taking immense care, he set about re-creating Ford's "Wonder Car", now using a chassis of his own design and powering his creation with an XR3 Turbo unit. The fibreglass body was made dimensionally as close as possible to the original, but featured a number of modifications intended to ease maintenance and allow for detachable bodywork.

As soon as the hand-built car appeared on the scene, it immediately attracted a good deal of media coverage, the result being that Ken was quickly deluged with enquiries and requests for a full-blown kit version. As a result, the KVA company came into being.

Two chassis options were offered by KVA, one being a basic unit which was suitable for engines up to 3.5 litres, and the other being a "Type C", for greater capacity units. The latter was a type of space-frame, consisting of twin upper and lower perimeter rails of 40 mm square-section steel, with cross-members and roll-over protection. Naturally, the unit came fully-drilled and bracketed. The front suspension consisted of a Ford Granada cross-member, this supplying the disc brake assemblies, hubs, shock absorbers, uprights, and steering rack. Cortina uprights and rack are other possible options. At the rear, Granada hubs, drive-shafts and brakes are used.

In 1984, Phoenix Automotive became involved with KVA, becoming the only UK licensee. Phoenix built up a GT40 clone using the KVA body, but with a chassis and running-gear of their own. A space-frame chassis was used, with Mk III/IV Cortina front suspension and steering

Ford based kit cars

5
Clone cars

rack. At the rear, was a wishbone system, with Granada hubs and Spax coil-over units. Jaguar drive-shafts and disc brakes completed the picture. Phoenix offered an engine choice of either a Ford V6 or V8, driving through a Citroen SM 5-speed box via an adaptor plate, the engine being cooled by a front-mounted Sierra radiator.

There is sometimes confusion concerning KVA's relationship with GT Developments, the latter having entered the arena as agents for KVA. They produced their own chassis but used the KVA body. After some time (in 1986), there was trouble between the two companies, and GTD's sole agency was formally ended. GTD (South) Ltd was then formed, new moulds produced and their own version of the GT40 put into production.

The first GTD car used the KVA Mk I body but with their own chassis and suspension arrangement, power coming from a 5 litre Ford V8. Much of the initial design and construction was carried out by Ray Christopher, a name well-known to the Street Rodding fraternity, who is a director of GTD. Their comprehensive chassis kit contains springs, shock absorbers, hubs, brakes, wishbones and so on. It is largely constructed from 40 mm square section steel tube and is similar in design to the original KVA unit, with the exception of the use of Ford Scorpio (Mk III Granada) discs at the rear. The body is of good quality fibreglass, both inside and out, and comes supplied in a gel-coat finish. There are a number of minor differences in the bodyshell, such as cut-outs in the front wings and some alterations around the rear section. Unlike the KVA, which requires a certain amount of aluminium fabrication work, the GTD body comes with floor, sills and bulkheads in situ. Not

surprisingly, a good supply of additional parts is available from both sources.

KVA have not been inactive throughout this period, as they have now teamed up

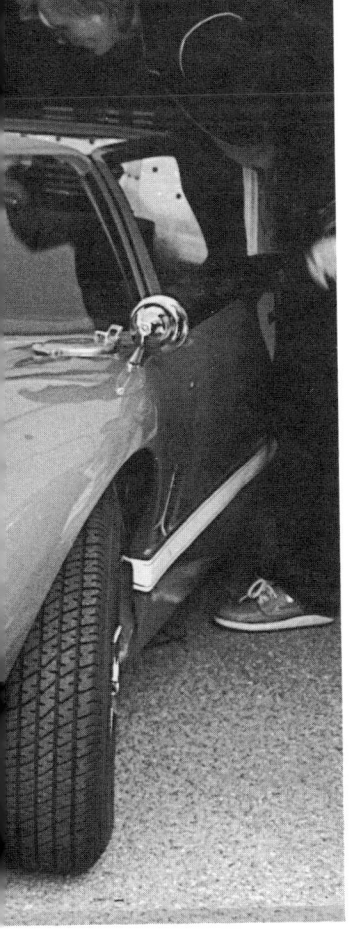

with DJ Sportscars (of DAX Cobra/Tojeiro fame), and have produced a KVA 2. This body is much lighter than the original, now being available in Carbon fibre and Kevlar. The new chassis is a further development of the Type C spaceframe, Granada parts being used for the front uprights and brakes, rear hubs, rear brakes and drive shafts. A 289 or 302 ci Ford V8 or V6 makes a suitable choice of engine, driving through a Renault 30 four- or five-speed gearbox.

A further newcomer to the scene, is the engineering company of High Tech Welding, whose version also uses a body based on that of the Mk I KVA. They have produced a chassis that is very strong, well-constructed and, overall, is a very impressive piece of work. It is constructed from 16 gauge steel tube, of 40 x 25 mm, with 80 x 40 mm section cross-members. The unit is TIG welded and comes with seat belt mountings, roll-over protection and the numerous other fixtures and mounting points, all in place. The suspension system is similar to that of its rivals, but uses polished stainless steel for such parts as wishbones. The body comes complete with its aluminium panelling ready-fitted. A long list of additional parts and accessories including fuel tank, laminated wind-screen, Perspex side and rear windows, lights, and dashboard, are also available. As with the other GT40 clones, a Ford V6 or V8 makes a suitable power-plant.

One further alternative currently available, is the GT40 clone of Cheetah Cars. Their kits are undoubtedly the cheapest on the market, although some reservations have been expressed as to the overall finish of the fibreglass. Although it seems likely that more time would need to be spent on body preparation before spraying, however there

should be no major problems. The Cheetah kit may well be the only alternative for those working on a tight budget, the lower cost being the main factor involved. Cheetah's engineering is quite impressive however, their space-frame using Cortina front suspension and Renault 30 front suspension, mounted at the rear. Their cars are designed, in standard form, to take either the Renault 30 or Rover V8 engines, although Ford V8 or V6 units could doubtless be persuaded to fit without too much trouble. Their kit is offered in a number of different forms, such as the Economy version, which includes chassis, front and rear body sections, sills, doors, floor, bulkheads, bonnet and dashboard. The Deluxe kit contains all of the above, plus a full glass kit, roll-over bar, and many other parts. The body is fitted to the chassis, Spax adjustable coil-over units in place, the customer's drive-train installed, and Cheetah's own front and rear suspension systems in position.

An additional option is that of a fully rose-jointed chassis, featuring Cheetah's double 4-link suspension system at the front, and their 2-link upper/3-link lower set-up at the rear.

The general comment is that the Cheetah car requires more detail work to be carried out by the customer, but clearly, this is compensated for by the lower price. The choice of kit, as is so often the case, is dictated by the customer's abilities and bank balance!

With this range of alternatives, that unattainable dream now becomes much more of a distinct possibility. Although a good deal of time and effort is required with most of the cars mentioned, once complete, the builder has a car that is a clone of one of the most charismatic cars to ever hit the streets!

Left: **Late 1986 saw the initial outing of the High Tech Welding multi-tubular space-frame chassis. The front and rear wishbone suspension is fabricated in house using polished stainless steel, and uses coil-spring damper units. Ford engine options include the 289, 302 and 351 ci V8s mated to a Renault gearbox and transaxle, and driving through Granada drive shafts. The company's high quality single piece fibreglass body shell is based on that of the Mk I KVA.**

6
Jeeps and off-roaders

For years, the off-road and four-wheel drive fraternity traditionally consisted of farmers, foresters and builders and those few who genuinely needed a vehicle with four-wheel drive capability. Four-wheel drive was largely limited to the long-running, ubiquitous Land-Rover that, as well as its continued use by the armed forces, was put to use on farms and building sites from one end of Britain to the other. It was a different matter in the United States, where a thriving off-road market had always existed, catering for the many hunters, fishermen and weekend "backwood" explorers. This market was amply catered for by such vehicles as the Chevrolet Blazer, the Ford Bronco and of course, the Jeep. As a result of the obvious sociological and geographical differences between Britain and the United States, an equivalent market for "leisure" four-wheel drive vehicles did not exist. Britain lacked the equivalent of the Apalachian Mountains or the Mojave Desert for weekend sorties!

The American interest in off-roading was, however, to have an effect in Britain, largely as a result of the host of American television programmes that were continually being screened. The rugged, even brutal, looks of these vehicles, soon caught the imagination of a whole section of society who, before long, began to look around for comparable British vehicles. All they found was the Land-Rover!

Some time during this period it became clear that a market for a rather more sophisticated and luxuriously equipped Land-Rover-type vehicle was developing in Britain, the gap in the market ultimately being filled by the arrival of the V8-powered Range Rover. As with its humbler brother, the Range Rover achieved success worldwide and was also beginning to be seen in suburban driveways as well as on the farms and large estates of the countryside. The Range Rover was more of a "dual purpose" machine, equally at home taking the kids to school as well as making its way up a muddy track. In many cases, the former use often dominated the latter! The Range Rover achieved the dubious distinction of becoming something of a trendy status symbol, a vehicle to have parked in the drive next to the Jaguar! This is, to a certain extent, still the case today.

Clearly the rugged looks of the Land and Range Rovers, coupled with the undoubted influence of the television, helped to create a great deal of interest in such vehicles. The result was a tremendous upsurge in the demand and a huge increase in the interest in what had previously been a specialised and comparatively small section of the market.

What actually happened when people went out to actively look for such a vehicle, was that they were faced with a very limited choice. The American Jeeps, Blazers and Broncos were expensive to buy and maintain, expensive to run and expensive to insure, as well as mainly left-hand drive. The British offerings, apart from right-hand drive, suffered from the same drawbacks. What many people wanted, largely because of the "looks", they were in no position to afford.

Any four-wheel drive machine is obviously a lot more complex than its two-wheel drive counterpart, this resulting in a much higher price tag. Perhaps surprisingly, there were a fairly large number of people who were prepared to pay these high prices, merely for the status of owning such a vehicle, never putting it to any real use on the terrain for which it was really intended.

It did not take long for a number of, mainly Eastern, manufacturers to realise that here was a potentially valuable section of the automotive market that was not being tapped. Consequently, various four-wheel drive cars/trucks began to appear on British roads. Toyota brought out their Land Cruiser, clearly aimed at the traditional Land and Range Rover market, with more up-market offerings coming from the likes of, Mitsubishi and Subaru. Some of these were aimed at the Range Rover end of the market and their prices clearly reflected this. Nonetheless, they were readily accepted by the British public and sold comparatively well. Four-wheel drive was the order of the day and rather remarkably, even the four-wheel drive version of Fiat's little Panda sold in surprisingly large numbers.

The majority of these vehicles were comparatively large and it became apparent that there was also a public demand developing for something smaller, this eventually manifesting itself in the form of, for instance, the diminutive Suzuki Jeeps. These proved to be immensely popular and, once again, were to be found in abundance in suburban driveways as well as in the countryside. Their looks and styling endeared them to many however, the little 970 cc engine did not. Various comments were made about their poor petrol consumption low gearing, road noise and poor creature comfort, amongst others. They were however, a supremely practical and moderately priced little vehicle and did have four-wheel drive, with all of its attendant benefits. It is debatable how much real use this was put to in most cases!

One other vehicle worthy of comment is the Matra-Simca Rancho. This was basically a rugged-looking fibreglass body grafted to a Simca pick-up. It certainly had the looks of the off-roaders, with chunky wheel-arch and side mouldings, scuttle mounted spotlights and raised rear roof section. Underneath it consisted of a Simca transverse engine, front-wheel drive layout, a system that many people were not over enthusiastic about. A high insurance rating, mediocre performance and uncertainty over spare part supplies persuaded some prospective buyers against it. However there is no denying that the Rancho and its counterparts had a lot of fans and did have some influence on the design and styling that was later to be adopted by a number of the kit car manufacturers.

By the early 1980s there was a wide range of four-wheel drive machinery available to the buying public. Despite this, there were still a number of factors that dissuaded many people from buying one. In many cases it was simply that they were too expensive, in others, the problems of fuel consumption and running costs were a source of concern. Whatever the reasons, there were still a lot of individuals who were very appreciative of the off-road look but not of the inherent problems of buying and running such vehicles. Once again, the kit car manufacturers were left to provide the answer.

The first kit-based off-roader to appear was the Jago Geep. This was the creation of Geoff Jago who, at the time, was busily engaged with a number of hot-rodding ventures. Realising that the company needed to diversify into other areas, he took a set of moulds from a battered 1942 Willys Jeep and began producing passable fibreglass replica bodies. This was fitted to a simple but substantial steel box chassis designed to accept the major mechanical parts from the, then plentiful, 105E Anglia. This supplied the drive-train, suspension, wiring, instrumentation and many of the smaller necessary parts needed. Jago's move into this sphere of the market proved to be an unqualified

success with the Ford-based Geep kits proving to be immensely popular as well as providing the inspiration for a number of other Jeep-type kits that were to come in later years.

Probably as something of a spin off from the Jeep lookalikes, a market began to develop for a vehicle that could be more comprehensively equipped, had better weather protection but still retained something of the off-road image. Jeeps were fine for carrying a couple of adults but were sometimes less than practical for the family man. His requirements were obviously different and eventually came to be met following the introduction of a number of kits that, to varying degrees, resembled the style and proportion of the Rancho, but made use of the tried and tested Ford mechanical parts.

Jago Geep

Of all of the off-road kits currently available, the Jago Geep is the most popular and longest running. It has been around in various forms, since 1971 and clearly owes its looks and dimensions to the World War II Willys Jeep. Originally based on the 105E Anglia mechanicals, 1975 saw the arrival of the Mk I Escort-based version. From this time, sales really took off and the company never really looked back.

Like its Anglia based predecessor, the Geep uses a fibreglass body and a rugged box-section chassis. This is designed so that virtually all of the main mechanical components of the Escort can simply be bolted into place. Assembly of the rolling chassis is straightforward, the main components only requiring installation of no more than a couple of dozen bolts!

The body consists of a main structure that comes complete with a floor bonded into place, wings, screen, grille and dash panel. This is supported by the well built Jago chassis the design of which ensures that the panels remain unstressed. The fibreglass body panels come self-coloured and are available in over 200 different colours.

With the passing years, the Geep has been quite heavily restyled although it has never completely lost the characteristics of its Willys forerunner. Early versions sported a large US military style star moulded into the bonnet, flat wings and a fairly clumsy treatment around the screen area. Since those early beginnings, the bonnet has been restyled, the wings updated and rear arch extensions made available, all this resulting in a vehicle that, like the "genuine" Jeep, has successfully matured from its 1940s origins to one that looks quite appropriate for the 1980s.

The kit will handle any of the range of Ford engines, from the humble 1300 right

A pair of Jago Geeps, first introduced in the Mk I Escort-based form in 1975. This was followed later by the version based on the Mk II variants. The fibreglass bodies are colour impregnated and are available in over 200 different colours. The 1300 ohc powered example in the foreground, of Philip Rogers, has the soft top option, with opening doors, and the other, the hard top. Like the majority of other Geeps, both run on white 8-spoke wheels.

up to the 3 litre V6. The most popular choices seem to fall in the 1600–2000 range, this giving a very healthy performance in this lightweight machine.

Virtually all of the Escort mechanical parts, wiring and so on, can be transplanted without modification. Even the suspension doesn't require uprating, standard springs and shock absorbers being more than capable of coping with most situations. Slightly worn units appear to work the best. Braking is adequately handled by standard disc brakes units rather than the earlier drums, however no servo is used as this tends to over-brake the Geep.

A long list of options is available from Jago, these including well fitting hard and soft tops, as well as detachable doors. Jago will also supply steel eight-spoke wheels although a range of 14 and 15 inch types are available from a number of sources. The choice of wheels and tyres will depend on the completed Geep's eventual use. To look the part, it really does need a fairly large wheel/tyre combination, 13 inch rims looking lost under the gaping arches.

How does the little Geep perform in the rough? Unlike the original Willys, the short wheelbase Geep handles remarkably well and is capable of being pushed into corners with surprising rapidity and lack of body roll. Clearly the aerodynamics come into play at higher speeds however, performance can be decidedly brisk depending upon the choice of engine. For off-road use, the Geep has proved to be remarkably agile despite its lack of four-wheel drive. Its rigid chassis, light weight and short wheelbase, especially when coupled with reasonably large tyres enabling it to get out of mud and over the sort of terrain that would have most two-wheel drive and even certain four-wheel drive vehicles struggling. In short, its off-road performance is remarkably good and on a par with many purpose-built vehicles.

1985 saw the production of the limited edition "Geep 85" built as a celebration of the firms 25th birthday. The 25 specials built, had special paintwork with graphics and numerous additional parts such as lights, roo bars, gold eight-spoke wheels and tan hoods. The models will probably

This 1600 cc ohv-powered version, owned by Tony and Laura Crockford, clearly shows the differences to the earlier Anglia-based type. Over the years, the screen pillars were slimmed down, the bonnet redesigned, the front wings widened and improved, and the rear wheel arches extended. This all helped to update the Geeps appearance. 1987 saw further changes to the grille, wings and chassis.

become quite sought after with the passing years.

1987 saw the launch of the Jago 1987 which had improvements such as return flanges on the front wings, redesigned grille, bonnet and chassis. The number of donor cars can now be more than one. Jago is also now a member of the Specialist Car Manufacturers Group of the SMMT.

As a result of its looks, ease of construction, and all round performance, the Jago Geep has firmly established itself on the scene and certainly looks set to remain there for a long time to come.

The Eagle RV

The Eagle RV is another vehicle that owes much of its style and character to the World War II Willys, although, like both the genuine Jeep products and the Jago Geep, it has been suitably restyled and updated to transform it into a vehicle more in line with the times. Its current styling reflects more rounded, less angular lines, similar to those adopted for the present day range of Jeeps, rather than to those of the original Willys. Its size is also comparable with that of the Jeep Renegade, being larger than both the Geep and the Willys and with the capacity to carry four adults with ease. There is also a reasonable amount of space left for luggage. In this respect it certainly scores over the opposition, although to be fair, it does seem to be aimed at a slightly different segment of the market. The RV, with its longer wheelbase and greater carrying capacity, makes it a more practical proposition for the family man, and it is here particularly, that it seems to find great favour.

The RV in its current form, can trace its roots back to 1982 when it was being produced using VW components. Then, Alan Breeze of Eagle Cars, bought out the project as a stablemate for the Eagle SS. The kit was redesigned to accept Ford running-gear, re-emerging late in 1983 with a tubular steel chassis designed to take the main components from the Mk III and IV Cortina range.

The new chassis was of a straight-forward ladder design and featured 80 x 40 mm main rails with 40 x 40 mm cross bracing in the appropriate places. With a few modifications, this is still largely the same today. The unit comes fully drilled, ready to take the Cortina drive-train, and features bolt-on front and rear bumpers, useful should repairs be necessary. The chassis is well made and experience has shown it to be a very strong assembly, quite capable of taking a severe off-road battering! Apart from the engine and gearbox, the Cortina supplies the majority of the other necessary parts such as braking and suspension systems, lights, electrical parts, wiring harness, wiper motor, radiator, heater and pedal assembly.

Right: **This bright blue RV is powered by a Ford V6 and uses a de-caged and fully chromed Jaguar IRS, an uncommon arrangement for such a vehicle. In addition, it has many individual touches such as wide alloy wheels with BF Goodrich radials, and GT Cortina instrumentation. Weather protection is provided by the soft top with fibreglass doors option.**

Below: **A remarkable example of an RV, here in six-wheeler form! Notice the extended double length rear wheel arches and the lengthened soft top. Truly a unique vehicle.**

As with many kit cars, virtually any of the range of Ford engines up to the 3 litre V6 can be accommodated, the final performance clearly being dependent on this choice.

The assembly of the rolling-chassis is quite straightforward, the majority of the assembly consisting of bolt-in jobs. A few parts such as the exhaust system, steering column and propshaft need altering, however these are all fairly basic modifications. The front springs can be left as they are, however there is some opinion that suggests that they sometimes need softening slightly. It largely depends on their age.

As with the Geep, to adequately look the part, the RV really needs fairly large wheels and tyres of the 15 or 16 inch variety. Anything smaller looks completely out of place.

The main body moulding comes complete, with the floor ready bonded in, and shows obvious signs of good workmanship and attention to detail. The general opinion is that the RV certainly represents good value for money. Inside, there is

plenty of passenger space, with a good driving position and excellent all-round visibility, even with the weather equipment on. Instrumentation and access to the controls is also good.

Numerous options are available from Eagle; these include an excellent hood and side-screens, hard top, 8–spoke wheels, rear spare mount and roo bars.

In conclusion, the RV has shown itself to be a winner, with its easy construction and solid workmanship. It has proved itself to be a very practical multipurpose vehicle and one that has made a welcome addition to the Jeep-type ranks in recent years. The similarities in styling to the Jeep Renegade are obvious. One major difference is the price!

Rickman Ranger

Anyone with an interest in motor cycles will undoubtedly be familiar with the name of Rickman. For many years the company was heavily involved with the motor cycle industry, however unlike

many of the other British manufacturers who fell by the wayside as a result of the influx of Japanese machinery, Rickman's are still alive and kicking. Sensibly, the company, which is now in the hands of Don and Derek Rickman, had diversified into other areas of manufacture. Their activities ultimately led them into the kit car field, the first vehicle to bear the Rickman logo emerging from their comprehensively equipped workshop in 1987.

Their first, and very impressive, initial offering was the Ranger, similar in style and proportions to the Suzuki SJ410, and oozing professionalism in every aspect of its design and manufacture. The Ranger is based on the ever-popular Escort, using most of its mechanical parts, a fact that will undoubtedly endear it to many potential buyers. Popular as the little Suzukis undeniably are, as a result of their dual-role capability, a number of compromises clearly had to be made in order to cater for both on- and off-road use. The Ranger on the other hand, although only two-wheel drive, does not suffer from these potential drawbacks as it was clearly designed mainly with road use in mind, with the occasional sortie into the wilds, well within its capabilities. Like the Suzukis, the vast majority will find them-

selves on city streets rather than muddy tracks.

The Ranger scores over the Suzuki in respect of cost, availability and maintenance of its running gear. The latter does have four-wheel drive although this, in most cases, constitutes an expensively unnecessary item. As with some of the other Jeep-type kits, the Ranger, as a result of its light weight, good ground clearance and reasonably sized tyres, is likely to go over the top of rough or boggy ground, rather than sink into it. This is often worth as much as four-wheel drive.

The Ranger's main body shell is not manufactured as a single moulding, being carefully jig-assembled from a number of separate pieces. Rickman's experience with fibreglass is clearly apparent in the high quality finish and good attention to detail of the moulded sections. The three doors are hung on sturdy external hinges, the rear one having the option of carrying the spare wheel a la Suzuki. The doors come ready hung and gapped from the factory, thereby avoiding an area that many amateur builders find difficult. The glass also comes fully fitted, further simplifying matters.

The backbone of the little runabout

A newcomer to the scene is the thoroughly designed and well constructed Rickman Ranger. The Ranger's steel ladder chassis is designed to accept the mechanical parts from the Mk I and II Escort range. Rickman's workmanship, both in terms of engineering and fibreglass quality, is excellent. Virtually all of the Escort parts can be transferred without modification, the finished vehicle appealing to a wide cross-section of people. A very neat and practical little vehicle.

consists of a steel ladder-frame chassis, designed to take the running-gear from either the Mk I or II Escort range. Once again, Rickman's workmanship is in evidence, the well made chassis coming fully drilled, bracketed and hot-dip galvanised to ensure longevity. As a result of minor differences between the Mk I and II Escorts, there are corresponding differences in the Ranger kit, Rickman's needing to know which type of donor car has been selected at the fabrication stage.

Because of the Ranger's careful design, virtually all of the Escort parts can be transferred without modification. The few exceptions are the propshaft, that requires ten inches taking out of its length and the exhaust system which needs to lose the same amount. Hardly major problems!

Inside, a substantial steel cage is in evidence, this featuring a roll bar that also carries the seat belt mountings. A further steel hoop runs across the top of the dashboard, both this and the cage, tying into the main chassis, forming a very strong, safe unit. The Escort supplies much of the internal equipment including facia and instruments, pedal box, seats, door catches, heater assembly, handbrake and seat belts, as well as numerous small trim parts. The rear of the Ranger is surprisingly roomy and features a ribbed floor, the latter adding stiffness as well as making it easy to keep clean.

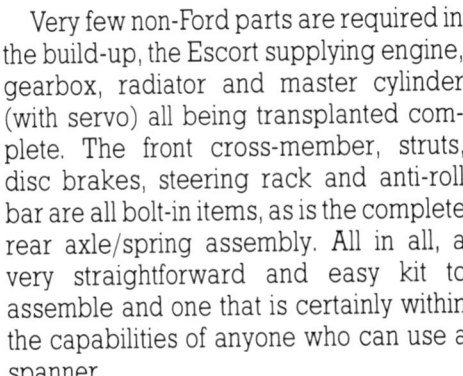

Very few non-Ford parts are required in the build-up, the Escort supplying engine, gearbox, radiator and master cylinder (with servo) all being transplanted complete. The front cross-member, struts, disc brakes, steering rack and anti-roll bar are all bolt-in items, as is the complete rear axle/spring assembly. All in all, a very straightforward and easy kit to assemble and one that is certainly within the capabilities of anyone who can use a spanner.

Although a recent arrival, the Ranger looks set to make a sizeable place for itself on the kit car scene. It is not a direct rival for vehicles such as the Geep or Eagle RV, being more likely to prove popular with those who had perhaps been considering a Japanese "mini Jeep" but who has been hesitant largely on grounds of cost. The Ranger really is a multipurpose vehicle, doubling as both car and van as well as an occasional off-roader. Its overall quality, value for money and variety of potential and uses should ensure that it has a rosy future.

Carlton Commando

If such vehicles as the Range Rover or the Simca Rancho fail to appeal, or if the cost is a little too prohibitive, then in some cases the Carlton Commando could prove to be a viable alternative. The men behind its creation were Dave Peasent and Stuart Allatt, with Dave Peasent being responsible for much of the styling work. The car made its debut at Hindhead during the latter half of 1983 and has proved, by its sales, very popular ever since.

The main donor vehicle is a Mk III or IV Cortina. For the power plant, most UK Ford four-cylinder and V6s will fit, as well as the Cologne V6. A Ford V8 can be fitted as an option. Which ever engine is selected it now exhausts through rear exit pipes as opposed to the earlier models which had side pipes. Stopping power is provided by the standard Cortina system of front discs and rear drums, one further option being a Granada servo unit.

The entire, four-seater body shell is constructed from fibreglass and sits on a

The rugged off road-inspired Carlton Commando makes use of the Mk III or IV Cortina as its donor vehicle. This supplies virtually all of the necessary mechanical parts, as well as numerous trim and electrical components. Numerous smaller parts such as window mechanisms are also re-used. The completed Commando is supremely practical, carrying 4/5 passengers, with a large luggage capacity. The Commando was first introduced late in 1983 and has proved to be very popular.

Ford based kit cars & Jeeps and off-roaders

ladder chassis. This is produced by Carlton and is predrilled for every component of the Cortina's running gear, including suspension mounts.

The front wings, main tub and front and rear bumpers simply bolt on and once constructed, results in one of the longest kits on the market, "measuring in" at a length of 14' 6". One very good design feature is the Commando's tailgate which is divided into two pieces. The top section hinges upwards and the lower one down, forming a flat platform, level with the floor of the vehicle. This is clearly an advantage when loading and carrying large objects, a logical, and seemingly obvious apsect that some of the "mainstream" manufacturers could do well to emulate.

The Cortina supplies its complete dashboard plus glovebox, windows (with all of the winding mechanism) and door trim panels. If they are in a suitable condition, the donor vehicle's seats, front and rear, and carpets can even be reused.

Supplied with the kit are the front indicator housings and the rear light clusters, a steering column extension to mate to the Cortina unit also being supplied. The glass is supplied together with the necessary seals and hinges. The donor supplies virtually everything else. Extras include a sunroof, gas struts, tow bar and light pack. Recommended wheel size is 205/70 x 14 or 225/70 x 14, on 6 inch rims.

On the road, the Commando is a large impressive "estate" with an extremely large payload capacity. With the car riding high as it does, a sill mounted step is a nice touch, and for that extra "mean" look, as well as protecting the front and rear light clusters, a set of nerf bars completes the picture. The final result, is a multipurpose, practical vehicle with a very spacious interior.

The car has been compared in some quarters with such vehicles as the

The Dutton Sierra was first introduced in 1979 and has proved to be immensely popular ever since. It has been top of the kit car sales league for some years and is still the UK's top selling kit. The Sierra is now in its Series III form, its popularity showing no signs of waning.

Chevrolet Blazer. This is, perhaps, a little pretentious, however the Commando certainly makes a very sensible and much more cost effective alternative to such vehicles.

Dutton Sierra

In the late 1970s Dutton's Phaeton was enjoying unrivalled sales and paved the way for the continuation of Dutton's development work. After a move to larger premises, in 1980, Dutton launched the Sierra, a car aimed primarily at the family man. This four-seater Sierra estate, like the Melos and Phaetons that were to follow, were all based on the easily available Ford Escort. The Sierra proved to be a best seller and has been top of the kit car sales for many years. In addition, the estate range is complemented by four other models. A van, which is a standard Estate with fill-in glassfibre panels in place of the side glass, whilst the pick-up version is an open-bodied truck, incorporating a drop down tailgate. The third is a Sierra chassis/cab which is basically a running chassis with a Sierra cab upfront with modifications to the rear being entirely at the discretion of the builder. The fourth option is a drophead convertible.

Since 1980 there have been a few model changes to the Sierra, the latest version being the Series III. This model is not merely a facelift of the Series II, but a completely new car with an all new body moulding and now, as with the Carlton, a completely flat rear loading area.

The chassis is built from MIG welded 80 x 40 x 3 mm square-section steel, complete with all brackets and holes ready to accept the Escort components, and comes supplied painted black. Built into the chassis is a roll-over bar which houses the seat belt mountings, which, incidently, conform to Type Approval Regulations. The front suspension is by the usual Escort McPherson struts located by an anti-roll bar, although earlier versions used radius arms. The track control arms are standard and the hubs and steering rack are all a la Escort. In short, the front is almost an entire transplant of the Escort components and likewise, the rear, with the usual springs and live rear axle. Engine mounting points can be fitted by Duttons for a variety of engine options, including all of the Escort engines as well as other Fords up to the 3 litre V6. It is suggested that most of the mechanicals are taken from a Mk I Escort saloon, Estate or van, but only a van or an Estate if a Mk II Escort is selected. The petrol tank is again Ford, the lie-flat variety, taken from a Van or Estate. Stopping power is via. Escort brakes with servo and discs at the front (rear drums) if a Mk I GT donor is opted for.

The body panels supplied, consist of a fully trimmed central tub, bonnet, front wings, front bumpers and integral grille, with assembly points for round or rectangular headlight options, internal mouldings and door skins. The latter are attached to transplanted Escort doors. The rear door is supplied, although there is a choice of a one-piece vertically hinged, or two-piece, split unit with hinged rear window. All of the panels are supplied with a gel-coat, self-coloured with the options of sand, yellow, black, green or brown. Other options include side-mounted swivel spot lights and a good range of wheel types. All of the necessary hinges are jig-mounted, thus eliminating one of those tricky tasks. At the rear, flush fitting light clusters are fitted together with a number plate light. All the glass required is supplied, as are the usual Dutton pack of fasteners, etc that are always needed. Dutton also supply one of the most comprehensive sets of instructions that are available.

The dashboard, instruments and heater (like just about everything else) come straight out of the Escort. The forward visibility is similar to that found with the Escort Saloon although some owners have commented that the rear visibility is a little restricted.

On the road, the steering is light and, presumably due to the height of the ride there is usually some body roll, although it should be made clear that this is only encountered when driving harshly. Acceleration and top speed, with any of the Escort options is comparable with the

Mk I Escort 1300 GT and is certainly adequate, presenting no real problems with four up and with luggage on board.

In comparison with, say, the Carlton Commando the Sierra is quite short, stepping in at 12' 6", a good two feet shorter, although it will handle a surprisingly large load. One slight problem encountered is the optional "spare" position. Mounted on a hinge at the rear, it needs to be moved out of the way for the loading of "larger items".

The design and finish of the Series III is an improvement, in quality, on previous models. There are still large gaps by the Escort doors and some of the panels are badly trimmed, but as this is one of the cheapest kits of this type on the road, there are plenty of benefits to make up for what are, after all, minor pitfalls. All in all, a very good estate and one which will undoubtedly continue to be a best seller.

The GRS Tora

The Tora was originally designed by Ginetta Cars to have a donor selected from Hillman Hunters, Sceptres, Humbers, Rapiers and most of the Chrysler/Rootes selection.

A novel option, and perhaps one that should have been available from birth, was that of Ford power. The Ford-powered Tora was developed, with help from Ginetta, by Pitstop of Maidstone, who offer a build up service for Ginetta Cars. At first glance, one may be forgiven for thinking that the Tora is of East European origin, as it greatly resembles the new Lada "estate" (The Tora was launched first, incidently). This large, boxy vehicle has, as its base, a MIG welded 4 x 2 inch ladder-type, box-

section chassis, extending upwards at the scuttle and, advantageously, providing door hinge locations. The front is strengthened to take the tall supports needed for the Chrysler McPherson struts and springs, and is panelled for extra strength. The struts are mounted on stabilising arms, running forward, and the rear suspension is via semi-elliptical leaf springs. As with most other kits nowadays, the chassis comes pre-drilled with all of the necessary brackets welded in place. The usual finish is in black paint, but for longevity there is the option of a galvanised finish.

The Tora's main bodyshell comes supplied, ready fitted to the chassis, complete with glass and gas struts. There is a bonded-in steel roll-hoop plus steel tube reinforcements, which all increase the strength and safety, as well as providing strong anchorage points for the seatbelts. The bonnet and tailgate are of very rigid construction. Additional layers of fibreglass are added in areas of the body, where extra strength is needed, the overall unit being very strong.

The bumpers are also made from fibreglass and although very strong, it is probably sensible to invest in a set of nudge bars, which are an optional extra. The bonnet opens with the aid of gas rams (as does the rear) revealing a large engine compartment which will easily accept the ohc engine, radiator and other necessary standard Ford components.

The Sierra, here in its estate form. This example runs on a set of GB alloy wheels and sports the optional rugged nudge bars, complete with extra lights. Notice the use of sliding side-windows, a feature of later models.

The olive-green Geep of Peter Burr of Woldingham, is powered by a 1600 ohc engine. He, unusually, built his Geep in World War II guise. His unusual treatment included many authentic details such as large diameter, narrow steel wheels.

This Escort-based Geep is typical of the high standard often encountered, and features the optional front roo-bars and soft top. The well padded roll-over bar is a sensible addition to any open vehicle. Notice the differences around the front wings and bonnet, when compared to the earlier version.

The Eagle RV is really the Geep's main rival however. Introduced in 1983, the RV uses the running-gear and suspension from the Mk III or IV Cortina. The chassis is an extremely strong unit that has proved itself both on- and off-road. There is a choice of engines, these including the Ford 1600 or 2 litre ohc or 1600 ohv units. The engine bay will also hold any of the Ford V6 engines as well as the Rover V8. The RV is now in its Series II form.

The Carlton Commando is based on the mechanical parts from the Mk III or IV Cortina. This supplies the drive-train and suspension systems, all fitting with few modification. The fibreglass body is of very sturdy construction and comes with bolt-on front wings and door-skins (to re-skin the Cortina doors). The Commando is a supremely practical vehicle and will carry four adults plus their luggage, with ease. Its rugged, off-road inspired looks make it a possible alternative to the GRS Tora or the Dutton Sierra. This well built example has steel Weller wheels and a contrasting black top.

This Commando has been given a contemporary theme by the use of graphic paintwork, its colour-coded nudge-bars and 8-spoke wheels completing the picture. The Commando looks equally at home on the city streets, as well as the backwoods.

An example of the versatile NCF Diamond, shown here in estate form. The Diamond is available in a variety of guises, each using an aluminium body with a very strong steel chassis. The Cortina is adopted as the donor car, this supplying much of the suspension and drive-train, largely unmodified. In long wheelbase form, the Cortina propshaft is even of the correct length. A four-wheel drive version based on Sierra parts is scheduled to join the ranks in the near future.

Despite its unusual styling, the Jago Samuri has been selling well over the past few years. Taking the majority of its running-gear from the Mk I or II Escort, this practical, four-seater, features a combination of full weather protection equipment and a large, lockable boot. There is a wide range of options available for the Samuri, including such things as roo-bars, wheels and crash-bars, as well as, of course, a huge range of colours. This immaculate all black example sports a number of the options.

It takes a brave manufacturer to do this, however, with the quality to be found in Rickman products, why hide it. This meticulously finished Ranger chassis regularly forms part of the impressive Rickman display at major kit car events. It gives prospective kit car buyers the chance to examine Rickman's engineering at close quarters. The high quality kit takes much of the running-gear and suspension assemblies from the Ford Escort range. This small "off-roader" could easily make a viable alternative to the little Suzuki Jeep.

The, almost brutal looking, Henson M30 uses the Granada as its donor car, this supplying the engine and gearbox, plus front and rear sub-frames. The backbone for the project is an immensely strong chassis/roll-cage, as well as substantial door-intrusion beams. The angular fibreglass body shell is constructed to exacting standards and features a foam-filled nose section, this increasing frontal impact resistance. Although no lightweight, the car performs in true sports car fashion, courtesy of its V6 and full independent suspension system.

Originally based on the mechanical parts from the VW, the Bonito was later redesigned, under the Seraph banner, to make use of Ford components. This particular ten year old example is the 1600 cc Ford-powered car of Bill Battey. Having bought the car as a half-built project, he completed it using parts from a long list of donor cars. The car reflects the high standards applied by the owner, during its build-up.

The Westfield 11 was modelled on the 1950s Lotus on the same nomenclature. The little track-inspired projectile uses much of the running-gear from the Midget or Sprite, but can accommodate a number of Ford engines and gearboxes. Examples are regularly seen on the roads, as well as scoring great successes in kit car racing.

Well over a thousand Marcos cars are now on the roads, scattered to all parts of the globe. The Peter-Adams designed beauty has faced the test of time, and passed with flying colours. With only minor restylings, the car has never really dated. A real classic!
(Marcos)

The ultra-swoopy, gull-winged Eagle SS is now in its Series III form. The Ford-based kit consists of a box-section steel chassis that accepts much of the Ford running-gear with ease. The opinion amongst owners is that, despite its exotic looks, it is not unduly difficult to build. The Eagle kit is one of the few economically viable routes to owning such a car, the end-result certainly being eye-catching and always guaranteed to cause a stir!

The legendary Marcos has been around now for over a quarter of a century and really needs little description. Over the years, the car has been systematically refined and improved to its current high standard. The engineering and fibreglass quality is, as would be expected, excellent. Ford components are to be found in the shape of Ford power-plants and rear axle. The front suspension is Triumph-based. Available in different degrees of completion, the comprehensive kits include everything necessary to complete one of Jem Marsh's wonder cars.

The very impressive Ava RS in its natural habitat! The RS version differs from the road-going KI in that it uses a lighter and stronger body shell, plus a lightweight version of the stainless steel chassis. The handling and performance of the contemporary looking machine is excellent, with a top speed in the region of 170 mph. The RS uses a small aero screen as opposed to the full sized unit of the KI.

The Melos is certainly a straightforward kit to build, some having been built with remarkable rapidity. The lightweight body helps to give the car much improved performance and handling over the Escort donor, and all at a remarkably economical price. Notice the use of upmarket alloy wheels on this spotless example.

Two fine examples from the Dutton stable. The car in the foreground is the Dutton B-Plus, Series II, recently brought back to the fold after many customer requests. The other vehicle is a Series IV Phaeton. These two cars have been built to a very high standard and, like the rest of the Dutton range, are Ford Escort based. They are displaying the optional weather protection and are seen here forming part of the owners display at Castle Coombe.

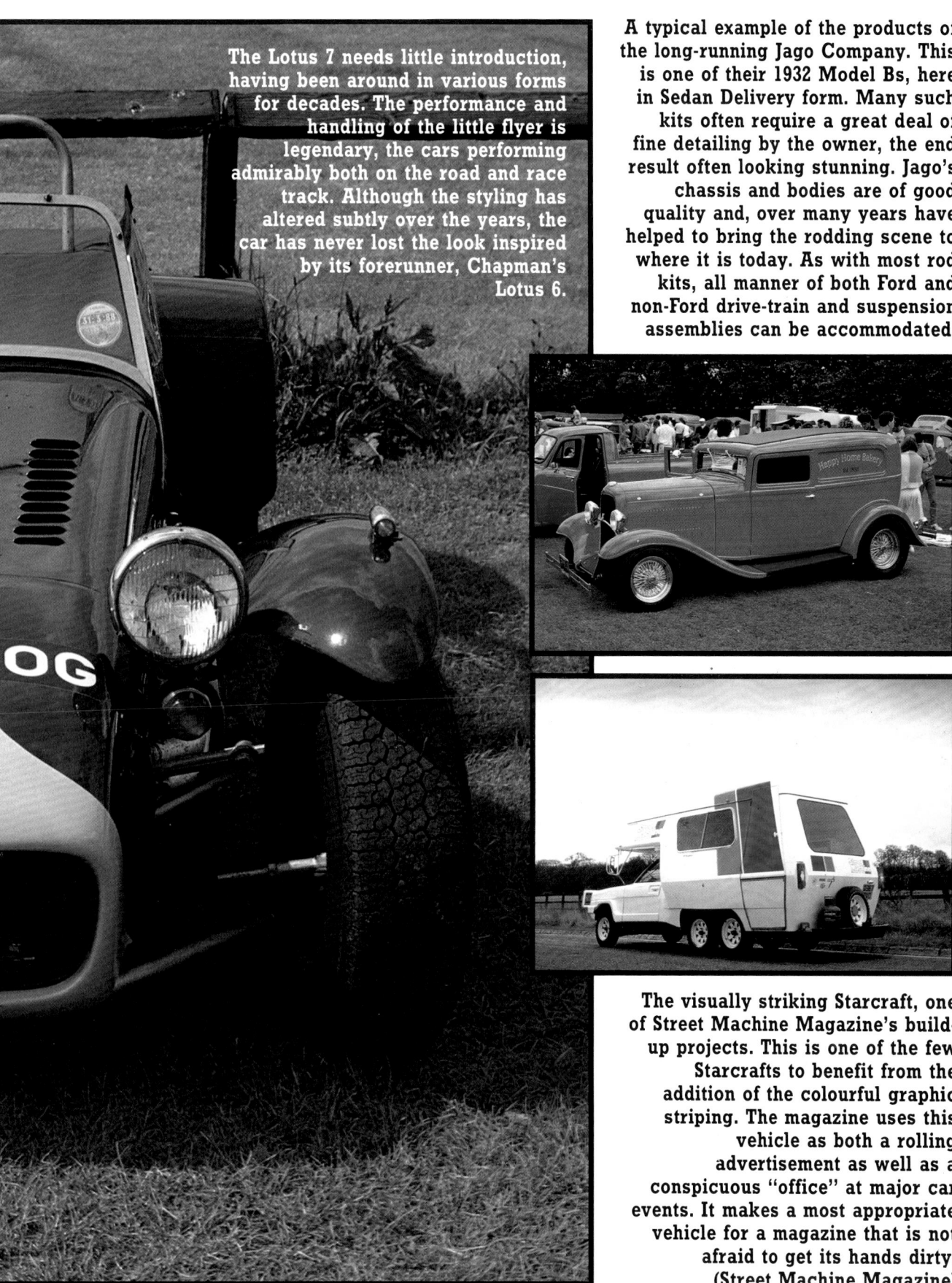

The Lotus 7 needs little introduction, having been around in various forms for decades. The performance and handling of the little flyer is legendary, the cars performing admirably both on the road and race track. Although the styling has altered subtly over the years, the car has never lost the look inspired by its forerunner, Chapman's Lotus 6.

A typical example of the products of the long-running Jago Company. This is one of their 1932 Model Bs, here in Sedan Delivery form. Many such kits often require a great deal of fine detailing by the owner, the end result often looking stunning. Jago's chassis and bodies are of good quality and, over many years have helped to bring the rodding scene to where it is today. As with most rod kits, all manner of both Ford and non-Ford drive-train and suspension assemblies can be accommodated.

The visually striking Starcraft, one of Street Machine Magazine's build-up projects. This is one of the few Starcrafts to benefit from the addition of the colourful graphic striping. The magazine uses this vehicle as both a rolling advertisement as well as a conspicuous "office" at major car events. It makes a most appropriate vehicle for a magazine that is not afraid to get its hands dirty! (Street Machine Magazine)

The reborn Falcon Shells-based Gemini of Anthony Taylor. This piece of kit car heritage is now powered by a Lotus twin-cam and has a Ford Escort rear axle, Cortina parts making up much of the front suspension. The car was built with kit car racing in mind although it can double as a road car. It was caught here in full race trim giving prospective customers the chance to try the car on the Castle Coombe Racing Circuit.

Inset below:
The now fully developed 164LM Ferrari clone of Classic Replicars, here shown are Castle Coombe race track ready for on-track testing. The various engine options available ensure that the car can be built primarily for either road or track use.

This is the Nyvrem Nirvana, the first kit car from Nyvrem Cars Ltd. It features a full space-frame chassis and carries an angular, yet stylish two-seater fibreglass body. The car is available in numerous stages of completion, taking much of its running-gear from the Mk III, IV or V Cortina. Virtually any of the range of Ford engines, up to the V6 units, can be accommodated. Great things are expected for the UK market in the near future.

The GRS Tora, by Ginetta, uses a high quality fibreglass body shell and makes use of a pair of doors from the Hillman Hunter/Sceptre range. The Tora also uses the front and rear suspension systems from the same source and will accept the Hillman drive-train. A recent alternative is the use of Ford power, in the shape of virtually any of the four-cylinder Ford engines and gearboxes. The quality of the chassis and body, as would be expected from Ginetta, is very good.

Many would consider this to be the better engine option to the Chrysler range for availability of spares, fuel consumption and of course performance.

The front wings are bolt on units with Hunter doors being used complete and unmodified. The instruments and facia can have a touch of class about them as they can be taken, complete with wood veneer, straight from the more upmarket Hillman models. The Hunter seats can be used at the rear and there are many after-market options for the front. The luggage area is large and reached via the gas-rammed hatch. The main criticism is that, unlike the Carlton Commando or Dutton Sierra, the luggage has to be manoeuvred over a lip, which is quite a drawback for a vehicle aimed at the estate market. In its defence, it must be said, that once inside, there is plenty of room and if the Hillman rear seats can be hinged down, then the rear area would be positively cavernous.

The visibility, when driving, is good, but as with most estates, the rear view is rather limited, so care is needed for parking. The length of the Tora is about the same as a 1600 Escort Estate (Mk IV) and with the Ford engine option the performance is about the same.

Options include carpets, headlinings, tow hook, roof rack, and sporty looking nerf bars and spotlights. The styling of the Tora may be said to be practical, but not really that stylish. The lines are not as smooth as say the Dutton Sierra, or even the Carlton, but it is tough, strong, and represents very good value for money. One thing is certain, if Ginetta have designed and built it, the quality is going to be second to none.

The NCF Diamond

The Diamond was the brainchild of Nick Findeison who spent two years working on prototypes before its launch in early 1985. Unlike most of its competitors, the Diamond's body is not built from fibre-glass, thus the possible cracks, crazing,

ripples and undulations do not appear.

Having looked around, he decided that, as most of his competitors used Escorts as donors, they were somewhat limited to making "small" cars. As a result, he went one up to the Cortina. The Cortina Mk III through to Mk V can be used as a suitable donor, allowing a wider track and a selection of more powerful engine options.

The kit comes as a complete, integral steel chassis/aluminium body unit. The chassis is made from 80 x 40 x 3.2 mm steel and is of the ladder type with cross bracing, and incorporates front and rear bumpers. Welded to this is a roll-over bar, outriggers and supporting structure for the aluminium body and steel floor. A galvanised bulkhead is supplied, pre-drilled for wiper motor, servo unit, accelerator pedal, steering column, heater and with all the holes conveniently punched, ready to take all the necessary cables. The complete assembly is supplied in a black paint finish.

The body parts are constructed from 16 gauge aluminium sheet cut from patterns so, in the event of that major knock, replacement panels actually fit! Glass is supplied for the windscreen, side and rear panels. The lower rear panels are supplied smooth, so the builder can

"french" or bolt on any rear lighting system of his choice. The front wings accept Transit indicator units with blank plates in place ready for headlight mounting. The lower half of the tailgate is hinged and attached at NCF (another difficult job you don't have to do). An Allegro or Marina supplies burst-proof locks and the bonnet release. The hinges and doors are also fitted by NCF, together with all of the necessary sealing.

If the donor Cortina is post 1974, then the dashboard can be transplanted complete. For power, a 1600, 2 litre or 2.3 litre engine can be lowered into place (NCF consider that the 1300 engine is not really up to the job for this particular kit). Due to the long wheelbase (not the case on the original version) the Cortina's propshaft can be used unmodified. The result of this combination (with a 2 litre engine on board) is a maximum speed of over 100 mph.

The standard Cortina exhaust system, can be reused in its entirety, as can the front and rear seats, the quality of these obviously depending upon the age and trim of the donor selected for the job.

For the wheels, the choice is up to the builder. NCF recommend 205 x 70s for road use or 185/195 x 15 for off-road applications. NCF themselves use Kelly Safari A-Ts, a la Daihatsu.

Optional extras include painting of the finished kit, nudge-bars, swing-away spare wheel and roof rack. One additional option definitely worth buying, is the NCF petrol tank (of 9 gallons capacity) complete with filler pipe and the appropriate aperture for the Cortina gauge unit.

At the end of the day, the result is a four-or five-seater which is a lot cheaper, and may out-perform many a Daihatsu or Datsun. Other models in the range include a pick-up, a soft-top and a chassis/cab unit. Mid 1987 brought the arrival of the 4 x 4 Diamond, utilising the 4 x 4 mechanicals from the Ford Sierra. Thus, the Diamond range of cars looks equally at home, shopping, carrying vast amounts of luggage, taking the kids to school or even across (with the 4 x 4 option) the tougher off-road terrain. With a price tag not too dissimilar to that of its fibreglass competitors, the NCF Diamond offers real value for money.

Jago Samuri

It's very difficult actually defining what type of vehicle the Samuri is. From some angles it has a distinct Beach-Buggy look about it and from others, it shows some similarities with its stablemate, the Geep.

Whatever bracket it falls into, with its rugged, utilitarian, off-road inspired looks, it has proved to be a very popular machine.

The Samuri came into existence in 1983, as a result of repeated customer requests and pressure for a fun-to-drive, practical, full four-seater, plus luggage, machine that could be built easily and at a reasonable cost, and be Ford based. With the wealth of experience to be found within the walls Jago's Chichester factory, it was not long before the Samuri was unveiled, designed to make use of the cheap and easily available mechanical parts from the Mk I and II Escort.

The chassis is a MIG-welded, pre-drilled affair, the design and construction of which was based upon many years of experience building chassis, not only for their own products, but also for other manufacturers. Not surprisingly, the final product is both well-designed and well-made. It accepts the majority of the Escort mechanical parts, largely unmodified. This includes the McPherson struts, steering gear, engine and gearbox, and complete rear suspension and axle assembly. As the wheelbase is the same as the Escort, even the propshaft can be left unaltered, being of the correct length.

As would be expected, not only does the Escort supply the main mechanical parts, it also donates its instrument package (this must be from a Mk II), handbrake, seats, wiring harness, radiator and so on, the end-result being a very straightforward build-up. Estimates of effort required vary enormously, however the general consensus of opinion seems to put it in the 100–150 hour range.

A number of special parts are included in the kit, such as steering column extension and support bracket. The remainder of the kit includes the main eleven body panels comprising the main tub, front panel, boot lid and rear panel, bonnet and wings. In addition, a Targa bar and complete screen assembly is included, as are all of the necessary fasteners. The fibreglass is of good quality as is the way that the panels fit together. The major advantage of the multi-panel configuration is that, in the events of accident damage, repairs are much easier. The drawback is that a good fit is sometimes lacking, however the Samuri does not suffer from this. The panels are, like the Geep, available in over 200 different colours.

Practicality is one of the Samuri's strong points and it certainly scores here in a number of areas. The bodywork and chassis are virtually maintainance-free. The drive-train and suspension is simple and easily repaired, and the interior is roomy and quite capable of holding four adults. There is also the additional bonus of a large lockable boot.

How does this rugged-looking machine perform? The most popular engine choices seem to fall in the 1600–2000 range, this ensuring brisk performance from this comparative lightweight. The ride qualities, even with unmodified Escort suspension, are excellent, as are the cornering characteristics. The driving position is comfortable with good all-round visibility. Despite its off-road looks, the car is a nippy, agile performer on the road and overall great fun to drive. Options include a hard top (a hard top plus soft rear top is also available), eight-spoke wheels, roo-bar, seat belts and so on.

Although the Samuri's styling is not to everyone's taste, there is no denying that it is practical, drivable, easy to build and comparatively cheap. As a result, it looks as if it will be around for a long time to come.

The Sherwood

The Sherwood is an interesting, multi-purpose vehicle that should not only appeal to kit car aficionados, but also to those of the business community, farmers,

The Samuri's rear end, showing the large lockable boot space. This will accommodate the targa panels when not in use. The twin tube rear bumper is a sensible and well made option from Jago. This fine red and black example is the 1300 cc powered car of Steve and Clare Barber of Weybridge.

builders and so on. As well as converting into a good-looking utility vehicle for domestic use, it also has great potential as a general purpose workhorse for any of the above uses. In one guise, it can be a large estate which, in a matter of minutes, can be transformed into an equally-useful pick-up.

This concept is not a new one, frequently being encountered with a number of the Japanese mini pick-ups, however, the obvious advantages of the Sherwood are both its initial cost as well as the easy servicing and availability of Ford parts. It therefore has a wide appeal.

The donor vehicle is the Mk III, IV or V Cortina (1970–82), this supplying most of the necessary mechanical parts. These slot neatly into the Sherwood's sturdy, twin-rail, pre-drilled chassis, ensuring that the rolling-chassis stage can be reached without any real problems. All of the necessary mounting brackets for the drive-train, suspension and body, are all in place. The Cortina's front and rear suspension assemblies bolt simply into place without modification, however, unusually, the propshaft needs lengthening. The Sherwood must be one of the few kit vehicles that requires this, virtually

every other, requiring a shortening operation. The chassis rails are open at the ends, but these can be plugged using plastic, or possibly heat-shrinkable caps. The chassis comes with a protective coating of red oxide paint applied. The rear section has a built-in tow hitch, merely needing the addition of the ball, as well as the appropriate bracketing for the Cortina petrol tank.

The fibreglass body is constructed from no less than fourteen separate pieces, which should make accident damage easier to repair, although this concept can sometimes lead to problems of panel fit. Fortunately this does not seem to pose a problem with the Sherwood. The panels are used to build up the front end and cover much of the existing Cortina sheet metal, and include bonnet, front panel, door skins, wings, cab roof, quarter panels, rear wings, back panel, tail-gate and hard top, all coming supplied in a white gel coat. White 8–spoke wheels are supplied, this adding to the rugged looks. Also supplied is a full set of glass and sealing rubbers, and a strong roll-over bar. The hard-top is fixed in place with four quick-release fasteners, although the builder has the option of bonding it permanently into position.

The drive-train option will probably be influenced by the particular donor car used, although the Sherwood will take any of the range of Ford engines, from the 1300 cc up to the V6 units, if a spare Capri or Granada happens to be lying around. The Cortina also furnishes numerous other parts, such as radiator, dashboard, interior fittings and windscreen. If an Estate version has been used, the rear seating can be installed, giving a full 4/5 seater, with extra luggage space. Clearly, the cab section from the Cortina should be in relatively rust-free condition in order to avoid too many problems of bodywork repairs. The Cortina's bulkhead is cut out, however, many of the internal parts are reused, such as floor, instruments, door pillars, and seat-belt mountings. Wiring the Sherwood is straightforward, as the Cortina loom can, with a few modifications, be used intact.

At the rear is a two-piece tail-gate, the upper section being opened with the assistance of gas-rams. This gives access to the cavernous interior, however, some care is needed when lowering the bottom section.

Once complete, the Sherwood forms a very practical, versatile, and useful vehicle. Its large interior makes it suitable for substantial load-carrying duties. An interesting comparison has been made between the Sherwood and a Volvo estate, and although the former is nine inches shorter than the Volvo, at 114 cu.ft., its carrying capacity is around 20% greater.

On the road, although the smaller engines will fit, at least a 2 litre ohc unit is really necessary to give anything like satisfactory performance. The driving characteristics, handling and road holding, are, perhaps not surprisingly, like those of the Cortina.

The Sherwood is an immensely practical vehicle that can be transformed from an estate, to a pick-up, and by fitting fibreglass covers to the side windows, into a commercial. Its sheer versatility should ensure that it is put to many good uses.

A further alternative for the Sherwood is that of a commercial. In this case, the body side-glass has not been installed, thus creating a roomy, multipurpose vehicle. The rugged looks are enhanced by the use of graphic striping and tinted glass. Notice the smooth lines created by the absence of door handles etc.

7 Modern performance saloons and coupes

There are relatively few cars currently on the market that fall into this category, which is rather surprising in some respects, as practical, family transportation vehicles make up such a large percentage of cars on the road.

This section of the market is largely composed of full-bodied cars and this can clearly pose a number of problems during the manufacturing stage. This fact alone, probably accounts for their lack of numbers. The manufacture of, for instance, a small, two-seater sports body, can be a fairly straightforward procedure, and even the addition of full weather protection in the form of a clip-on hard top, fairly simple. When it comes to a full saloon body, complete with doors, roof, boot and bonnet panels, this obviously becomes a lot more complicated. With complication, comes specialised expertise (not always available), and with this, comes expense. A small sports body need not have doors, roof or boot area, and hence its often fairly rudimentary design can be undertaken by someone with only limited experience in the field of fibreglass technology. Additional skills are clearly involved in the design and manufacture of a saloon or coupe body. Because of its greater size and complexity, the styling sometimes assumes a greater importance. In addition, careful design of such diverse aspects as door mechanisms, hinges, window assemblies and weather sealing around the door openings, have to be considered. Clearly,

the design and production of a saloon body is not something to be tackled by the fainthearted!

It is an undisputable fact that the greater and flatter the body area, the more pronounced any ripples, flaws or imperfections will be. Whereas it may be possible to get away with such things, to a certain extent, on small, curved sections, on the large relatively flat areas of a saloon body, such as the roof, bonnet, doors and boot lid, the overall finish of the fibreglass assumes a much greater significance. Fortunately this fact has not escaped some of the manufacturers, the overall quality of the fibreglass of, for instance, Ginetta and JBA, being excellent.

A far more comprehensive chassis is often necessary to carry this more complex body structure, a number of extra forces being placed upon it. As well as having to handle all of the stresses involved in daily driving, it also has to include adequate roll-over, front, rear and side-impact resistance. Although these factors are clearly important in any kit car, they assume even more significance where the car may have up to five occupants.

From the manufacturer's point of view, there are obviously a number of potential technical problems involved in this area. In addition to his engineering, styling and quality of manufacture, the kit car manufacturer finds himself competing head-on with many of the major, conventional car producers. There are plenty of cars already available in this area, many of them at second-hand prices far below that of a kit car, and it is in this forum that the kit car has to compete.

There are many people who ideally would like more from their car than mere daily transportation, however practical and reliable it might be. Admittedly, there are a number of sports-oriented saloons and coupes in production, however their prices put them well out of the reach of many "family" men. For them, it usually means settling for a mundane, run-of-the-mill saloon. There is now something of an alternative in the shape of a number of practical, 4/5-seater sporting-saloons, that have been brought into being by the kit car industry. For a reasonable cost, it is now a practical proposition to recycle the family Capri or Cortina into a stylish sports-oriented vehicle, that still has room for the family and their luggage. Add to this, cheap and reliable Ford running gear, and it really does give the best of both worlds!

This section of the market is now receiving increasing attention from the kit car industry, not because there has been a sudden increase in demand for such cars, but really because it has always been there, largely untapped. It is into this void, that the industry is now beginning to make headroads, with a number of remarkably sophisticated products.

Ginetta G26, G28, G30, G31

When the Ginetta G26 burst onto the scene in 1984, it added a number of new and important dimensions to the world of the kit car. Looking at such a professionally designed and built car, it is hard to realise that what we are referring to is a "conventional", home assembly car that, almost unbelievably, uses the running gear from the Mk III, IV or V Cortina. It seems out of the question that such a sleek, stylish projectile would house the commonplace mechanical components from Ford's run-of-the-mill Cortina, but that's what it does. An equally important fact was that this was the first genuine five-seater sporting saloon of such quality to appear, clearly aimed at competing head-on with the mass produced products of the motor industry. It does this remarkably well, both in terms of quality and workmanship, the overall result being a car that looks more as if it were the product of some major manufacturer's design exercise. This is quite an achievement for a comparatively small company such as Ginetta but, remembering that the Walklett brothers have been designing, building, racing and producing road-going vehicles for three decades, this is perhaps not so surprising. The variety and wealth of experience to be found within the walls of the Ginetta factory has given rise, over the years, to a range of

Ford based kit cars
**7 Modern
performance
saloons and coupes**

innovative and sophisticated cars that any manufacturer (both kit or otherwise), would have been proud to put their name to, one of the latest in the line being the G26.

The car represents something of a change of direction for the Walkletts, being a real alternative to some of the high-performance "family" saloons that make up so much of the motor industry's turnover. It is the sort of car that would not look out of place almost anywhere, standing comparison with the best products of the European industry as well as some of the sophisticated cars currently coming in from the East.

Styling is such an esoteric concept to pin down and it is difficult to find an equivalent car with which to compare the G26. Many people mistake it for a Lotus or some kind of Honda or Toyota (however, the car has a uniqueness all of its own) and it is only when they notice the Ginetta badge, they realise their mistake. They also fail to realise the significance of this, the fact that such a comparatively cheap car, based on Cortina mechanical parts, can stand alongside similar looking cars that cost maybe five times as much, and still compare favourably.

The chassis is a steel tube construction, that comes fully drilled to accept the main mechanical assemblies from the Cortina, mainly in unmodified form. It is constructed from 3″ x 2″ box-section and is, in essence, of ladder frame configuration. It is one of the most carefully designed chassis of this type currently to be found on the market and comes as a result of the Walkletts extensive racing activities over the years. As well as being a very strong unit, it is also a very safe one, for the engine-bay is surrounded by a steel cage and the rear, similarly protected by cross-bracing. Side impact protection is provided by twin side-rails, all of this being in

addition to the roll-cage. This impressive feat of engineering is also available in galvanised form, thus ensuring its longevity.

The body, which is of excellent quality, is strengthened by a bonded in steel framework that runs around the windscreen area and along both sides of the roof. These sections are tied together at the rear and central areas, thus forming a substantial roll-over protection system. Despite this framework, the interior is very roomy, with sufficient space to carry four/five adults. The doors are from the Ford Fiesta, complete with remote control mirrors, speakers and the standard integral pocket. Anyone used to driving a Cortina will feel instantly at home in the G26 as the seats, pedals, steering column, facia and instruments, as well as a number of minor trim pieces, are transferred from the donor. The overall layout is very similar, apart from the fact that the column is positioned slightly differently.

The boot is positively cavernous, a fact that will undoubtedly appeal to many. The passenger and luggage carrying capacity is on a par, and in some cases, even better than, many comparable production cars.

The performance of the G26 with a 2.0 litre ohc engine fitted should prove to be more than adequate for most people, however, the engine bay has sufficient room to take the 2.8 litre V6. The weight, at 1020 kg is slightly less than that of the donor. The cornering ability, roadholding and ride qualities are all good, the car being a real pleasure to drive under almost any conditions.

It should also be mentioned that there is now also a G28 model. This has been developed to cater for the sportier end of the market. It is shorter than the G26 and is really a 2+2 saloon. The rear quarterlights are ex-XR4 units and a Peugeot supplies the front lights. The bonnet line has also been raised to "easily" accommodate the 2.8i V6 unit. Other than these differences the kit is still Cortina-based, and late 1987 saw the option of the independent rear suspension (courtesy of the Sierra), to improve handling. The G31 followed, which is a G28 with a G26 front end (i.e. with pop-up headlights).

The Tarragon was one of the first sports saloons to appear on the scene, having been around in various forms for over a decade. Much of the running-gear is supplied from the Mk I or II Escort range, with the option of virtually any of the four-cylinder Ford engines. The stylish fibreglass body is carried on a very strong ladder frame chassis, the design of which was arrived at as a result of experience gained during rallying. The fibreglass quality is good, the body coming with the doors ready hung and a number of other components in place.

Overall, the Ginetta cars represent one of the few viable alternatives to the far more expensive sports saloons currently on the market, and whatever G number is chosen, they are all good value for money.

Tarragon

The Tarragon is one of the small group of genuine four-seater, sports saloons currently available however, unlike, the Ginetta G26 for example, the car has been around in various forms for over a decade. Remarkably, with only a few restyling features, it has managed to avoid looking dated. Its looks have been compared by some writers as being similar to those of the Reliant Scimitar and although it does have some similarities, it is no more than a passing resemblance.

The Tarragon TXR is visually similar to its partner, but uses most of the mechanical parts from the Capri. This car is one of the company's demonstrators and is powered by a BDA 1600 unit. Not surprisingly, the performance is impressive, the body and chassis being quite capable of handling such powerful engines.

The car definitely has its own distinct looks and character.

The story of the Tarragon really began in 1969, when Steve Johnson set up the company known as Lightspeed Panels. Out of this, Magenta Cars eventually emerged, producing a kit car called, not surprisingly, the Magenta. This could be based on a number of different donor cars. In 1975, Steve produced a chassis for another hopeful manufacturer but when their dreams of production faded in 1977, he took over the half-completed project and brought it to fruition. The fruits of his labours were to appear as the Tarragon. Various modifications followed, including a nine inch increase in the body length as well as changes around the headlight and frontal areas.

The body and chassis were designed to take the vast majority of the components from the Mk I and II Escort, only few modifications being necessary. The Estate version was the best choice mainly because of its horizontal petrol tank, the Saloon requiring some extra modifications.

The chassis, in line with many other kit

**Ford based kit cars
7 Modern
performance
saloons and coupes**

manufacturers, is a box-section steel affair. A simple ladder configuration was adopted, this being substantially strengthened by the use of a hefty X-frame centre section. The front end incorporates a pair of towers to take the McPherson struts, which are used unmodified except for a switch to softer springs. The chassis is a very strong and rigid unit, owing much of its design to experience gained in off-road and rally situations. Consequently, it is quite capable of withstanding plenty of hard driving, however for serious competition use, a tie-bar between the strut towers is recommended.

The sleek-looking body is of fibreglass and features well-fitting, ready-hung doors. This avoids an area that many amateur builders often find something of a problem. The body is fairly light and features extra strenthening in areas of high stress such as around hinge points. When fitted to the chassis, a very strong and rigid unit is formed. A roll cage is available although this is not fitted as standard. The quality of the fibreglass is considered to be very good with return edges on a number of panels and around the wheel arches, all adding to the body's strength. The slippery front end sports a shallow air-dam and a fibreglass bumper that blends in well with the overall frontal styling. The headlights reside behind hinged panels although simple Perspex covers are another possibility.

The interior is fairly spacious, being quite capable of holding four adults. The instruments and facia are provided by the Escort, as are a number of the trim parts. A deluxe option includes a carpet kit, headlining and door trim panels, as well as wind-up windows.

The basic kit is composed of the body (complete with doors), side glass, softer springs and, of course, the chassis. A number of other options are available such as a brake pipe kit, quad headlights and a sun-roof.

The car weighs in at 15 cwt, a light weight for a full sized four-seater, hence the performance with even a standard Escort engine is brisk. With a 1600 or 2 litre ohc unit, the car is decidedly nippy. Magenta's demonstrator is powered by a 16 valve BDA engine, the result being a *very* rapid car!

The Tarragon's driving position is comfortable and its handling, quite adequate for even high powered engine options. An interesting addition to the range following on the heels of the Tarragon, is the Tarragon TXR. This uses the same stylish body shell with a chassis suitably modified to take the mechanical parts from the equally available Capri. Visually there is little difference between the two except for the TXR's wider track. Whichever option is chosen, the result is a very contemporarily styled and practical car. It is yet another example of the ever-flexible kit car industry plugging one of the gaps left by the major manufacturers.

The Excalibur

Excalibur Cars are a relative newcomer to the scene, the West Looe-based company being formed in 1986 by Clive Clark. Their first product is a well-styled and thoroughly designed vehicle which the company describe as a roomy "2+2 Sports Coupe", known simply as the Excalibur. The frontal area looks remarkably like one of de Tomaso's 1500 cc Ford-engined Vallelunga coupes.

The car was originally designed around VW components, this being followed by a full-chassised, Ford-based version. It will come as no surprise to find that the well-proven Mk III and IV Cortina was adopted as the donor vehicle, this providing virtually all of the necessary mechanical components.

The chassis is constructed from box-section steel of 50 x 76 x 3.5 mm dimensions and features substantial cross-bracing and side rails. The unit comes pre-drilled and bushed where

Excalibur Cars were founded in 1986, their first car being VW-based. This was redesigned to make use of the Mk III/IV Cortina as the donor car, although it will accept any of the four-cylinder ohv and ohc engines. The very strong body/chassis unit features substantial roll-over protection and makes use of Kevlar in its construction. The front screen comes from the Renault 5 and the rear, from the Capri. For a first product, the slippery car exhibits a high degree of sophistication.

necessary, ready to accept the Cortina engine, gearbox, front and rear suspension assemblies complete. Most of the mechanical parts will slip into place without alteration, however, in common with many other kit cars, the propshaft needs shortening and the steering column, an extension piece fitting. Both of these modifications can be carried out by the manufacturers on an exchange basis. In addition, the Cortina also supplies most of the ancillaries and electrical parts needed.

The choice of the power-plant depends upon the builder and the donor vehicle, however, the Excalibur will accept any of the Ford range, from the humble 1300 up to the V6 units.

The swoopy, performance-inspired body shell is a very complex piece of moulding technology and despite its obviously sporting lines, is remarkably spacious inside. As well as making use of the more normal fibreglass materials, high strength Kevlar fibre is also used in the construction. Kevlar has a very high strength to weight ratio and its properties

are much loved by racing car constructors. In areas requiring extra strength, the thickness of the lay-up is increased and in the roof section, additional Kevlar and woven roving are used. A steel cage structure, made from 20 mm diameter steel tube, is integrally bonded in around the roof and door openings, this greatly increasing the shell's strength and rigidity as well as doubling for seat-belt attachment points. It also obviously offers a good degree of roll-over protection.

The body's rigidity is also further increased by the bonding in of various internal panels such as the front and rear inner sub-sections, the rear seat panel, dashboard/scuttle section and the air ducts at the rear. In addition, the floor sections are also laminated in, the overall structure being very strong. The quality of the finish is very good and certainly on a par with the best to be found in the kit car industry. Excalibur proudly proclaim that their body is both strong and safe, the amount of work going into the body's construction clearly giving credence to this.

The glass is supplied in the form of a Renault 5 front and a Capri rear screen. The old bugbear of door-hanging has been avoided, as the company, in line with a number of other manufacturers, supplies the double-skinned doors, ready hung on specially made hinges. The windows and winder mechanisms are also ready fitted. The quad headlight system uses 5.5 inch units, these residing behind neat Perspex screens. Overall, the body is a most impressive piece of work. Its design is not based upon any particular car although the lines do have a certain familiarity about them. There is definitely a hint of the GT40 and perhaps a touch of Ferrari, but whatever, the design works very well, the car having its own individual style and characteristics.

Inside, there is plenty of room for the driver and front seat passenger. The rear seats would comfortably hold two children although could conceivably become a little cramped for adults on a long journey.

Although the car has not been around for long, most reports are complimentary about its ride and handling characteris-

tics. Its performance depends on the drive-train selected although, as usual, the full range of Ford engines in various states of tune are obviously available.

For a first product, the Excalibur is a most impressive machine, both in terms of its construction and styling. It looks like it will have a bright future!

The Mirage

Autotune is run by Anthony Taylor who, for more than twenty five years, has been involved in motor engineering and racing. He has competed in Sprint Championships and has achieved National Sports car Championship awards. Autotune is one of those rare breeds of independent engineering companies that has lasted through the years, being formed in 1969. They have specialised in all types of automotive competition and preparation including historic, classic and modern sports cars as well as a more recent diversification into power boats.

Their first sports car was the Aristocat, a two-seater sports kit car having a single Jaguar donor. This was very successful and Autotune saw a gap in the market for a four-seater saloon, the result being the sleek-looking Cortina-based Mirage. The Mirage combines modern styling, a drag factor of 0.35, with the option of a high-performance GT or an economical four-seater tourer.

The backbone of the project is a jig-built, MIG welded, space-frame chassis constructed from 1.5 x 1.5 inch 14 gauge steel, pre-drilled for seat belt mountings, suspension points, a steel body hoop and two aluminium door frames. The front suspension can be from a Mk III, IV or V Cortina, transferred from the donor complete, the only alteration being up-rated springs, which are supplied by

Autotune. The rear suspension has the same donor options using the original Ford radius arms. A Panhard rod alleviates sideways movement while brackets for the complete assembly are welded in place on the chassis. The Cortina axle is suspended by Jaguar shock absorbers, bolted on with brackets included in the kit. The propshaft is also from the Cortina but needs shortening, a service that Autotune will also carry out. For braking power, the usual Cortina combination of front discs and rear drums slip into place, although with a large power-plant installed, extra stopping power can be supplied using Granada units. The recommended wheel/tyre options are 5.5 inch rims shod with 165/SR13 or 6 inch rims, with 205/60/HR13 tyres.

The wiring harness is taken complete from the donor, as are all of the instruments, cooling and heating being supplied via a Toyota unit. The electric windows come from an XJ6, with slight modification to the lifting gear. Other non-Ford components include Avenger rectangular headlights, Viva HB front indicators, Daimler rear lights, with reversing and number plate lights coming courtesy of a Midget or MGB. Any front-engined Ford power-plant can be fitted (also many non-Ford engines are options, eg. Rover V8) and is cooled, preferably with a 3 litre Capri radiator. Steering is

The Autotune Mirage makes use of the Cortina Mk III, IV or V range as the donor, this supplying the complete drive-train and suspension assemblies. The Mirage space-frame chassis will handle a variety of engines as well as the Ford units, even up to the Rover V8. The body can be supplied ready fitted, complete with all of its high quality fibreglass panels in place.

handled by the Cortina rack, the column being extended using an adaptor and a Triumph steering-link.

The sleek body is supplied in six sections; main body tub, bonnet, boot lid, two doors and floor section. The main body and floor section can be supplied ready fitted to the chassis as a monocoque unit, all of the fibreglass panels being finished in gel coat. The bonnet hinges from the front giving good access to the engine.

All the hinges and glass/Perspex are included in the kit, whilst extras include such things as propshaft, brake and petrol piping, interior moulding kit, roof lining and carpets.

With the optional extras fitted, the Mirage is an exceptional car, having a high standard of finish, inside and out. This high standard is also reflected in the back-up service Autotune offer. On the road, it is a pleasure to drive, with good all-round visibility. A great deal of thought and effort has obviously been given to producing one of the better examples of an "original" modern, sports saloon, with low drag, high performance and excellent fuel consumption. A car that should sell well and become increasingly more popular as the years go by.

Camino

The Camino was launched at the South West Custom Car Show, held at Bristol Docks in October 1984. It is manufactured by Delkit, a company formed by John Rock and Dereck Allen. What they have produced between them is a very stylish 2+2 Cortina-based coupe.

The backbone of this car is a ladder-frame chassis, with extensive bracing, which has been designed to accept the mechanical components from a Mk III, IV or V Cortina. The transmission tunnel and floor also add to the overall strength, being constructed from mild steel plate. Additional box sections add strength to the rear as well as being connected to a roll-over bar (bonded into the roof section). The engine is contained in a steel cage whilst the front bulkhead has two cross-members located on chassis

uprights for door attachment. A similar construction is also present at the rear. The mechanical parts from the Cortina transfer across completely without any modification, although if required, specially designed Spax shock absorbers are available.

The bodywork is ripple-free and of very high quality, the thick fibreglass body being supplied ready fitted to the chassis, if required. Opening the bonnet reveals the donor engine, a 1.6 or 2.0 litre ohc being recommended. Behind the engine, a steel bulkhead is shaped to accept the Cortina's heater, wipers and other assemblies. Access to the interior is via thick, well-hinged doors. The doors are trimmed to match the leather grain of the dash and hide the standard Cortina window mechanisms, door latches and locks. There is a one-piece moulded, leather-look console (with centre section) which fits well, and has apertures ready cut to accept all of the Cortina's dashboard instruments plus a host of extras.

The driving position is good for drivers of most shapes and sizes, although the "2+2" may seem a little exaggerated to all but rear "midget" passengers. The front passenger and driver also benefit from dash-mounted air vents.

The rear of the car is of very modern design. Vauxhall Cavalier light units are used in conjunction with a "Camino" tailblazer which all adds to the contemporary look. The rear bumper is made from fibreglass and finished in black, and as with the front, has a number plate recess. The front bumper also has recesses for BL sidelights and indicator units, Mk IV Cortina headlights providing the main lighting power. The boot lid opens on exterior hinges (depending upon the age of the kit), not to everyone's liking, revealing a spacious carpeted area complete with floor recess to take the Escort van or Estate flat tank, hidden with a plywood cover. The Camino uses 13 inch wheels although a larger diameter can give a more aggressive look.

On the road, the ride is very comfortable, and due to the weight difference between this and the Cortina, acceleration is very good. All around vision may be a problem for some people, particularly

Ford based kit cars
7 Modern
performance
saloons and coupes

with the long nose and small three-quarter rear windows, although later models have since appeared with full rear windows. In addition to the kit and the donor, a pair of Cavalier rear light clusters and BL front indicators and sidelights are required.

All in all, the kit so resembles the Cortina in dimensions that it is relatively easy to construct without any major modifications.

At the end of the day, the Camino is a very stylish car and, with its flared arches, side-skirts and deep valances, would not look out of place next to any of the smaller "body kit" styled Fords. It must be born in mind that the cost of a Camino kit is only slightly more than body styling kit for some new Fords!

JBA Javelin

The JBA Javelin is one of the few four-seater kit cars currently available, and was designed by John Barlow of JBA

Engineering. The initials 'JBA' are an amalgamation of the surname initials of the company's founder members, Ken Jones, John Barlow and David Ashley, all three coming originally from Leyland Trucks.

The donor car selected for their creation is the Mk II or III Capri, this becoming an increasingly popular choice for kits, the price and availability now beginning to make them an attractive alternative to the Cortina. The Capri supplies virtually all of the necessary mechanical assemblies and drive-train, this including engine, gearbox, steering, braking, and front and rear suspension. Not only does it supply the mechanical parts, it also donates numerous interior parts, such as seats, dashboard and trim panels. If a Ghia model is selected as the donor, the wood-grain dash, door-cappings and trim, will endow the car with a very up-market interior at a very reasonable price. Heating and demisting is carried out by the normal Capri systems, unmodified.

JBA's chassis is a rectangular-section steel structure of 100 x 50 x 3.2 mm dimensions, the design of which offers good passenger protection in the event of an impact from almost any direction. Roll-over protection is also included, as are all of the necessary structures for mounting the Capri's front struts and rear axle assembly. Unlike many other kit cars, a

Right and below: **The stylish JBA Javelin uses the main mechanical components from the Mk II/III Capri, an increasingly popular choice as a donor. The Capri supplies virtually all of the necessary parts, that, when added to JBA's excellent kit, results in a very well made, practical four-seater. The box-section steel chassis takes the Capri running-gear, virtually unmodified, and will accept any of the usual range of Ford engines. The 2 litre ohc unit makes an ideal compromise between performance and economy, and is an increasingly popular choice. This Javelin features quad headlights, black grille and a tastefully trimmed interior, complete with wooden dash panel.**

hints of the latter can still be detected in the Javelin's styling although the front end and grille styling, bear some similarities to that of the current Daimler models. Overall, it all works very well. The body comes as a single main moulding, plus the boot and bonnet lids, both of which fit well. The grille is also supplied, black, in its standard form, although available in polished stainless steel as a worthwhile option. Also supplied by JBA, are floor panels, a fuel cap cover, bonnet support, badges, hinges, roof locking mechanism and body cappings.

The choice of power-plant is clearly wide open, all of the usual Ford range fitting, the 2 litre engine making a good compromise between performance and economy. If performance is the main requirement, then one of the V6 engines would neatly fit the bill. The braking system of the Capri is retained in its normal servo-assisted disc/drum configuration, this being more than adequate for most driving conditions.

One of the few non-Ford items needed are the Toyota headlights, Capri light clusters being used at the rear.

The Javelin, as well as being a very well designed and built car, is also a supremely practical one. It has a full, four-seat capacity, a sizeable boot, as well as

This Javelin was based on a 3 litre Ghia Capri. Amongst the individual touches are rectangular headlights, bonnet air-intakes, boot spoiler and steel four-spoke wheels.

good deal of steel is used in the Javelin's construction, being utilised for the inner wings, transmission tunnel and bulkhead, all adding to the overall strength and rigidity of the unit. As would be expected, the chassis comes fully drilled and bushed, ready to accept the Ford components. The quality is very good, JBA having established something of a reputation in this sphere.

The body is of fibreglass and is of similar proportions to the Capri. Certain

Ford based kit cars
7 Modern
performance
saloons and coupes

the option of nicely-fitting soft and hard tops. Safety features high on its list of advantages, as does the easy maintenance afforded by the use of the Ford components. It really does offer a relatively easy answer to the problem of what to do with that rusty Capri, transforming it into a very contemporary-looking, open-top car. With an ohc engine or similar, the car has more than enough performance for most road-going conditions.

It is also a very pleasant car to drive, the Capri suspension, even in the unmodified form, giving excellent handling and road-holding.

JBA have managed to produce a practical, easy-to-build, "sporty" car, of very good quality. It appeals to a broad spectrum of buyers, from the person who merely wants to recycle his old Capri, to the family man wanting a stylish car that can be used to transport his brood throughout the year. Like its equally well made stablemate, the Falcon, the Javelin manages to score all round.

The Rico Saloon and Shuttle

The four-seater Dutton Rico sports saloon was launched in 1984. By 1985 the Series 2 Rico was on the streets, featuring much cleaner lines, with flush fitting headlights, door handles and indicators. The donor vehicle, as for most Duttons, is a Mk I or II Escort, although the windscreen and doors have to be taken from a two-door Mk I. Prior to leaving Duttons, the Rico is fitted with Escort doors to check on the alignments, so when the kit arrives at its new home, the doors from the donor should fit without too many problems. The kit is supplied with the body attached to the chassis (square-section steel tube of dimensions 4″ x 2″) which has a roll-over bar and seat belt mountings, front and rear. The body edging comes fitted, together with a hinged bonnet and boot lid. The boot houses a bracket to hold the spare wheel. The front spoiler, bumper and grille come as a one-piece unit and house the number plate, fog lights and halogen headlights (the Series One had double DeLorean headlights, the Series Two, Escort units). Similarly, at the rear there is an integral bumper/spoiler unit, which houses the rear fog lights, number plate and light; the rear light clusters (Mk III Escort units) are also provided with the kit. The rain gutters are self-adhesive. Also supplied is all of the glass (with the exception of the windscreen). One useful option is a heated rear screen, this being a must, and with the rear wash/ wipe that is supplied, ensures adequate rear vision in all winds and weathers. There are many other "bits" included in the kit, such as badges, hinges and all of the usual nuts and bolts. There are many

As with most of the Dutton range, the Rico uses the running-gear from the plentiful Mk I/II Escort. The body, shrewdly uses the doors from a Mk I Escort, this supplying such necessary items as locking and wind-up window mechanisms. This approach obviously avoids the expense of specially made doors. The kit comes as a body/chassis assembly, complete with roll-over bar. The power-plant can consist of any of the 1100–1600 cc Escort engines, or even the V4 and V6 units. The Series 1 Rico used DeLorien headlights and the Series 2, more easily obtainable Escort units.

additional options including such things as tow bars and brake pipes.

With the many Escort variations, the engine and gearbox can be taken from anything from an 1100 cc to 1600 cc, with even the option of the V4 or V6 units. It is of course necessary to decide well in advance of purchase on the engine option, so that any modifications can be made prior to the kit leaving the factory.

1986 saw the launch of the Rico Shuttle. This is based on the Rico Saloon styling, front-wise, but has a very large load carrying area at the rear. As with the Saloon, the Shuttle is Escort-based although in this case, if heavy loads are to be carried, the larger Cortina engine options may well be the ones to go for. The 1.6 and 2.0 litre seem to be the most popular choices. The chassis is similar to the Saloon, being jig and MIG welded, and is really a modification of the very successful Dutton Sierra chassis. The main differences are the reduction in ground clearance and the extended length, by four inches. All mountings are ready fitted for the engine, gearbox, McPherson struts etc. The roll-bar and seat belt mountings are the same as the saloon and conform to the Motor Industry Research Association Regulations, a test which is designed to determine the overall strength of the chassis structure and the integrity of its welds. The Shuttle

also uses the doors from a Mk I Escort, the remaining mechanicals coming from Mk I or Mk II versions. The front bumper, lights and spoiler arrangement is as for the Saloon, and colour-coded to match the bodywork. The rest of the "bits" are as for the Saloon, except for the rear windows (all glass fitted) and of course the large rear opening door. The rear lights for the Shuttle come courtesy of an Escort van. One useful addition is the lockable filler cap, the tank position and filler, incidently, being well designed and positioned and easy to fill, something often forgotten in other kits. The dashboard for both models depends on the donor selected. Obviously a basic Mk I Escort dashboard looks less attractive when compared to a Mk II Sport of Ghia version. The demisters are also taken from the donor. With the rear seat down, over 20 cubic feet are available. A further useful feature is that with the rear door open, the whole loading area is flat, a great advantage for load carrying. Overall the Shuttle makes a good stable-mate to the Saloon and is competing well in the estate market. One design area that is sometimes criticised (for both models) are the two front pins for the bonnet release. These don't really aid either security, or the smooth lines.

On the road, the degree of comfort is really up to the builder. There are some very comfortable versions and some, that have been far less successful. The ride is smooth, but when heavily laden, the bumps can sometimes be felt. The acceleration is very good, particularly when powered by the 2.0 litre Cortina engine option. Overall visibility is very good, better than the Saloon, and the Escort heater is as good as ever. In the wet, the rear screen wash/wipe is a necessity, as is the heated rear screen, features that are definitely worth the extra expense.

This is probably one of the cheapest estate kits currently on the market but one which manages to match up to most of the expensive competition, in many respects. It's a vehicle that appeals to a wide range of people and uses, and one which will undoubtedly be on the roads for many years to come.

8
Sports and performance cars

For a long time, kit cars have provided an economical answer to the quest for high performance motoring. In its infancy, the industry turned out countless fibreglass replacement bodies and chassis, to take the ubiquitous Ford running-gear. By today's standards, many of the "sports" cars thus created, were not exactly fast, nor did many of them handle too well as a result of the antiquated Ford suspension that many of them still retained. Their performance was considerably better than the saloon that had supplied the mechanical parts, and that in itself was enough for many people.

At the extreme, there were enthusiasts and racers who were prepared to pursue the development of such cars much further. Gradually, a proportion of these cars were reworked to a high degree of sophistication. Engines were tuned, suspension improved, and aerodynamic lightweight body shells adopted. Despite their humble beginnings, these cars were often a match for "real" sports cars of the period. There were plenty of home-built, inexpensive kit cars, based around ancient Ford running gear, that were capable of showing a clean pair of heels to, for instance, the little MGs of the period! Many kit cars had a number of advantages (apart from their cost) such as aerodynamic shape and light weight, the latter effectively being the equivalent of extra horsepower. Over the years, as true sports cars gradually disappeared from the product lists of most of the major

manufacturers, the kit car often provided one of the few viable alternatives in the quest for performance. Although recent years have seen something of a change of attitude, with a number of sports-type cars appearing, most still fail to capture the raw, exhilarating feeling engendered by many of the earlier cars. Their other big disadvantage, is their price!

Clearly the kit car industry still has an important role to play in this area and although few of today's kit-based sports cars are as cheap and cheerful as their predecessors, they can still offer excellent handling and exciting performance for a lot less money than many of today's, so called "sports cars". Recent years have seen true sports car virtually disappear from the scene. A number of vehicles have appeared that purported to be "sports cars" but in truth their performance has often been mediocre. With the increasing activities of the kit car industry, significant changes have started to occur.

Some new cars such as the Tripos and the Maelstrom, really manage to put the performance back into motoring. Even in full road trim, they would be a good match for some of their racing predecessors. As major manufacturers have largely turned their backs on this section of the market, it has been left to a few small independent producers, and the kit car industry, to step into the gap created. From a performance point of view, Ford drive-trains make a good choice because of their strength and reliability, plus a huge amount of tuning equipment that is readily available. In this way, it is possible to build a sports car using a standard Ford drive-train, then systematically upgrade it as required.

Straight line and top speed performance is not the only consideration. More important for a road car, is performance in terms of handling and general "driveability". Such terms are very hard to define, but anyone who has stepped from the driver's seat of, for instance, a Lotus 7, into a typical production saloon, will understand the meaning! Suspension systems have come a long way from the early days of performance-oriented kit cars. The limitations imposed by the old Ford chassis, even when equipped with such things as swing-axle conversions and IRS set-ups, have long been left behind. Today's cars have purpose-built chassis, the design of which is often as a result of race track experience. Likewise, the suspension systems now include special components such as adjustable coil-over shock absorbers, adjustable front and rear anti-roll bars, lightweight wishbones, and so on. In reality, today's road cars are not far removed from yesterday's racing cars. The results on the road are obvious, such cars being able to "out-drive" the vast majority of others. Not surprisingly, the performance and handling of a number of cars of this type, is on a par with some track-only vehicles. The "Kit Cars and Specials Challenge" has spawned a number of highly competitive cars, their increasing sophistication, with the passage of time, being clearly evident. This has led to an inevitable spin-off effect, refinements being developed for the track, finding their way into road-going equivalents. Such is the case with many of today's performance-oriented kit cars.

A number of the cars in this bracket, have put all-out performance (in all senses) at the top of their list of priorities. Hand in hand with this, has gone safety, the advanced chassis, braking and suspension systems, ensuring that such cars are capable of being driven hard, but also safely.

Practicality, is not necessarily a word that can be applied to some of them. Luggage space is limited or non-existent, as indeed is passenger space, and weather protection often minimal. In addition, the interiors can also be very cramped. It is obvious that cars of this type are not intended for the more mundane tasks of ferrying passengers and cargo about. Such vehicles are one of the most cost-effective ways of owning a car that is capable of holding its own with even the most advanced products of the major motor manufacturers. A lightweight body shell, a track-bred chassis and suspension, coupled with an affordable and easily tuned Ford drive-train, can create a car that is capable of showing a clean pair of heels to all but the most expensive and sophisticated cars. The cars that fall into this group, are aimed at the section of the motoring public who want nothing more from their cars than the ability to drive them to the limit, but in conditions of safety, and who are prepared to accept a few compromises in pursuit of their aim. They want cars that are capable of leaving 99% of all others in the dust! Clearly, this must also be at an affordable price.

A number of other cars in this category, have placed performance near the top of the list, but have made it available with a high degree of comfort and refinement. Such cars as the Marcos, have managed to combine many of the elements of the true sports car with a degree of luxury only to be expected in a well-appointed saloon. In the case of Marcos, years of refinement and development have resulted in a car with a high degree of comfort, coupled with sporting ability and all year round practicality. Quite an achievement! Despite their high level of creature comforts, cars such as the Marcos, Carrera and Hensen, are undeniably "sports" cars. Whereas cars such as the Tripos and Maelstrom are tremendously attractive for summer driving, cars that compose this latter group are clearly more suited for all-weather use.

The choice is clearly up to the buyer. If he wants wind-in-the-hair, all-out performance, there are a number of Ford-based/powered kit cars that will fit the bill. If weather protection and a degree of comfort, perhaps at the expense of a certain amount of overall performance, is wanted, equally, there are plenty of options to choose from. Once again, the wealth of experience and great adaptability of the kit car industry manages to produce a range of products that cater for a whole spectrum of requirements, and still at an affordable price!

Hensen M30

There were a number of different routes that Hugo Henrickson could have taken when it came to producing his first kit car. With a long list of Sports, American and kit cars behind him, his experiences could have led to almost anything. What it ultimately led to was the Hensen M30, a performance-orientated kit car that has been likened by some, to a modern day equivalent of the legendary Cobra.

The M30 first saw the light of day late in 1983, emerging from Henrickson's Milford Haven factory. The car caused a reaction wherever it was seen, some loving it and others being less sure about some of its very individual styling characteristics. Reservations were voiced concerning the frontal styling, the rear wheel arches, the rear window and so on, but at the end of the day, most had to concede that the car definitely had a special charisma of its own.

Whatever unfavourable comments were passed concerning its looks, only praise was heaped upon it with regards to its engineering and overall quality. The superbly-made fibreglass body shell clothes an equally well made chassis and roll-over protection system, one which probably offers unparalleled passenger protection. The main rails are of 4 x 2 inch steel box-section with additional 2 x 2

inch bracing. The roll cage is built from 2 x 2 inch and 1.5 x 1.5 inch steel, the whole structure being immensely strong. Another notable safety feature is the use of hefty door intrusion beams offering excellent protection in the event of a side-on impact.

The kit is designed to accept the running gear from the Granada, the front and rear sub-frames being solidly mounted to the Hensen's chassis. As well as the suspension, the Granada also supplies the engine and gearbox.

The fibreglass body, like the chassis, is superbly constructed and is almost certainly one of the strongest kit car bodies ever made. The fibreglass is very thick, especially in critical areas, and of excellent quality. Another feature not commonly encountered is the use of polyurethane foam, used to fill the front 18 inches of the body section, this increasing the car's impact resistance and giving even greater passenger protection. The body is constructed from lower and upper sections, these being fitted together around the chassis/cage structure, the final product being exceedingly strong. The double-skinned doors contain, as well as the intrusion beams, the Granada glass, electric window mechanisms

The latter day equivalent of the Cobra? The Henson M30 features numerous innovations in its construction, the body being one of the strongest and safest kit car bodies ever constructed. The hefty door-intrusion beams, roll-cage and polyurethane filled front body section all combine to provide a high degree of passenger protection.

Although not universally admired, there is no denying that the Henson's angular lines do have a certain brutal appeal. The mechanical components come from the Granada, this supplying the engine, gearbox and complete front and rear sub-frame and suspension assemblies. Even though the car is no lightweight, the Granada's V6 will push it to 125 mph, with a 0-60 time of 8 seconds. Any reservations concerning its styling are soon forgotten when in the driving seat! The all round performance of Henrickson's meticulously designed road-burner is excellent.

(depending upon donor model) and lock assemblies. The Granada also supplies the front screen, the other glass being specially made.

The interior features the Granada instrument package as well as a single additional rear seat. The overall feeling is one of surprising space and comfort, combined with the feel of a luxury sports car.

The M30 kit is fairly expensive but is equally comprehensive in its content. Apart from the body/chassis unit (painted to colour of choice), the package includes a sun roof, steering wheel, stereo system, all additional glass, seats, indicators and aluminium petrol tank. In addition, 8 x 14 wheels are included, as well as quad headlights. A further worthwhile option is a full stainless steel exhaust system.

Not surprisingly, the car is no lightweight, but at 25 cwt, it is a full 3 cwt lighter than the Granada. It is also a totally different car to drive! The handling and road holding are excellent, as is the cornering ability, very little body roll being noted. Uprated shock absorbers are used, this clearly helping matters. The steering is considered by some to be a little on the light side, however, it is both quick and responsive as a result of the Granada's PAS system (again depending on the donor).

Despite the car's weight, a respectable 0-60 time in the region of 8 seconds is obtained, with a top speed somewhere in excess of 125 mph. Clearly the Granada's V6 is quite capable of making this comparative heavyweight perform as a real road-burner.

The M30's manufacturing rights have recently been taken over by Eagle Cars who initially intended to market the kit. A change of Company policy has led to the plans and moulds, once again, being put on the market.

The Hensen M30, not withstanding any reservations about its styling, is an incredibly well-built car that is fast, practical and very safe. The tough, almost brutal looks of the M30 may well indeed make the car come to be regarded as a latter day equivalent of the Cobra!

Seraph 115 and 215

Seraph cars was set up by John Grosart, formally Girling's chief design engineer, who originally became involved in the kit car scene in the form of a company known as "Motor Style". This offered a build up service for various types of kits. John was later joined by a grass-track racer, Steve Langford and out of this union came the Seraph SS. This was built around a

complex space frame and featured an integral roll-bar system and complex suspension arrangement. It was powered by a mid-mounted Lotus twin-cam, weighed a mere 14 cwt and made an impressive circuit racer. It obviously lacked practicality for road use, but out of it, the Seraph 115 and 215 models were ultimately born.

The two models were virtually identical, the difference being in the drivetrain, the 115 housing the range of four-cylinder Ford engines, and the 215, the V6 units.

The chassis was a complex, fully triangulated space frame, constructed from square-section steel tube, and carried all of the necessary mounting brackets for the seat belts, steering, engine, gearbox and body. The chassis was designed so that none of the stresses were passed onto the body, thus avoiding any problems of crazing or cracking of the fibreglass.

The front suspension was mainly Cortina, this supplying the uprights, hub assemblies and upper wishbones. The lower wishbones were specially made, and independently tested, Seraph units.

The rear axle was located by four radius arms and a Panhard rod and sprung by a pair of Spax coil-over units. The company did investigate the use of the Sierra independent rear end however this was deemed to be too wide.

Although parts were required from a number of sources, the majority of the main mechanical components could conveniently be taken from the Mk II Capri. This supplied engine, gearbox, propshaft, radiator, exhaust system, steering column and rack. Various other parts were required such as an Escort petrol tank, pedal box and handbrake cables. In addition, a few non-Ford items were also needed such as Vauxhall Viva HC headlights and Marina wiper assembly, doorlock mechanisms and bonnet lock.

As well as the chassis, the kit included the body shell, doors, boot lid, bonnet, front screen, quarter lights, aluminium window frames, window winder mechanisms, rear bumper and dash panel. The body came complete with the doors, window frames and glass fully fitted, and fully prepared and finished in self-etching primer. The quality of the body mouldings was excellent, their

This is the uncommon Bonito of Bill Battey. He bought the car, now over ten years old, as a half-completed project. During the construction, parts were used from over 28 donor cars! The power for this low-slung projectile is now provided by a 1970 Mk II Cortina engine, in a high state of tune. If sufficient interest is created, there is the possibility that the car may reappear in kit form.

The Seraph 115 was designed to accept a variety of four-cylinder Ford engines, the performance and handling of the track-bred missile being second to none. The car used a complex space-frame chassis that came with all mountings for the major components, including the Cortina-derived front suspension and the 5-link live rear axle set-up, in place. Although a number of donors were required for the necessary parts, the Capri could be conveniently used to supply most of the major components.

One of the few 215s, shown here under construction at the factory, the engine and gearbox coming from a Capri. The 115 and 215 were visually very similar, however the use of the V6 engines meant that the stronger 3 litre Capri rear axle was necessary. The Cortina/Seraph front suspension was identical for both. The cars excellent handling came as a result of a great deal of race track experience, coupled with computer-aided studies. Although the cars were of excellent quality, the company unfortunately went out of business in 1986. Rumours concerning the future of the body moulds, jigs etc. continue to circulate, and there is the distinct possibility that the cars could reappear at a later date.

manufacture being carried out by Avondale Mouldings of Radstock. An option included the use of Kevlar for the body, an excellent but expensive choice!

A number of the Ford engine range were available new, for fitting in the Seraph, including the XR3, XR3i, 2.8 and 3 litre V6 units. Alternatively, the donor Capri's engine could be used. Seraph could also supply four- and five-speed gearboxes as well as a range of Capri back axles.

The use of the V6 engines meant that a number of differences in chassis construction were required. In addition, the use of the V6 meant that the rear axle from a 3 litre Capri was needed in order to cope with the high power output. The front suspension was identical for the two models.

The handling of both cars was superb, their track-bred heritage being most evident. The car cornered almost flat, with virtually no body roll, with a firm, but nonetheless, comfortable ride. Performance with a 2 litre ohc engine usually gave a top speed in the 110–120 mph bracket, with the top speed, when fitted with a V6, being around 140 mph.

The 115 and 215 models were later joined by a Ford-based Bonito, somewhat similar in both looks and styling. The Seraph cars were of good quality, good design and workmanship, and performed superbly on the road. Despite the un-

doubted excellence of their products, the company ultimately foundered and went out of business towards the end of 1986. Surviving Seraphs are now becoming quite sought after machines although, only a few people will now be in a position to sample the delights of their performance.

Carlton Carrera

At first glance you could be forgiven for thinking that this is a Datsun 240Z Sports, but a close inspection reveals that it is the two-door hatchback of Carlton Auto-motive, known as the Carrera.

It was originally launched in 1985 (by Carlton Mouldings) and is based on a Mk III, IV or V Cortina. Another further option offered uses Cortina parts but with a Capri or Jaguar rear axle, this wider combination allowing for four full-sized seats inside. For Jaguar fans, a version is now available which uses the complete front and rear suspension assemblies donated by Jaguar.

The chassis is of a very sturdy con-struction made from 10 gauge steel, MIG and jig welded. The chassis can be supplied to the customer either as bare metal or with a black Hammerite finish. It is pre-drilled, so that the front and rear axles are in the same alignment and geometric position to that of the Cortina donor. All of the necessary fittings are supplied for brake pipe supports, and flanges are provided to anchor the fibreglass body into place. Outriggers provide extra support as well as pro-viding anchor points for a roll-over cage. A tow bar can also be welded on if required. One very thoughtful addition

Often mistaken for a Datsun sports car, this is, in fact, the Carrera from Carlton Automotive. This tough-looking, two-door hatchback uses much of the running-gear from the Mk III, IV or V Cortina, this fitting the Carrera's substantial steel chassis with little modification. The body is constructed from fibreglass, and features a distinctive rear hatch mounted spoiler.

and not encountered in most other manufacturer's products, are mounts for baby seat supports, which are added to the kit if required, free of charge. The chassis can be bought separately in order to get the project cheaply underway and when assembled, can be returned to Carlton for the body fittings (free of charge).

The bodyshell consists of a forward hinging body assembly, complete with inner and outer wings and air intake scoops. The locking mechanism utilises the rear door locks from a Cortina, together with a modified bonnet release cable. The main tub is of a one-piece construction, providing a sealed bulkhead and rear floor section (also weather resistance). A steel roll-over cage is moulded into the fibreglass. It is constructed from 40 x 40 x 3 mm square-section, forming a hoop behind the driver's head, and extends down to the rear of the chassis. The hoop also carries the seat belt mountings. Additional protective rails also protrude from this

construction, providing adequate protection for the Cortina or Capri petrol tank. The doors are constructed from fibreglass and utilise internal steel tubes to increase their side impact resistance. Locking is via the standard Capri or Cortina units. The doors mount onto steel posts and house the complete Capri window mechanisms. The rear tailgate is also a one-piece moulding, the rear glass coming courtesy of an MGB GT.

The bulkhead is designed to take all of the standard Cortina parts such as heater, windscreen wiper assembly, air ducting and all of the necessary dashboard instruments. The entire Cortina dashboard and equipment can be installed complete if required. An option is Carlton's own fibreglass dashboard which is designed to hold Mk II Escort instrumentation. The choice really depends on the model and quality of the donor vehicle, for either choice.

Every attention to detail has been catered for, extra box-section being added where necessary, providing

Marcos

To many people, the name of Marcos is synonymous with high quality component cars. Of all of the manufacturers of this type, Marcos is one of the oldest, well respected producers of quality cars, and has been that way for nearly three decades.

The year 1959 saw the start of the partnership of Jem Marsh, who was active manufacturing and supplying Austin 7 Special parts, and ex-Vanwall man, Frank Costin. Out of their alliance, came the first innovative, wooden-chassised cars to bear the Marcos logo. These cars were built using marine ply and fibreglass, and structured in a similar fashion to an aircraft fuselage. The radical concept was successful and before long, Marcos cars were making a name for themselves on the race track. 1960 saw Costin moving on, to be replaced by Peter and Dennis Adams. With the coming of 1964 came a new model, the 1800 Coupe, still using the plywood/fibreglass monocoque system.

The lengendary Marcos, a car so well established, that it needs little further comment. There are now well over a thousand cars world-wide. Over the years, there has been a wide range of power-plants adopted, including the Ford 1500, 1600, 2 and 3 litre units. After a decade out of production, the car was reintroduced in 1981, looking better than ever. The quality of the body and all aspects of its engineering, is very high.

strength around all of the potential "pressure" points. One good additional touch, is a special box-section above the windscreen to house a rear view mirror and sun visors. The rear tailgate has a built in whale-tail spoiler, providing that "sporty" look. It is hinged on Talbot hinges opened via gas rams, and is locked by a standard Cortina boot lock attached to a suitable bonnet release.

As well as all of the parts already mentioned, the Cortina supplies the engine (anything from the 1.3/1.6 saloon through to the 3.0 litre V6 Ford), gearbox, propshaft, wiper system and the wiring loom. Also needed are a Capri windscreen (with rubbers) and, from the same vehicle, three-quarter windows. An Escort Mk II supplies the front indicators, a Mini the headlights and a Cavalier the rear light clusters.

Other options include a tow bar, gas struts for the bonnet, sunroof and rear valance. To produce a four-seater, modifications are needed to the chassis and main body tub, and these are carried out before delivery by Carlton. Clearly this must be planned well in advance.

The road holding is very good and the car on the move is amazingly quiet. It corners well (better with Jaguar suspension) and the overall ride is good. A softer ride can be achieved by using 1.3 or 1.6 Cortina suspension. For a firmer ride the 2.3 Mk V Estate is a good option and one which is needed if the intention is to carry heavy loads, rather than with performance in mind. Visibility is good all around, although for shorter drivers, the rear spoiler can cause problems when reversing. All in all, a very well designed car that can be a sporty performer for either two or four passengers and one which would undoubtedly find favour for the family driver who wants something more than an ordinary saloon.

This was ultimately replaced, in 1969, by an easier to manufacture, steel space-frame chassis. Over the following years, the cars were powered by a variety of engines such as the 1800 Volvo, the Triumph 2.5 and Ford 1500, 1600, 2 and 3 litre units. It came as something of a shock when, in 1971, Marcos stopped producing cars, deciding to concentrate solely on the repair and maintenance of those cars already on the road (there were now somewhere in excess of 1000 at this point!).

This was the way things remained for a decade until, in 1981, it became apparent that the market was now in a much healthier state, and the decision to relaunch the Marcos was taken. How would the public take to the car after such a long break? The company need not have worried!

The "new" car was basically the same sleek, Peter Adams-designed road-burner but updated with innumerable detailed improvements and refinements. Before long, cars were beginning to flow from the Marcos Wiltshire base, having rapidly re-established itself on the scene. The Marcos was back!

The space-frame chassis was retained and like virtually everything else associated with the car, is made in-house. It is a beautifully made unit of 1.5 x 1.5 inch square-section steel of 16 gauge. This accepts most of the mechanical parts from a number of donors, perhaps the most convenient of which are the Mk I and II Cortina or Capri. One of the best choices is probably the 3 litre Capri, this supplying its engine, gearbox, propshaft and back axle, as well as a multitude of smaller parts. The front suspension is non-Ford, being mainly composed of Triumph Vitesse/GT6 parts. To overcome the problem of different bolt patterns, Marcos can supply new hubs with Ford pattern studs to fit the Triumph stub-axles. The back axle needs brackets welding on to accept the radius rods, this service being offered by the factory. Alternatively, well-detailed plans are available for the home-builder to carry out this himself.

The styling of the body really needs little description, its race-bred lines being so well established on the scene. What

does bear reiteration, is its overall quality and panel fit, both of which are excellent. The body comes with the doors ready hung, the front screen in place, and the bonnet and boot lid in position. Also supplied are the rear screen, a rose-jointed steering linkage, instruments, and adjustable pedal-box assembly.

Marcos will build the car to any degree of completion, from basic assembly, up to virtually complete cars, less drive-train. They also offer an impressive selection of options including seats and trim package, headlight covers, spring set, bumpers, Panhard rod, and adjustable shock absorbers. Additional items include headlining, fuel tank, electric window mechanisms, and so on.

Assembly of the Marcos is considered to be a straightforward operation, somewhat dependent on the degree of completion selected by the customer. Body preparation is minimal, the quality and fit ensuring that little time needs to be spent on this aspect.

The fully-assembled car weighs around 17 cwt and with a V6 fitted, a 0–60 time of around 8 seconds can be expected, and a top speed of somewhere in excess of 120 mph. The Marcos is a comfortable car to drive and, after a brief period getting acquainted with it, is a confidence inspiring car.

Marcos is one of the small handful of manufacturers whose products can stand comparison with some of the best cars produced by major producers, but at considerably lower prices. What you do get for your money, is one of the most stylish, well constructed "home-build" cars currently available anywhere in the world. Even after its long life, the Marcos has lost none of its appeal, if anything, it has matured into an even better looking car than the original. The car has now been around for nearly a quarter of a century and who knows, it may well be around for another!

Tripos R81

The diminutive R81 has only recently arrived on the scene, and is the first commercial product of Tripos R & D Ltd.

For the first car, the R81 is quite an innovative and remarkable little car for a number of reasons that will become apparent.

The car is not strictly based on a single donor, but makes use, in conjunction with a number of specially fabricated parts, of Ford components for many of the main assemblies. In true racing tradition, a full space-frame is used. This was constructed from one inch square steel tubing and was designed by Bob Eggington. A very nice piece of work it is too! The front suspension also betrays a race track heritage, consisting of a double wishbone system, most of which is specially built. The remaining parts consist of an adjustable anti-roll bar and Spax adjustable coil-over units. Cortina components are to be found in the shape of modified uprights, hubs and disc brake assemblies. Steering is handled by a special column, connected to an Escort steering rack fitted with extension pieces.

At the rear, a Cortina axle is used, this being located by radius arms and a Panhard rod, and mounted an another pair of Spax coil-over units.

The engine bay will accept a number of engines, although because of its very low lines, this is limited to engines such as the 1300 and 1600 X-flow units. As a result of their greater height, the ohc engines will not fit, and neither will any of the V engines. The wheels used are 6 x 15 with 195 x 15, 60 profile tyres, these tucking neatly beneath the mudguards and matching their radii perfectly.

What about that exquisite body? It was designed by Laurie Abbot and is produced, by Protoco Mouldings, in fibreglass of excellent quality. Its looks are quite unlike anything else currently available and although they have a definite race track character about them, it is difficult to pin them down to any one particular car. There is a hint of Vanwall about it from certain angles and yet the nose section and grille opening bear some resemblance to the D-Type Jaguar. There are certainly styling lines reminiscent of the 1954 Frazer Nash Sebring Sports, especially around the rear wheel arches and cockpit, although only a passing similarity. Some have even likened it to the Allard J2 Sports, although the R81 lacks the brutal looks of the J2, being a much more petite and civilised machine. It is virtually impossible to narrow it down, and yet the car has a certain familiarity about it. It may simply be that it manages to look ''correct'' and purposeful from every angle. Whatever,

The remarkable little R81, the first car from Tripos R and D Ltd. The race-bred car uses a complex space-frame chassis, constructed from 1-inch square steel tube. The front suspension consists of a number of specially fabricated parts, coupled with Cortina uprights, hubs and brakes. Steering is handled by an Escort rack. The limited engine bay will only accept such engines as the 1300 and 1600 crossflow units, the ohc units being too tall. Performance and roadholding of the R81 are quite exceptional.

there is no denying that its heritage lies on the race track rather than the road.

The kit is offered in two stages. Stage 1, which includes the body, chassis, nose section, fuel tank, pedals, steering column and screen. A number of specially made adaptor pieces for the steering rack and the front uprights, as well as a number of engine pieces, such as thermostat housing, are also supplied. In Stage II form, the kit also includes dash panel, boot floor, Spax coil-overs, springs, wiring harness, lights, instruments, exhaust, propshaft, seats, tonneau, hood and side screens. Clearly this is not a cheap option, but it certainly supplies virtually everything needed to complete the car, less drive-train.

Not surprisingly, the performance, handling and road holding are superb, almost akin to driving a small racing car on the road. With a 1600 Ford engine providing the power, the performance is every bit as good as the car's looks. Rapid acceleration, superb characteristics, and confidence inspiring handling can all be relished. As expected in a true sports car, the ride is firm, but not uncomfortable. The R81 is a true driver's car!

The R81 has been very professionally designed and built and, naturally the price reflects this. This puts it in the Lotus/Caterham 7 class, with no-compromise performance being the number one priority. Since Chapman's first Lotus 6, in terms of styling, little has changed, most sports cars of this type content to follow in its foot steps. Perhaps the R81 (at last!), is a fresh development of it, or perhaps it is the start of a new line. It is possible that the R81 is an indicator of the shape of things to come. It may well be that the next three decades will see a whole string of clone cars emulating the looks of the R81, as has happened with the Lotus. Future generations may well look back on this as the first of a whole new breed of no-compromise sports cars, which put the excitement back into motoring.

Eagle SS and 2 Plus

Like their other well-established product the RV, Eagle Cars (under the guiding hand of Alan Breeze), have over the years, systematically improved and upgraded the SS. Alan, originally in conjunction with Tim Dutton, was responsible for bringing the SS to the UK, the car then being produced in the US by Amore Cars and marketed as the Cimbria. It used the VW floor-pan, however like many other kits, it was only a matter of time before a major rethink occurred and the SS also became available with a Ford-based option. Although the VW option is still available, the newer Ford-based kit now predominates, the reliability and availability of Ford components being second to none.

The SS was launched on an unsuspecting public in 1981 and for such an exotic-looking, gull-winged projectile, the prices were very favourable. The result was a rapid market acceptance for the car. With the passing years, the car was continually refined and improved, both in terms of quality and styling, this ultimately culminating in the Series III.

The donor car is either the Mk III or IV Cortina, any of the range of Ford engines up to the 2 litre ohc being suitable. The V6 units will fit, although Eagle suggest that the 2 litre engine is probably the best compromise. As well as its power-plant, the Cortina also donates its gearbox, electrical system, steering column, suspension and steering systems, all fitting

The swoopy Eagle SS first saw the light of day in VW-based form in 1981. This was later followed by a switch to Ford components, the Mk III/IV Cortina being adopted as the donor car. This supplies the drive-train, steering, front and rear suspension and electrical systems. The car has been continually refined during its life, now being in its Series III form. The Ford-based version of this exotic, gull-winged car features a redesigned interior and lower floor line, this greatly increasing available space.

neatly into place with few modifications.

The chassis is fabricated from box-section steel of 3 x 1.5 inches, substantially crossbraced by 1.5 x 1.5 inch steel tube. It is of conventional ladder design and comes fully drilled, ready to accept the Cortina's mechanical parts. The Cortina front subframe bolts directly into place, complete with suspension, steering rack, hubs, brakes and uprights, without modification. Assembling the rear end is equally as simple, the complete set-up bolting into place. As would be expected, the Cortina propshaft needs shortening, the actual amount being dependent on the engine/gearbox chosen.

Undoubtedly the most commented part of the car is not its mechanical parts, but its ultra-low, swoopy bodyshell. Very few cars on the road resemble the SS and those that do, are only to be found in the expensive, exotic sports car bracket. The body comes supplied with the front screen already in place as well as a purpose-built dashboard fitted. The quality of the fibreglass is now considered to be good, although earlier cars did tend to suffer a little in this respect. Successive improvements in manufacturing and quality control have eliminated these problems. The body is strengthened by the use of steel reinforcing around the window and door pillars.

The impressive gull-wing doors come complete with gas-rams, locks, hinges and handles. The rear and side glass is also supplied. The massive, specially made screen can be swept by either a standard single-arm wiper or by a pantograph system, both being available from Eagle. The body is available in six standard colours although non-standard ones can be supplied at extra cost.

The "basic" kit includes the chassis, bodyshell, screen, bonnet, boot lid, rear bumper, dash, nose section, complete doors and pop-up light system. Various other parts are also available. The kit is also offered in a less fully prepared form, known as the "economy" kit, and provides a possible solution for those operating on a tight budget. Eagle are very flexible in this respect.

The Series III is the latest in the line, and scores over its predecessors in a number of ways. As well as a redesigned chassis, it features upgraded interior options, lower floor line, and a number of other cosmetic and mechanical refinements. Clearly Eagle listen to customer feedback and act upon it.

The Eagle SS is yet another car that has matured and improved over the years, the 41 inch high projectile finding its way into the hands of many people who would have liked a Ferrari or something similar, but who couldn't run to the astronomical prices. The SS has offered them the chance to own an exotic, glamorous sports car but at a sensible price.

Following the undisputed success of the SS, came the topless version, the Eagle 2 Plus. Mechanically, this is nearly identical to the SS, the obvious difference being the open-top, plus-two bodyshell. Apart from the lack of roof, the car uses conventional doors and a Granada front screen, set at a relatively steep angle. The car is supplied with a roll-over bar, this also carrying the seat belt mounts. As its name implies, the car now has additional seating in the form of a limited rear seat.

Other obvious differences (with the new 2 Plus Series II) include the frontal styling and use of rectangular headlights instead of the pop-up variety.

There is now an Eagle to meet most people's requirements. For a couple, the SS would be the choice, or for the small family or the "wind-in-the-hair" brigade, perhaps the 2 Plus would fit the bill. The Eagle cars are undoubtedly glamorous and real crowd-stoppers wherever they park. To their credit, most people assume that they are some form of Italian flyer, never realising that humble Cortina parts lurk beneath their sleek bodyshells. These two cars really do offer the chance of a very impressive-looking sports car at a reasonable price. Hundreds of satisfied customers would probably agree with this.

The Maelstrom Lancaster One

The Maelstrom Lancaster One is one of those cars set to join the exclusive ranks of the true, no-holds-barred, sports/racing cars of which the new Tripos R81 and the fabled Lotus/Caterham 7 are members. These are cars where "drive-ability" and performance are of paramount importance, yet still retaining a degree of comfort and a good measure of safety. Such vehicles give true meaning to the term "Sports Cars". Like the Tripos, the Maelstrom is a relative newcomer, coming into existence as a result of the efforts of ex-Ford man, Mike Eydmann. He called on the services of the talented Bob Eggington of Automotive Systems Development, for the chassis and suspension design, and Neil Hirst of Expresso Design, for the car's styling. This combination of talents has produced one hell of a road car!

The donor for this projectile is none other than the Mk III Cortina, this supplying the engine, gearbox, front stub-axles, hubs, disc brake assemblies, rear axle and brakes, and handbrake mechanism.

The chassis is a fully triangulated, jig-built space-frame, constructed from 18 gauge steel tubing and semi-stressed sheet steel. Over 170 individual parts are used in the construction, the result being a very strong, as well as very safe, unit. Its design and manufacture is such that it provides a large safety margin, enabling it to cope with considerable amounts of horsepower as well as anything that a driver might throw at it. The chassis is available with a black powder finish and is also available in a lightweight form, primarily designed for racing purposes.

It is the suspension that helps endow the Maelstrom with its superb handling characteristics. In the words of the company, it is a "no compromise" system, the front-end featuring a race-bred, rising-rate design, which is commonplace on racing cars, but probably unique on the UK kit car scene. Under normal suspension movements, the ride is comparatively soft, but under more extreme conditions, the suspension system tightens up, having the safe effect as if stiffer springs had been fitted in the first place. Adjustable Spax gas dampers, concentric springs actuated by pull-rods and control arms, as well as Cortina uprights and ball joints, complete the package. The steering is handled by a specially made column and an Escort rack fitted with extended arms.

At the rear, the Cortina axle is modified to accept four trailing arms and a Panhard rod, this, plus a pair of Spax coil-over units, comprising the rear suspension set-up.

The engine choice is limited to the Ford X–flow series, namely the 1300, 1600 or 1600 GT units. The ohc engines will not fit under the low bonnet line as a result of their greater height. Things are so tight for space that even the X-flow engine's rocker box requires some modification. Carburation is best handled by the use of side-draught units, these increasing the power as well as reducing the overall height of the engine. Cooling is handled by a Dolomite Sprint radiator and exhaust gases, by the special side-mounted system.

The body has been variously described as "purposeful" and "functional", its sleek, wedge-shaped profile undoubtedly reflecting the influence of the racetrack. It is constructed from fibreglass and features extra reinforcement in the necessary areas. The body is unstressed and hence should give no problems of crazing, even under hard driving conditions. Apart from the main moulding, the body is made up from a nose section, bonnet and boot lids, and the Grand Prix inspired side-pods. The left-hand pod houses the exhaust system. The other parts consist of four cycle wings, a boot liner, transmission tunnel cover, and a pair of radius rod covers, all finished in black gel-coat. Additional items, such as grilles are also included. Limited weather protection is provided in the form of a tonneau cover and a small detachable wind screen that can be removed for racing purposes.

The kit is broken down into seven different packages, namely, chassis, body, steering, brakes and transmission, cooling and exhaust, carburation and fuel, and trim. Each package is very comprehensive, supplying virtually everything that the Cortina does not. As a result, the Maelstrom should present no real problems during construction. The company's extensive list of parts does not appear to exclude anything!

Impressive as the car looks, it is on the road that it really comes into its own. In full flight, it is a joy to behold, its handling being superb! Track-experienced drivers have commented that the handling is certainly on a par, or possibly even better, than that of the Caterham 7, a car that others are often measured against. Its ride characteristics, cornering, braking and steering, put the car firmly in the Sports Car bracket. It will be interesting to see how, in the future, this low-slung, innovative little car fares on the race track. In all probability, it will do very well! Even if it is limited to road use, the car's builder will be assured of having a car that will out-handle virtually anything else that it is likely to meet. There is no doubt that the Maelstrom is a true driver's car, one that is a sheer thrill to drive. It may well prove to be something of a threat to the more well established cars, such as the Westfield or Caterham 7.

The Ava K1 and K1 RS

Whereas such cars as the Tripos and Caterham 7 are undeniably "modern" sports cars, their character and styling clearly have their roots way back. This was clearly in the mind of Nick Topliss, the man who created the Ava K1, a car that also falls into the modern sports car bracket, but is a vastly different vehicle to the majority of its brethren. There are no cycle wings or cramped interiors to be found with the Ava, the car being a practical, comfortable, and very contemporary-looking creation, its looks clearly reflecting the styling currently found in a number of expensive, sports-orientated vehicles.

The donor car for the Ava is the front-wheel drive Mk III and IV Escort. These have now been around long enough to be

This is the "standard" version of the K1 from Ava Cars. The donor for this road/track car is the Mk III, front-wheel drive Ford Escort. The chassis is very strong, well designed, and constructed from stainless steel. The body shell is made from fibreglass and has a very low drag factor, the overall quality and finish being excellent. The front section of the body (bonnet with wings attached) tilts forward to reveal the cvh engine compartment. The most common engine options seem to be from the XR3 and XR3i. The interior of the vehicle is also Ford Escort, the seats, dashboard and instruments being easily recognisable. Weather protection is available in the form of a soft top. The rear of the car is the view that most people will see!

considered as a comparatively economical base vehicle. The Escort supplies the mechanical parts, including the McPherson front suspension set-up, as well as the complete rear suspension assembly. The Ava is one of the few kits currently available, that makes use of the Ford front-wheel drive assembly, using the cvh transverse engine, gearbox and transaxle, complete. The whole assembly makes a very neat, compact, and relatively easily transplanted drive-train, one that will undoubtedly find greater acceptance in the future as its availability increases. Not only does the Escort supply the afore mentioned parts, it also donates such things as its wiring loom, instrumentation, seats and trim parts. If required, the Ford anti-lock braking system (ABS) can be transplanted.

The chassis is of stainless steel construction and will accept the majority of the Ford parts without modification. In this case, there is not even a propshaft to shorten! It consists of a central monocoque structure, with tubular front and rear sections. The centre section includes the floor pan and front bulkhead, the overall design being the result of a computer-aided design study, which ensured that optimum strength and stiffness was obtained. Large sill beams are a feature of the chassis, as are a number of other tubular structures that support the steering assembly, pedals, door hinges, and engine and suspension mounts. The

This Ava RS was caught at Mallory Park circuit, where incidently, it was launched in 1986. It was taking part in a Kit Cars and Specials "Action Day", an event which gives prospective owners a chance to drive a wide variety of kits. This lightweight, Ford cvh-powered car has a top speed of around 170 mph. When compared with the K1, the RS has a strengthened body shell, a lightweight version of the stainless K1 chassis, plus attachments for a full racing harness. Here, the side windows have been removed, the car now sporting a small aero screen. This particular car has taken part in a number of hill-climb events, as well as showing off its prowess on the race track.

rear section carries the mounting points for the rear suspension, courtesy of a new cross-member, as well as the petrol tank, exhaust, and spare wheel fittings. Naturally strong seat belt mountings are also included.

The body essentially consists of four parts, the fibreglass being of excellent quality and finish. At the front, is a forward-hinging bonnet section, which includes a radiator air intake duct, air dam, and headlamp mounting panels. The main body moulding is of one-piece construction and also includes the complete rear section, side sills, and the scuttle/dash board section. A pair of doors completes the body, these coming with door handle recesses, and accepting the locking mechanisms from the Escort. Each of the double-skinned doors has a tubular steel framework inside, helping to increase side-impact protection. The panel fit of the various parts is very good.

A number of options are available from Ava, including a well fitting hood assembly and side screens, which does not detract from the car's sporting appearance. Creature comforts can be further enhanced by the use of an interior trim package, which includes carpets and side and door trim panels.

A further development from the K1 is the RS version. Whereas the standard car is capable of around 130 mph (depending upon engine choice), the RS version will approach 170 mph! Clearly the RS version has been developed with competition use in mind, however it can still double as a road car. Wind tunnel development featured in the design of both versions, the K1 having a drag factor of only 0.295. Further minor body refinements were made in order to clean up the RS version even further. The RS features body mouldings that are lighter, but reinforced with carbon fibre, and uses a lightweight version of the chassis, this carrying the necessary mounting points for racing harnesses. A moulded-in aero screen and a roll-over bar are also used.

The car handles remarkably well, and much better than the original donor. This is due in part, to a number of refinements

to the front suspension. The castor and camber angles have been altered by repositioning the struts, and the anti-roll bar positioned in a higher location so as to overcome any tendency for the car to lift or dive. The K1 is substantially lighter than the Escort and consequently the acceleration is fairly rapid. The ride is comfortable and the steering, very light and predictable. Cornering presents no problems, the car remaining virtually flat even under hard driving conditions. Overall performance is dependent upon the drive-train, any of the cvh engines, from 1300 cc up to the 300 php turbo being acceptable.

In a sphere that tends to be fairly heavily populated with cars that exhibit a high degree of nostalgia, the Ava cars stand out as a completely fresh approach to the demand for performance motoring. Their contemporary looks are well in advance of many of their major manufacturers, giving them something of a "novelty" value. This, coupled with their design, quality and performance, make them a very practical proposition, and one that looks set to establish them firmly on the scene in increasing numbers.

The Dutton Melos, Phaeton and B Plus

Dutton Cars really got started back in 1968, due to one man's enthusiasm, Tim Dutton. He initially built Specials, his first major project being a Mantis, based on Lotus 11 and Sunbeam Alpine parts. He was then commissioned to build a Lotus Seven kit and from there, his interest blossomed. The Dutton Company really started in earnest in 1970, early models being based on the Spridget. 1971 saw the emergence of the B-Type and the company developed and grew. The B-Type used Triumph 1200 parts and had a tubular steel chassis. By 1972 a chassis was constructed to accommodate a Ford 1600 unit. Other variations included BMC and Alfa options. The kit specification was uprated in 1973 with the introduction of a Ford solid rear axle located by a Panhard rod and three trailing arms. This, together with a stronger steel chassis, led to the B-Plus which was capable of taking any Ford engine up the V6. 1975 and 76 saw the appearance of Duttons Malaga, and in 1978, the Cantera. Later in the same year, Dutton brought the Phaeton into the world. This initially used a Triumph front suspension with the rest of the mechanical parts coming from the Cortina. The Phaeton (Series 1) was soon established and became a best seller. The Melos Two-Plus (Series 1) followed, after a successful launch at Motor Fair in 1981. The Melos was the chance for all of the family to get into racing. This kit was Escort-based with enough room for four passengers, a large boot, yet still managing to retain that racing look.

With the body edges of the kit tidied up and a general improvement in quality, the kits soon became the Phaeton S3 (series 3) and the improved Melos Two-Plus.

The Phaeton is currently in its Series 4 form and accepts all if its components from the Ford Escort. The chassis and body units now come ready assembled. The chassis is of a rigid box-section

This exotically-styled 2+2 is the Mistral, designed and built by Ben Sparham. The donor can be any Mk III, IV or V Cortina, all of the mechanical parts being utilised without modification. The engine choice is also Ford, and includes anything from the 1300 cc, right up to the 2.3 litre V6. This very comprehensive kit is supplied in a white gel coat and fits onto a sturdy 3 x 1.5 inch tubular steel chassis. The car features gull-wing doors and, despite its sporty ground-hugging looks, can accommodate four people.

top which can be fitted with fixed windows. The Escort Mk I or II Saloon or Estate is the usual donor but as with most Escort-based kits the petrol tank has to be from a van or estate. The engine choice is Ford and can be any unit up to the large Ford V engines.

The Melos kit, now in Series 2 form, (with colour co-ordinated bumpers and redesigned bonnet) comes with all of the parts already mentioned for the Phaeton. It has a similar chassis to the Phaeton but the body is slightly wider and has a modified front end, the kit overall, being a 2+2. For both kits, modifications have to be made to some of the donor items, which are modified by Dutton, free of charge. These are the propshaft, steering column, McPherson strut and lower link, and the wiper motor assembly. Both the Melos and the Phaeton have seat belt anchorages (to the standard required by Regulation 14) a full length chassis and safety glass.

Due to popular demand, the B Plus has been brought back to the range, now appearing as the B Plus Series 2. The kit parts and specification are similar to the Phaeton, but with a redesigned front end.

As for driving, the car's performance depends on the engine option. The overall

The lack of colour co-ordinated bumpers and rectangular bonnet cut-outs identifies this as a Series 1 Melos. Notice the use of a well padded roll-over bar and the unique grille treatment.

construction and has a braced roll-over bar. It also has side bracing to protect from side impact. The chassis comes complete with top wishbone, front coil-over units if required, or, these can be obtained from a Triumph Herald. The body, after bolting to the chassis, is ready cut to accept lights, fuel tank and so on. All of the spoilers, the bonnet, indicators, dashboard, radiator grille, the glass, boot lid, badges, hinges etc are supplied with the kit. Extras include a full length hard

This Series 4 Phaeton is seen here forming part of the impressive Club Dutton display. As with the Melos, a multi-tubular space-frame chassis is used to carry the purposeful-looking body which features a combination of fibreglass panels. Notice the bonnet cut-outs and integral bumper/spoiler unit that distinguishes this as a Series 4.

low weight of the vehicles means that with, say a 1.6 ohc installed a 110+ mph is achievable together with sub-10 second 0-60 time. The ride is good, not exceptional, but then these are sports cars. It should be stated though that, over the years, and with the various subtle changes from series to series that have been made, there have been definite improvements in the cornering and over-all ride.

Presumably, with even more Series and refinements to come, the Phaeton, Melos and B-Plus will be with us on the road, track and hill climb for many years to come.

The Lotus and Caterham Seven

The Lotus Engineering Company was formed in 1952 by Colin Chapman. He initially ran the company in his spare time, the rest of the time being run by his partner, Michael Allen. Most of these early cars were Austin-based and Chapman decided to produce kits en-abling customers to fit their own engine and gearbox combinations. From this idea the Lotus 6 was born, based on a multitubular chassis with either Ford or MG supplying the motive power. The firm got into financial trouble in 1953 (when unfortunately Allen had to withdraw) but by 1955 the company was gradually fighting back and the Lotus 6 was selling well. By this time over 100 Lotus 6s were on the track and hill climb courses. By 1958 the now famous Lotus Seven had replaced the 6 and this, as far as the kit car industry is concerned, is where the story really starts. The Lotus Seven (the Mk VII, S1) was in those days, referred to as the Lotus Super Seven. Lotus formerly produced "pure" racing cars, but with the

6 and the Seven, the business expanded, with the marketing of the Seven being aimed at a race/road going public, the company went from strength to strength.

The Seven was of an alloy construction and had a tubular space frame-chassis. Later years saw the emergence of the Series 2 (S2) and the S3 (the S2 from 1961-67 and the S3 from 1967-1970). They were similar to the S1 but now made use of fibreglass wings with a similar chassis design. Engine options of that time were virtually all Ford and the choice seemed endless. For power it was possible to use the 100E, Classic 1340, Lotus twin-cam, Cosworth 1500 and the Cosworth 1340, the latter with 40 DCOE Webers, unfiltered. All of the engines were mated to their standard gearboxes and later models used a rear axle from the Escort Mexico.

The first Seven to utilise a complete fibreglass tub was the S4, this being really the same as the S3 except for some improvements to the suspension set-up. By 1973 Lotus were winning virtually everything they raced in and the company was becoming very profitable. However, at this time, due to poor sales, Lotus decided to axe the Seven.

Graham Nearn of Caterham Cars however, had other ideas. He had, for many years been an agent for Lotus and continued to be so even through the "troubled times", when Lotus started their direct selling policy. This was a marketing ploy that caused most of the Lotus Dealers/agents, Caterham being one of the exceptions, to look elsewhere. There was some initial disagreement between Lotus and Caterham but by the end of 1973, this was sorted out and Nearn bought the rights and spare parts of the Seven, from Lotus. The Caterham Seven, Series 4 was born.

After a further year of mediocre sales, Caterham decided, due to popular demand, to return to the "look" of the old Series 3. Caterham started redesigning and produced a Series 3 clone, with modernised running gear, an altered chassis and suspension (with the Ford rear axle) which was called the Caterham Super Seven.

The Caterham Super 7 has been systematically developed over the years, for both the race track and the road. The chassis/body unit comes ready equipped with braking system, instrumentation and wiring, windscreen and wings. Over the last three decades the car has never fallen from favour and is now to be found world wide. As would be expected from one of the founder members of the SMMT Specialist Car Manufacturers Group, safety and quality rates very highly on the list of priorities. The styling is still reminiscent of Chapman's early cars, the power now, ideally coming courtesy of a Ford twin-cam or 1600 GT engine. Various options include a roll-over bar, tonneau cover, and heater.

Caterham have now been involved with the production or distribution of the Seven for over 30 years. The modern version has been updated and with Caterham being founder members of the SMMT Specialist Car Group quality will be assured. The Seven now comes complete with all of the safety and "difficult" items already fitted, such as brakes and wiring, and instruments.

As far as driving the beast is concerned, everything is set up for excellent roadholding even under the most severe driving conditions, something that would be expected after years of trials, on and off the race track. The only real problem is the lack of leg room for tall drivers, with little adjustment being available. The dashboard is well set out, and is also easy to read and use (unlike the older Seven where the switches and dials were almost randomly distributed about the dashboard with little, or no thought given to ergonomics and comfort). The latest Seven suffers none of these maladies and will continue to be a best seller in what is a very competitive area of the kit car industry.

The Westfield Seven SE

Following in the style of the Lotus/ Caterham Seven, is the Westfield Seven, built and marketed by Chris Smith of Westfield Sportscars. He started in the kit car business really by chance. He had an old, rotting, Lotus 11 chassis sitting in his garden and decided to build a car, the Westfield 11 ultimately being the result. This eventually led to the Seven, which first appeared in 1984. It was initially designed to take Midget components (with Ford engine options), however the kit now uses a combination of Escort and Cortina parts.

The backbone of this road-going racer is a fully triangulated space-frame

chassis, using a combination of tubular and box-section steel, and is jig assembled. The chassis differs from the original Lotus version in that chassis rails run right through the central tunnel, having extra cross-bracing in this area. This is supplied after being shot blasted and epoxy coated. In the earlier versions, most of the body panels were of aluminium construction, such as the transmission tunnel, bulkhead, sides, full floor, the rear section and the bonnet. Fibreglass was only used for the mud-guards and the nose cone. Nowadays, its a different story. Fibreglass in a choice of six colours is used for the rear tub, side panels, nose cone and bonnet, the remainder constructed from aluminium. The early models can be recognised by louvers in their aluminium bonnets, whereas the later versions have a bulge on their fibreglass bonnets.

The Westfield is available as a chassis or body kit, or a combination of both. The basic chassis kit contains the front wishbones, trailing arms, Panhard rod, bushes and engine mounts. The rest of the suspension and braking comes courtesy of a Mk III, IV or V Cortina. Modifications

have to be made to the rear axle (which is taken from a Mk I or II Escort, or Cortina) which are carried out free of charge.

Options include a new suspension set-up, hood with side screens and a trim and carpet set.

On the road, it is definitely a car for driving hard. It has a firm ride with excellent handling (no matter what you do to it), however creature comforts are minimal, but clearly, many find their way onto the race track.

As a clone of the Lotus/Caterham Seven, the early Westfields are very good, and some owners even fit Lotus badges! More recent models have the bonnet bulge and sport Westfield logos. This is a car of excellent quality and performance and one which will be seen on the road and race track, as often as the Lotus Seven, as the years go by.

Dutton Legerra ZS

The Motor Show held at the NEC in 1986, saw the launch of the Dutton Legerra. This is a car of the classic style (with a frog-eye look) and, in keeping with Dutton tradition, is based on the Ford Escort, Mk I or II. Dutton state however, that there are a few kits under preparation with cvh power, for racing. The chassis is based on that of the Phaeton and Melos and is supplied with Dutton's 5-link and coil-over shock adsorber competition rear suspension. The front suspension is as for the Melos and Phaeton and can be the unique Dutton system, or a set-up from the Triumph Herald/Vitesse range. The windscreen is unusual, being bonded into the body at the manufacturing stage. The shell is then supplied with the doors hinged and fitted. The body, with all parts such as bonnet, boot and floors, ready fitted, is then bolted to the chassis, complete with roll-over bar. The seat belt anchorages comply to Regulation 14, as do all of the Dutton kits. The engine choice is anything Ford, ohv, ohc and right up to the 3 litre V6. For racing, there are rumours of modifications that could include 1.4 or (with the five-speed gear-box) the 1.6 non-injected or turbo engines. All of the lighting for the kit is supplied fitted, and includes a five function rear lamp and number plate lamp, front indicators, front headlights and spaces cut for fog lights. The many optional extras include both hard and soft tops. The hard top can be in black or colour matched to the body (as are the bumpers) and can be fitted at the factory, with a sun roof. The side windows are of a sliding variety and can be completely removed, for any serious racing.

The prototype Dutton Legerra body on display, its first outing being the 1986 Motorshow. The donor vehicle, as with the other Dutton products, is the Mk I and II Escort, this supplying the majority of the mechanical parts. Any of the range of Ford engines from the 1100 cc to the 3 litre V6 will fit. The Legerra body comes as a fully assembled body/space-frame chassis unit, and features a laminated windscreen, bonded into the bodyshell. The rear suspension consists of a track-bred 5-link set-up. In addition, a roll-over bar, lights, dashboard and innumerable small parts are included in the kit.

9
Odds and rods

This chapter contains a number of kit cars that for one reason or another, do not fit neatly into any of the other classifications. The bulk of this section is made up of 'street rod' kits, an area that has gone through something of a quiet period, but now seems to be, once again, increasing in popularity.

The remainder is devoted to the Starcraft and the Jackal Van, both vehicles being out of the ordinary, even in kit car circles.

Street rod kits

Many of today's street rod "kits" have been around for a long time, although virtually all of them have been improved and upgraded with the passing years. Typical cars include the products of the long-running company of Geoff Jago, a man to whom the British rodding scene really owes a debt of gratitude. It was largely through the efforts of Jago, that street rods came to be seen in such profusion during the 1970s and 80s. Initially, he introduced his Model T, this comprising a chassis, fibreglass body tub and wings, and necessary hardware. These were fitted with all manner of drive-trains, and not surprisingly, many received Ford set-ups, ranging from the little four-cylinder pre X-flow engines, to ohc units, right up to small block Ford V8s. Suitable engine, transmission and axle mounts for such common options, were

available, enabling the cars to be assembled with a minimum of trouble. The Ts were systematically refined over the years and were later joined by such other cars as Model B variants. Likewise, these would accept all manner of Ford drive-trains.

A number of other companies were founded during the 1970s, some being short-lived, however, some of the better run concerns, who tended to concentrate on particular areas, survived and prospered. One such company is The Early Ford Store, founded and run by Paul Haigh. For some years, they have specialised in the manufacture of high quality Model A and B chassis, brake pedal kits and suspension set-ups, as well as fibreglass reproduction bodies. Their chassis are produced from 3 x 2 inch square box-section steel and are MIG welded and assembled on purpose-built jigs to ensure accuracy. Haighs produce both a Roadster and Tudor Sedan kits, these using similar mechanical layouts.

Engine options for their cars include 2 litre ohc, V6 and V8 Ford engines. A further option offered by the company is the use of their Granada-based independent front suspension system. Ford live rear axles are possible alternatives, these normally being located with a four-bar system, Panhard rod, and adjustable coil-over units.

The fibreglass bodies come with floor, bulkhead and dashboard all in place, the remaining parts consisting of double-

The Jago Model T bodies and chassis were one of the first rod kits to become easily available in the UK. Over the last few decades, hundreds have been built, making use of a wide range of drivetrains and suspension arrangements. Virtually every form of Ford engine, gearbox and rear axle has been used at some time. Mounting brackets for the most popular choices have been available, especially for the Ford engine options. The T body has always been made from fibreglass and has been greatly improved and refined over the years.

skinned doors, wings, splash aprons, grille shell and bonnet. Little pre-paint preparation is necessary as the finish of the panels is very good. A large variety of authentic reproduction accessories and parts is also carried, this enabling the finished car to include many of the little details often lacking in some other "kits".

The stablemate of the Model A, is the company's 1932 Model B 3-window Coupe. The high quality fibreglass body features steel reinforcement around the doors and hinge areas, and is virtually an exact copy of the genuine item, with the exception of the character-changing 3.5 inch roof-chop. The resulting car has the mean and purposeful look so beloved of street rodders.

The Early Ford Store also carries a large range of extras, including headlight bars, bumpers and reproduction petrol tanks, all adding to the finished car's authenticity. The company has built up a good reputation over the years, not only for the quality of their fibreglass, but also for their engineering prowess in general.

Clearly their attention to detail and overall quality has enabled them to survive where others have failed.

The Rod Shop is another name to come to the fore in recent years, this company specialising in a number of "component rods". Not only are their products of excellent quality, they are also some of the easiest of this type to assemble. They produce a number of 1929 Model A and 1932 Model B variants, the Cortina providing a sensible and economical choice of drive-train and suspension. Amongst their range is a Model A Delivery, a Tudor Sedan and a pick-up, as well as 5- and 3-window Model B Coupes.

The Rod Shop cars use substantial laser-cut chassis, which will accept the Cortina's engine, gearbox, front and rear suspension assemblies, as well as many of the smaller but equally necessary pieces of hardware. The bodies are constructed from fibreglass and come complete with floorpan and bulkhead. Assembling the cars can be fairly rapid, the Cortina components fitting with relative ease.

To make life even easier, The Rod Shop now offer a special "Superdeal" for customers who spend a minimum of £2,000 with them. They will now fit the customer's engine, gearbox and suspension, free of charge. In addition, they will also fit the body of choice to the chassis and even hang the doors, thus eliminating yet another time consuming stage.

A number of superbly built examples of the Rod Shop's products have appeared in recent years, real credits to both the company as well as the talented individuals who constructed and detailed them. Clearly, the chassis arrangement is flexible enough to accommodate a variety of drive-train and suspension assemblies apart from the Cortina. Rod Shop cars have now been built with various Ford engines including V6 and V8s, and alternative suspension arrangements such as drop-tube front axles and Jaguar independent rear-ends.

The Rod Shop Model As and Bs exhibit the smooth, uncluttered look currently in vogue in both the UK and USA and, when

based upon a Ford donor, can form a sensible and economical way to enter the often expensive world of street rodding.

One of the newest and perhaps most impressive arrivals on the scene, is the reproduction 1934 American 3-window Coupe of the Bournemouth-based 34 Corner. The 34 was, for a long time, the poor relation of the rodder's perennial favourite, the Model B, however recent years have seen a great upsurge in interest in the car which, until recently, was not available in reproduction form in the UK. Various American companies, such as Wescott, have produced countless examples in the US, but the 34 was denied to the UK rodder. Clearly, this has now changed!

The 34 really sprang to fame as a result of its appearance in recent years, as the "star" of the movie *The California Kid* and more recently, as a promotional vehicle for Texas rock band, ZZ Top (theirs was actually a 33).

The 34 Corner coupe body features a filled roof and cowl vent, and comes complete with bulkhead, double-skinned doors, rear deck lid, and with the floor and transmission tunnel bonded in

position. Completing the body is a set of wings, grille shell and 3-piece bonnet. A further set of mouldings, including the seat base, finishes off the inside. Further parts include a boot liner and a rumble seat kit. All the exterior panels are supplied in a red gel coat finish, the inner panels coming in grey. Other colours can be supplied as an option.

The backbone for the project is a chassis constructed from laser cut 3 mm replica steel profiles, with folded central cross-members. Following initial assembly, the chassis is transferred to a full chassis jig for boxing and final (double) welding. A full propshaft safety loop is also included. Front and rear cross-members are constructed from 1.5 inch square section steel. Options for the front suspension are either for a traditional solid axle or for a specially designed Cortina cross-member, three inches narrower than standard, designed for extra lowness. The rear axle can also be supplied from the same source or alternatively, can be a Jaguar independent unit. All necessary components are welded into place and protected with zinc primer.

Apart from the roof-chop, the 1934 American Ford 3-window coupe of 34 Corner is a faithful replica. As with most rod kits, the chassis will accommodate a variety of different drive-trains and suspension set-ups. Any of the range of Ford engines, from the 4-cylinders up to the American V8s, will fit. As well as traditional drop-tube and I-beam front axles, a special narrowed Cortina independent front suspension is also offered by the company.

handles, glass and door seals, replica knock-off wheel kits and cast aluminium dash panels.

The completed car looks superb, and on a par with any of the long-running American kits. The body is uncluttered, the quality is good, and the car's overall stance is just right. As each kit takes four craftsmen twelve working days to complete, 34 Corner estimate that a maximum of only twenty five cars a year can be produced. Clearly the car is going to remain a fairly exclusive beast, however, it forms a very welcome and impressive addition to the UK street rodding scene.

The Starcraft

It's not a caravan, it's not a car, it's not even a commercial, it's a Starcraft, designed and built by Jim Mcintyre (the head of Spartan), the only motor home available in kit form. Jim started making kit cars way back in 1969, the Starcraft being launched in 1985.

To build this beast, first select a Cortina donor and then add a jig-built chassis with front and rear mounting brackets, all the holes being pre-drilled. Body mounting brackets are already welded in

The completed cars are low, uncluttered and just plain mean-looking! The absence of unnecessary accessories and body trim parts helps to create the smooth, one-piece contemporary look currently in favour. In keeping with its image, this bright yellow example houses a large, GMC-blown American V8 under its smooth hood.

A wide range of additional options are available, such as I-beam and Super Bell dropped axles, as well as many other US-styled suspension related parts. A weld-on 4–bar set-up is also available for locating live rear axles.

Additional parts listed include lights, mirrors, wing mounting brackets, locks,

The 1929 Model As and 1932 Model Bs of the Rod Shop are some of the easiest of this type of vehicle to assemble. Like the 34 Corner's cars, the bodies are smooth and uncluttered, as shown by this red Model A Tudor. Various drive-trains can be accommodated, however much of the running-gear from the Cortina can be used, this forming an economical and reliable street rod. The chassis produced by the Rod Shop is laser-cut and based on a pair of reproduction side-rails.

place, and the whole thing is painted with primer. The chassis then accepts the components from all of the Mk III, IV, or V Cortina range of saloons and estates, from 1970 onwards. There is only one problem with the donor selection, and that is to avoid two-door Cortinas as the doors are too long for the kit. The front lights and frontal styling also depend on the donor, particularly the year of construction. Another variable is the dashboard. Obviously a better and more modern look can be achieved with a Mk V Cortina Ghia or Crusader, rather than a Basic "K" registered Cortina.

The normal body parts come as six pieces; two door skins, two wings, front panel and bonnet. The camper unit is of one piece construction and together with all of the other fibreglass panels, is supplied in a white gel coat (the colour that most stay with when they reach the streets). All the glazing is supplied, together with the rubbers and frames. The overall finish is very good and with the glazing kit fitted, the weather protection is excellent.

The whole unit sits on six wheels, all of which are supplied in the kit (its worth keeping one, or even two, of the Cortina's wheels as spares). It can use just four wheels, although an indespension unit (similar to boat trailers) and a few home drilled holes produce the six-wheeler. It is said that the extra wheels give more stability and traction when venturing across soft and uneven ground. The extra two are not driven or braked and are just there to cope with any extra weight. The tyres are extra, although Starcraft can supply low profiles at reasonable cost.

Nearly all of the Cortina's removable parts fit into the Starcraft, even the exhaust system. The propshaft is standard, as are the shock absorbers, wiring loom (which virtually stays as it is) and the complete front half of the car with seats, doors, bulkhead, seat belts, carpet, dashboard, instruments etc. This eliminates an otherwise very time consuming and often tricky operation. The fuel tank can also be transferred from the Cortina, although a larger one can be fitted if required. The engine options are anything from the 1.3 up to the 2.3 V6. For the more performance orientated camper there is a choice of Capri, Sierra, Granada and Scorpio engines and gearboxes. This

The remarkable Starcraft is currently the only motorhome kit available in the UK. The Starcraft's chassis accepts most of the mechanical assemblies from the Cortina range and also makes use of the front body section. The donor vehicle is limited to the two-door models as the doors are of the correct length. The fibreglass body consists of six panels, namely the door skins, wings, front panel, bonnet and camper unit. The Starcraft is available in both 4- and 6-wheeler form, the extra wheels remaining undriven. The use of the Cortina cab section enables the Cortina's interior, trim and instrumentation to be reused.

The Imperial Jackdaw Van is unusual in that it is aimed more at the business community rather than the kit car enthusiast. Its vintage lines and styling, coupled with the large advertising space on the sides, makes it an attractive proposition for many small businesses. Imperial Specialist Vehicles offer a choice of two different lengths, with the option of single or twin rear doors. The Jackdaw was originally introduced using the running-gear from either the Vauxhall Viva or the Magnum, but in line with many other kits, was redesigned to accept most of its drive-train and suspension from the Cortina range. As the company proclaims, "a superb mobile advertisement that works hard even when standing still!"

could give a five-speed gearbox, attached to a 2.8 V6, power steering, diesel options, air conditioning, the choice is limitless, even an automatic if the fancy takes you. Starcraft estimate that the camper can be built in around 100 hours and this does not seem unreasonable, assuming you have your clean "bits" already to go. The interior could take up to 200 hours!

The interior is amazingly spacious with plenty of room, even for the six-footer. This is very cleverly done as the total vehicle height is only 7' 5" (not too much of a problem under those tall bridges). Incidently, for those parking on a busy Saturday morning, the length is 17' 6". The interior layout (9' 4" x 6' 8") is up to the builder. Beds, kitchen, seats, the choice is again endless and at the end of the day, the only constraint is the cost (but at least there is a choice).

If you fancy owning a Starcraft, and kit building is too much for you, then Starcraft can supply one ready built, using all new Ford components. They will even put in cupboards, a sink, carpets, gas, beds, toilet, cooker etc., but not surprisingly, this version can prove to be expensive.

For family use, this kit is an excellent choice. It drives very well and is amazingly quiet considering the shape. The only extra that would be useful, and most on the road now have these, are larger tub mounted mirrors. The fuel economy is reasonable, the average, based on finished kits, seemed to be around 30 mpg, although this obviously depends on the donor. Whether boating, horsing, or just going on vacation, this is certainly one vehicle to choose and judging by the number now appearing at kit car shows, a choice that is becoming increasingly more popular.

10

Kit cars in action

Although the vast majority of kit cars built are destined for the road, a certain number of them inevitably find their way into various forms of performance or competition use. They clearly have a number of advantages over their mass-produced brethren and it is the influence from these, that has resulted in kit cars becoming very competitive in a number of fields.

Their light weight, when coupled with even a moderately tuned engine, results in a high power-to-weight ratio, an obvious advantage over heavier, steel-bodied competition. The weight advantage can prove useful in many different sports. For instance, being light is a definite advantage in drag racing, sprints and hill climbs, often gaining useful seconds. It also proves its worth in certain forms of off-road events, the tendency to sink into deep mud being replaced by an ability to "skate" over the top of it.

Another major advantage is that most kit cars have a separate steel chassis, a bonus not enjoyed by many modern cars. This means that it is a comparatively simple matter to fit alternative engine mounts, spring mounts and so on. Often this merely involves welding new brackets to the chassis, a much simpler exercise than for cars lacking a chassis. For instance, adding suitable brackets for a Panhard rod may involve welding on simple mounting tabs to a chassis rail. The same exercise in a typical unit-constructed production car may involve

the addition of complex reinforcement, gusseting and strengthening plates to the appropriate floor or wheel arch area. Consequently, modifications are more complex and time consuming. Having a solid substantial framework to work on, makes alterations and adjustments much easier for the kit car owner, especially as these are frequently called for in many spheres of motor sport.

If a kit car is being built up with competition use in mind from the outset, these refinements can be added at the construction stage. It is much easier working on a rolling chassis than on a unit-constructed vehicle. Access to the major components is also often easier with kit cars as the majority of the body panels may be lightweight and unstressed, hence easily removed.

There are a number of forms of motor sport that have come into being in recent years, specifically with kit cars in mind. Perhaps the most prestigious and popular form is that of the "Kit Cars and Specials" Challenge, sponsored by the widely-read magazine of the same name. The Challenge started in 1984 in the form of a twelve round championship, organised and run by the ever-popular 750 Motor Club. This long-running organisation was first formed in 1939 with the main aim of encouraging participation of Austin 7-based cars in various forms of motor sport. The club, which now boasts a membership in excess of 2000, organises various types of amateur motor racing,

one segment of which is the Kit Cars Challenge, which is a racing series specifically for kit cars. Since its conception, the Challenge has grown consistently in popularity, the result being very close racing and insufficient grid space to accommodate all of the hopeful entrants, especially in the lower classes.

The racing venues are well spread about the UK, being held at Castle Combe, Oulton Park, Mallory Park, Brands Hatch, Cadwell Park, Donington, Lydden and Snetterton. Many of the competitors take a very professional approach to the racing and in some cases, even manufacturers become involved. For instance, Dutton's have campaigned a 2.8i V6 powered Rico in the series. One of the great attractions of this type of competition is the great variety of cars competing. It is not uncommon to encounter such cars as JBA Falcons, Seraph, Bonito and Dutton Melos and Phaetons. Apart from these, Ford power-plants are frequently found in other, more normally, non-Ford kits such as the Sylva Star and the Westfield 11.

The general opinion is that the racing is tremendous fun for both competitors and spectators alike, many of the latter clearly identifying their own, more docile cars, with the race-bred versions on the track. The 750 Motor Club carry out an excellent job of organisation and still manage to retain the friendly atmosphere that they have long been famed for.

What do the competitors get for their stalwart (and often expensive) efforts? The Annual Racing Championship Awards consist of a trophy for 1st, 2nd and 3rd places overall, with a trophy for the first in each class. In addition, there is also the Westfield Trophy for the best prepared car, as judged by the Chief Scrutineer. These are considered to be adequate rewards by the majority of competitors, the main reward being the sheer thrill of competition!

To be eligible for kit car racing, the car must be recognised as a "Road-Going Kit Car" as listed by the 750 Motor Club. This excludes one-off specials and prototype cars. Competing cars must be fully road legal.

Clearly some form of classing arrange-

ments are necessary, these being based largely upon engine capacity. There are four classes, namely: up to 1330 cc, 1300–1600 cc, 1600–2000 cc and 2000 cc and over. Cars using supercharged or turbocharged engines up to 2000 cc compete in the latter class.

Naturally, safety requirements come high on the list of priorities, cars having to comply with a number of RAC MSA Technical Regulations. A roll-over bar is a mandatory requirement and a safety petrol tank, recommended.

The choice of engines is open, although they must be based on series production units. Tuning modifications are permitted, subject to a limit of only two valves per cylinder, and no forced induction (ie. no turbocharger or superchargers) on engines over 2000 cc.

The transmissions, gearbox and dif-ferential must have originated from a production car, specialist units such as the Hewland not being permitted.

The choice of wheels is fairly free, the only constraint being upon maximum width (6″ for class A and B, and 7″ for classes C and D). The tyres fitted, have to comply with the RAC MSA technical regulations, as applicable to Production Car Racing. The minimum tread depth is 3 mm and no deviation from the manufacturer's specification is allowed. The choice of suspension and brakes is free, on condition that no controls are fitted to adjust the brakes or anti-roll bars whilst seated in the cockpit. In addition, the lowest component of the track of the vehicle must be able to pass over a 3″ block (with driver aboard).

As far as the bodywork is concerned, the engine and transmission must be fully enclosed, for obvious reasons, with no adjustable aerodynamic devices fitted. Aerofoils are not allowed, front or rear, although spoilers are. The cockpit, in plan view, must be symmetrical about the cars longitudinal axis and contain two full-sized seats. The passenger area must provide as much room as for the driver, ie. the same leg, elbow and foot room etc.

Caught in action at Mallory Park, was this ten year old Bonito of Bill Battey, the car using a hot, rebuilt 1.6 Cortina engine. In the build-up, over 28 different donor vehicles were used, one even being a Rolls-Royce!

A Dutton Series 3 Phaeton in track-trim, ready to compete in a standing ¼ mile. Note the obvious, track preparation in the form of the single aeroscreen and the roll-over protection.

The Ava K1 about to take to the track. The drag factor is only 0.295. Primarily intended for road use (its brother the RS is aimed at more serious track use) this lightweight can still power past the much of the opposition!

The passenger space may be covered by a soft flexible tonneau cover.

A somewhat unexpected result of the very professional and highly competitive nature of the Kit Car Challenge, was that the cars competing soon became, in effect, "full-race" cars, as opposed to road-going. This situation suited many of the entrants, but not all. As a result, a number of individuals who found that the cost of remaining competitive were becoming prohibitive, approached the British Racing and Sports Car Club (BRSCC) with a view to starting up a second, lower budget series. The BRSCCA responded positively and set about organising a road-going series, *Kit Cars and Specials* magazine agreeing to sponsor it. New regulations were produced and a number of events organised, mainly at the same venues as those used for the 750MC–organised series. Although the BRSCCA series is still comparatively new, it looks set to appeal widely, the predicted "average" cost of competing cars being in the region of £3000.

Following the inaugural season's racing, a number of revisions to the regulations were felt to be in order. For instance, the use of full-width screens was expected to be made mandatory, as was the use of tuning restrictions in the form of an exhaust section of limited diameter. The BRSCCA's intention is that the series should remain as true "road-going" events, this helping to keep costs down and hence, attract more competitors.

To be eligible, cars must be bona fide road-going kit cars that are, or have been,

available in kit form to the general public. Where a car has also been available in fully-built form, the onus is placed upon the individual to prove that his particular car was built from a kit. The cars are required to display a current road-fund licence, have an MOT certificate, and are split into four classes, dependent on engine capacity. These are up to 1330 cc, 1331–1645 cc, 1646–2660 cc, and 2661 cc and over. Supercharging and turbocharging is not allowed in any class.

Clearly, entrants must comply with the appropriate BRSCCA and RAC safety requirements, the majority of these being similar to those required for the 750MC events. Engines, gearboxes and differentials are limited to those from series production cars, with engine tuning limited to only two valves per cylinder, with no forced induction or dry-sump systems permissible.

As with the 750MC events, the lower classes tend to attract the greatest numbers (classes are A–D), with classes C and D being dominated by such cars as Ford-powered Sylva Leaders. The general opinion seems to be that Ford engines and gearboxes have a great deal to offer. Remarkably, around 80% of the entrants of this series, are Ford-powered!

A second series, specifically for Caterham/Lotus Sevens in road-going form, is also organised by the BRSCCA. The BRSCCA Caterham Super 7 Race Series was designed so that road cars could be competitively raced, and yet still remain practical for daily use. Eligible cars are Lotus Super 7s, produced between 1957 and 1973 (series 1–4), and Caterham Super 7s, built between 1973 to date (series 3 and 4). A three class structure is used, this being dependent on the type and capacity of the engine used. Class A encompasses cars fitted with Lotus twin-cam, 1700 cc BDR, or push-rod engines (Kent ohv) up to 1800 cc. Class B is for push-rod engines between 1600 and 1700 cc, and Lotus twin-cam engines in basic guise, with Class C covering ohv and cvh engines up to 1630 cc. A number of tuning restrictions (such as limited carburation and no forced induction systems) are applied, however, steel engine internals, dry-sump systems, and competition exhausts are allowed.

A limited number of suspension alterations are also permitted, such as the use of negative camber wishbones and replacement springs and shock absorbers, however, most other modifications are banned. Naturally, there are a number of mandatory safety requirements that have to be observed. These

Below: **The K1 and the RS, "in the pits". The major visible difference is that the K1 is wearing its weather protection, a luxury not really necessary for the RS. The RS version has its bonnet open, revealing its cvh engine and suspension. The handling and overall quality of both cars is excellent.**

include FIA roll-bar, full harness seat belt, fire extinguisher, oil catch-cans, ignition cut-out, flameproof rear bulkhead and separate external throttle springs. Cars must also be taxed, tested and insured.

Eleven annual races are held at various locations, with competitors scoring points for each car beaten, up to a maximum of ten points in each race. Trophies are awarded for the first three cars in each class, with additional end of season awards for the overall champion plus the first three entrants in each category. The racing is often close as well as hotly contested, and as with the kit car series, a very professional attitude is adopted by the majority of the competitors.

It really is quite remarkable, just how much kit car owners and builders, are prepared to put into such forms of "no profit" racing, being content with the thrill of competition. This commendable attitude is not always to be found in certain other forms of motor sport!

An additional spin-off of this racing activity is that as well as providing a great deal of enjoyment, it also helps to increase public confidence in such amateur-built cars. If the race track is not the place to fully prove a chassis design and suspension, then nowhere is! Experience has shown that many road-going problems have been sorted out on the track.

As well as various track events, kit cars have recently begun showing up at such events as the Motor Cycle Club (MCC)

A Series 3 Phaeton taking part in a timed driving test. Cars have to complete a complicated course without hitting any of the cones, against the clock. Duttons frequently perform well in these tests, mainly due to their good handling characteristics.

reliability trials. These events have an off-road course (the muddier the better!) with very steep hill sections, some of which are timed. Not surprisingly, the treatment that trials cars get is usually much more severe than their road-going equivalents, despite the fact that the speeds encountered are not often very high. Having a substantial chassis is an obvious requirement, this, advantageously, being a feature of most kit cars. The peculiar requirements of such events means that ground clearance is of paramount

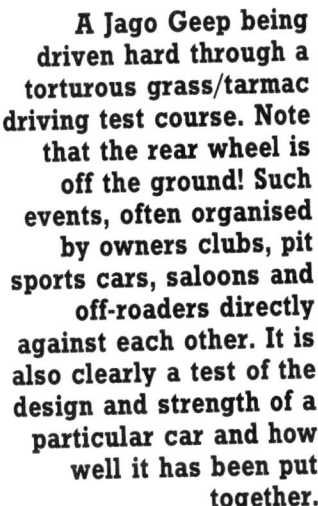

A Jago Geep being driven hard through a torturous grass/tarmac driving test course. Note that the rear wheel is off the ground! Such events, often organised by owners clubs, pit sports cars, saloons and off-roaders directly against each other. It is also clearly a test of the design and strength of a particular car and how well it has been put together.

163

importance, as are the use of such devices as Panhard rods, all of these features being easily built in at the construction stage. Kit cars also have the obvious advantage of light weight.

Many of the trials cars currently competing have been around for a considerable number of years and it would seem a distinct possibility that we may well see a whole new generation of such vehicles, based on some of the smaller, lightweight kit cars currently in production.

Because of the great diversity of types, kit cars tend to crop up in all manor of places. The drag strip, sprints, racing circuit, off-road courses, driving tests, reliability trials, in fact, virtually anywhere that a reasonable degree of performance is needed. As their popularity continues to increase, more events specifically for kit cars will almost certainly be organised, both on a local as well as a national basis. It is an undisputed fact that Ford components will feature predominantly in a great number of these cars, as a result of their obvious advantages of price, strength and availability, coupled with the vast amount of tuning and performance equipment available. Tuning parts are available for virtually every Ford engine ever built, from the 1172 cc sidevalve right up to the modern chv, V6 and American V8 units. As a result of the range of Ford engines and their allied performance parts, a home is ensured in many kit cars. Likewise, with the suspension systems, the rally scene in particular having resulted in many parts specifically for upgrading road suspension. Clearly Ford parts have many advantages to offer.

Top left: **The Sylva Leader SS came into being using much of the running-gear and suspension from the Vauxhall Viva. Over the years, it has been substantially revamped, largely as a result of racing activity, and now features a twin-rail chassis with substantial bracing around the passenger compartment and other stressed points. The car makes use of Viva or Firenza front crossmembers and rear axle assemblies, the further option of using Ford engines (especially the 1600 X-flow) now being available. The little cars have proved to be immensely successful in a number of forms of racing.**

Top right: **The 3 litre Ford V6-powered Eagle RV of Mark Barnett, launching hard on a ¼ mile time sprint. The standing quarter mile time for this vehicle was 18 seconds, certainly not shoddy performance for an off-road machine.**

Fortunately, an uncommon occurrence! This unhappy Spartan owner came to grief during a spot of hard driving during a timed trial!

The future?

Predicting the future is always a very tricky thing to do, however, there are a number of trends emerging in various parts of the industry. The course of events can often be changed as a result of outside influences and bearing this in mind, a number of general things are likely to happen. Firstly, kit cars will continue to become further refined, not only in the mechanical sense, but also in terms of their ease of assembly. Great strides have been taken in this direction in recent years, although there is still room for improvement in some cases. The kit car industry clearly cannot rely on the finite number of enthusiasts who possess the, albeit limited, skills necessary to assemble a kit car, but will have to continue its efforts to increase its sales area. This can be achieved by making its products even easier to assemble, in the hope that it can, as it is already tending to do, convince people who can barely hold a spanner that they are perfectly capable of assembling a kit car. In this respect, it will be necessary for some of the manufacturers to improve their after-sales care and assistance.

One field that seems to be increasing at an impressive rate, despite any potential problems of patent or copyright infringement, is that of "clone" cars, or replicas. There is no doubt that Ford engines will continue to play an important role in this area, an increasing number of them mounted in mid-engined configurations. The scene is now set for the appearance of such exotic clones as GT40s, Ferraris, and Lamborghinis, to arrive in greater profusion, now that a number of teething troubles have been ironed out and the cars are much easier to complete than many of their predecessors. It is likely that many of the cars in this bracket will be offered with, at least, Ford engine options, and possibly with a reasonably high Ford content in the suspension systems. Kits that previously did not offer the choice of a Ford power-plant, will probably be redesigned (as many others already have), to allow for this option. There are a number of exciting new cars set to emerge in this field, for instance, the stunning GT Developments T70 Lola clone. Kits such as these are not going to be cheap to assemble, but will offer the chance to those who are determined enough, to own a truly "exotic" clone car.

Another interesting new project (presently in the pipeline) that should see the light of day in the near future, is the Montana, currently under development by Carlton, the manufacturers of the Commando and Carrera models. The new car is based on the de Tomaso Pantera, a car that has been in production upwards of a decade and a half, yet still remains a very rare beast. Power for the Pantera came originally from a 351 ci Ford V8 engine, producing 330 bhp. Carlton are reproducing the bodywork in fibreglass, but using the running-gear from the Ford Granada. Once again, a

Ford based kit cars

??
The future?

sensible compromise between exotic styling and affordable drive-train. Hopefully, the Montana is set for a great future amongst the ranks of the exotic "clone" cars!

At the other end of the scale, it seems likely that there will be significant expansion in the area of 4/5-seater saloons and coupes, aimed at the family man. Although there are a few cars already on the market, such as the Ginetta G26, that fall into this area, the market still remains largely untapped. Here, the faithful Cortina will probably continue to be used as the donor car for the foreseeable future, as it forms a very economical base. One only has to look at the G26 to see what remarkable results can be achieved with such cars as the Escort and Cortina. For instance, Peter Hulse of Viking Cars is currently putting the finishing touches to his Ford-based 2+2. This uses a parallel steel backbone, 4-link/Panhard rod rear end and cut down Escort front struts. Escort, Cortina and Capri engines will all be possibilities. An interesting project and definitely one to look out for. There is obviously the possibility of a number of Sierra-based cars arriving in the near future, although these, because of their greater cost, will initially be limited to the more expensive "sporting" end of the range.

In the field of sports cars, it is likely that we shall see the arrival of a number of new products, making use of the Escort cvh engines, as well as some of its suspension system. Recent years have seen the appearance of several exciting new sports cars, such as the Tripos R81 and Maelstrom. There is the distinct possibility that similarly designed, race-bred cars will appear from a number of sources. One such beast is the Nyvrem Nirvana, a car which has sold well abroad but has yet to make its impact in the UK.

Ford drive-trains will continue to offer a sensible choice, although many will probably make use of specially produced suspension systems. For instance, sophisticated rising-rate set-ups are set to become more common. Some of these new projects will probably prosper at the expense of older, more well-established cars already on the market.

Remarkably, even in the heavily saturated field of traditionally-styled cars, newcomers keep arriving! Just when it appears that there is no further room in the market for any more good quality cars, along comes another! The newer ones are exhibiting not only good mechanical layout and quality of construction, they are also "correct" in terms of such things as stance and proportions, both very important parameters sometimes lacking in earlier cars. Clearly, up-and-coming designers such as David Pepper, have learnt a lot from their predecessors. In the case of David Pepper's latest project, he has managed to create a perfectly proportioned car, in the shape of the AF Sport. In all probability, such cars as the AF will take over a part of the market, at the expense of some of the other kits available. Conversely, their quality is such that they may well create a new niche for themselves. Another traditionally-styled sports car soon to hit the road is the Tripos XXX,

The stunning Lola T70 Mk III of GT Developments, of Poole. This will be the stablemate to the company's GT40 clone, Ford engines supplying the power for both. The Ford Motor Company has given its blessing to the project, thus avoiding any potential patent/copyright wrangles. There is a strong suspicion in certain quarters that this is one aspect of the law that may come to the fore in the near future, with a number of other manufacturers.

The Tripos Hunter, a 1930s styled 2-seater, is scheduled to come into production alongside the R81. Currently the car uses a Triumph TR2-TR6 chassis although there are indications that Ford power will be adopted. At present, there is a six month waiting list for Hunters in the USA. (Photo courtesy of Tripos)

which will initially be Triumph based although Ford based options are rumoured to be in the pipeline.

Other interesting arrivals on the scene in recent days, have been the Sierra-based Predator and Invader from Pike. These are some of the first cars to make use of the Sierra running-gear and it is perhaps surprising that this has occurred in this area of the market. This trend may well be followed by other manufacturers as they vie with each other for the public's attention. It is surely a sign of the times, that in a section where many cars rely on fairly simple and economical donor vehicles, such a comparatively expensive choice of running-gear has been chosen. Presumably the market is now ready for projects where cost is not the over-whelming factor. It will be interesting to see if other manufacturers follow Pike's lead in this respect.

One section that, perhaps surprisingly, does not seem to be expanding as fast as

might have been expected, is that of off-road styled vehicles. There have been a number of new projects, in recent years, that have foundered in their early stages. The one exception is the excellent little Rickman Ranger which looks set for great things. It appears that Jago and Eagle have got this section of the market well sewn up, future advancements probably being limited to the gradual improvement and refinement of their existing products. On the other hand, there will probably be a number of new off-road inspired ''utility'' vehicles, of the Sherwood and Commando type, appearing. The general feeling is that there is still plenty of scope in this area for new products. Quite possibly, these will continue to use the Cortina range as donors, however, we may well see the newer front-wheel drive Escort models, and even the Sierra, put to use.

The general picture for the kit car industry, at the moment, looks fairly rosy.

There will clearly be plenty of changes within the industry as companies merge and change hands, and projects move from one manufacturer to another. There will obviously be ups and downs at various times, however, certain aspects look as if they will go on for ever. The likes of Marcos, Ginetta, Jago, Dutton, Eagle, and so on, look set to take the industry well into the next decade, if not the next century. Sophistication is increasing as such companies as DJ Sportscars systematically improve their techiques with each successive product. This is a welcome trend throughout much of the industry and is an encouraging sign that a secure future for many of the manufacturers is assured.

Clearly, Ford parts will continue to be used in vast numbers in kit cars for as far as the eye can see. The Ford Motor Company itself, although it has no official policy, has become involved in an increasing variety of ways in recent years. For instance, they greatly assisted with parts and advice for various suspension aspects for the ill-fated Seraph, and more recently, were involved with the MIRA testing of the Classic Replicars LM164 clone.

Perhaps this is an indication that the kit car industry is being taken more seriously in high places. There is no doubt that the next decade could be very interesting indeed!

The now fully completed and developed 164 LM Ferrari clone of Classic Replicars. The sleek cvh-powered creature looks set to take off in a big way in 1988. (Classic Replicars)